HOW TO TALK WELL

Other books by JAMES F. BENDER:

NBC HANDBOOK OF PRONUNCIATION
PERSONALITY STRUCTURE OF STUTTERING
SALESMEN'S MISPRONUNCIATIONS
SALESMEN'S ERRORS OF GRAMMAR
COURTESY HINTS FOR SALESMEN
HOW TO SLEEP

In Collaboration with Volney R. Osha:

DO'S AND DON'TS OF THE SALES INTERVIEW

In Collaboration with Dr. V. A. Fields:

SPEECH CORRECTION MANUAL
PRINCIPLES AND PRACTICES OF SPEECH CORRECTION
PHONETIC READINGS IN AMERICAN SPEECH
VOICE AND DICTION

How to
TALK WELL

BY JAMES F. BENDER

McGraw-Hill Book Company, Inc.

NEW YORK : LONDON : TORONTO

HOW TO TALK WELL

Tenth Printing

PUBLISHED BY McGRAW-HILL BOOK COMPANY, INC.

PRINTED IN THE UNITED STATES OF AMERICA

To

ANNE *and* MOTHER

DEAR READER,

If you are like many of us, you're not satisfied with your speech, no matter how good it is. You know it could be better. You see the need to make it better. You have no doubt that good, clear speech is just about the best tool to influence others the way you want to influence them.

About the only fellow who can't improve his human relations through better speech is the lighthouse keeper. That is, if he's a bachelor and lives alone. Clear, pleasant speech gets things done. It makes communication easy; it boosts popularity; it can make or mar your fortune.

To learn to talk better is uphill work, but it's fascinating work. When Mrs. Eleanor Roosevelt became America's First Lady, she straightway sought a speech teacher, although she was already a good speaker. Winston Churchill, perhaps the greatest living orator, tells us about the long hours he spent to conquer a lisp and stutter before he made his first public speech. He still practices. Thank goodness, most of us don't have such tough handicaps to get rid of. Our job is pretty easy. But like Mr. Churchill, we can't rest on our oars. We need to check up every now and then on how we talk. Someone has said that the tongue is the only tool you can't dull with right use.

This book is the result of my twenty years in speech training. I began to earn a living as a tutor in public speaking and as psychological examiner in the Personnel Bureau of City College.

I soon met many stutterers. There was no place to send them for help. So the famous voice specialist, Dr. Victor A. Fields, whom I assisted, set up a speech clinic. There for nine years we tested and taught—at first alone, later with colleagues—an estimated ten thousand young men, women, and children. People with all kinds of mutilated speech—lisp, lall, stutter, voice problems, and so on—enrolled in the City College clinic.

In those years I went down to Columbia University in my spare time to earn my Ph.D. in speech pathology and psychology. My doctoral dissertation was *The Personality Structure of Stuttering*. I also had the good luck to work under Dr. Smiley Blanton at the New York Post-Graduate Hospital, later at Vanderbilt Clinic. That was another invaluable experience. There were adults and children who had lost their speech because of brain injuries—dysphasics. There were birth-injured or cerebral palsied patients. Some were cretins. Others had cleft palates. Many suffered from emotional tugs of the wrong kind.

Still later, I organized a clinic for children with speech and hearing disabilities. We called it the Queens Speech and Hearing Service Center because so many of my fine colleagues at Queens College and friends in the community made it a neighborhood venture.

My job was to examine each youngster, diagnose his disorder, provide reeducation, advise parents, write texts, and hold demonstration clinics for teachers. In the summers I sometimes taught at Columbia University, Mt. Holyoke College, Hunter College, and the University of Oregon. In the late afternoon and evening I served the Polytechnic Institute of Brooklyn as Adjunct Professor of Psychology.

During the past few years I have trained radio announcers and edited the *NBC Handbook of Pronunciation* for National Broadcasting Company. Among my duties at present is the training of salesmen. They know a good way to break down buyers' resistance is through persuasive speech.

On Monday evenings I conduct a course, Speech Training for Executives. Here men and women of ability and achievement sharpen their techniques of interviewing, conducting conferences, public speaking, etc.

The problems of the platform speaker are very close to my heart, since I lecture under the management of W. Colston Leigh, Inc.

From this varied experience come the ideas, quizzes, and drills in this book.

Psychologists have a law—*Appreciation precedes execution*. This is gobbledegook for, "You've got to know what to do before you can do it." That's why you'll find a lot of background material on speech, public speaking, and personality. I took some of this material from my own articles in *The American Magazine, The Christian Science Monitor, Good Housekeeping, Ladies' Home Journal, New York Times Magazine, Printers' Ink, The Reader's Digest, Sales Management, The Saturday Evening Post, Science Digest, The Scientific Monthly, Your Life.* Some of the practice material comes from my syndicated column to house organs, *How to Get Along with Others.*

I've tried hard to make the drills easy for you to give yourself. I wish you'd let me know how you make out with them. Are they easy to understand and apply?

Of course, you need to practice like a faithful friend. One hour a day for thirty weeks brings good returns. Fifteen minutes a day helps a lot—if you keep at it long enough. Regularity is the thing. It builds sturdy habits. You become speech-conscious that way, and you soon find yourself talking better.

The first chapter will help you to guide your own speech-improvement program. I hope you find useful hints there and in all the other chapters. Perhaps you may want to read the book through and take some quizzes to see how you measure up, before you really go to work. That's good. It gives you a bird's-eye view. It tells you which speech habit you need to build first—articulation, pronunciation, voice, vocabulary, conversation, or something else.

Good luck!

James F. Bender

THE NATIONAL INSTITUTE FOR HUMAN RELATIONS
NEW YORK 17, N. Y.

ACKNOWLEDGMENTS

The author of a book is a lucky fellow: he has so many collaborators to run interference for him.

Miss Virginia R. Frese, M.A., my former student and valued colleague at the National Institute for Human Relations, not only supervised the typing of the crabbed manuscript; she did all the tedious phonetic transcriptions and helped read the proof.

Mr. James Branch Cabell kindly gave his consent to quote from his illustrious book, *Jurgen* (see page 34). Mr. Frank Sullivan was generous too, as was *The New Yorker,* in permitting me to reproduce "The Cliché Expert" (see page 146).

Victor Fields, Henry Lieferant, Lyman Graybeal, Walter Hanlon, and J. F. MacGrail, fellow writers and staunch comrades in arms these many years, gave me many a pleasant and profitable hour at the wordsmithy.

My wife, Anne Parsons, was a constant source of inspiration and solace throughout the joys of composition. She aided me in the preparation of the Index and in many other ways. Thanks to her selflessness, I was able to spend many week ends on the book—week ends that belonged to her and us.

To all these nonesuch friends, I wish to say, "Thank you, from the bottom of my heart."

CONTENTS

Chapter 1: HERE'S HOW

A QUARTER-MILLION hours is a lot of hours. But at threescore and ten we've spent almost that much time talking or listening to others do the same thing. Man is a word animal. Speech conveys his thoughts. He needs to talk. It gives him confidence. It relieves his tensions. It makes way for good human relations.

Speech is the main arch between people. Over that arch travel thoughts and feelings (and also that odd stepchild of the two—snap judgment). Put a man alone—let him herd sheep, keep a lighthouse, serve a term in a solitary cell—and he soon talks to himself.

Psychiatrists everywhere use "the talking cure." They stretch the patient out on a comfortable couch and listen to him say whatever comes to his mind. After a number of visits he puts even his deepest conflicts into words. When that happens he's well on his way to better health.

Marriages have the best chance of success, Dr. and Mrs. Mowrer of the University of Chicago have discovered, when husband and wife talk out their problems as they arise. They must put their worries, their doubts, into words. They must share them with each other. And the earlier they begin to share them the happier their life partnership will be.

At Yale University's famed School of Alcoholic Studies, chronic alcoholics have confessed that as children they didn't—they couldn't—talk out their fears with sympathetic parents. Their fathers and mothers didn't know how to listen, how to say an encouraging word at the right time, how to bring out confidences.

Psychologists sometimes trace stuttering to early frustration in speech situations. Just think of it, one out of every 100 persons you see stutters. Almost all stuttering begins in early childhood. Therefore, we must conclude that parents, through ignorance or neglect, are responsible for this handicap.

So you see, you can make out a case for good speech as a means to a happy living. It's one of the best safety valves we have. For speech

1

was made to open man to man, not to put any barriers between them.

Good speech helps us to advance. Too few of us squeeze all the vocational possibilities out of our speech. Many of us don't talk well enough to become more valuable employees. "My knowledge of the open hearth helped me, of course," said Charles M. Schwab, "but if I hadn't been able to *persuade* Mr. Carnegie that I'd make a good right arm for him, I never would have landed the job of general superintendent." We're too often satisfied with a "good enough" standard. Like our walking, eating, and sleeping habits, our speech isn't as good as it could be.

When you ask successful men and women to list what helped them to get to the top, they place good speech first. I sent a questionnaire to fifty-five tycoons—presidents and board chairmen of General Motors, Baltimore and Ohio Railroad, American Telephone and Telegraph Company, Standard Oil of New Jersey, American Tobacco Company, Chase National Bank, Bethlehem Steel, etc. I invited them to name the abilities most helpful to junior executives in getting better jobs. Fifty-four of them put good speech first. The one exception—the president of a mail-order firm—put it second to good writing ability.

David Sarnoff, President of Radio Corporation of America, wrote in a representative vein. He stresses the many aspects of good speech the executive needs in the business world:

It has been my observation that one of the most important elements of success in the business world is the ability to speak clearly and forcefully. Words are tools by which we exchange ideas and thoughts, and when they are skillfully used, they can exert a powerful influence on the thoughts and actions of those who hear them.

This is true whether the words are spoken on the telephone, in private conversation, at a business conference, in a public address or broadcast. Clarity and conciseness, pronunciation and poise are attributes of good speaking. These factors show orderly thinking and command attention. Anyone who seeks advancement in business would do well to develop speech as an art. It is a fundamental of success in various fields of human endeavor.

You don't have to be brilliant to talk well. Anyone with common sense can increase the power and influence of his speech. Even those who stutter, lisp, or have weak voices can improve. They can often correct their speech defects entirely.

You can vanquish timidity. You can get rid of platform fright. You can learn to feel at ease when you preside or introduce a speaker. You can talk well standing before a formal group. You can hold your own in conversation. You can improve your interview technique. Of course, you must first want to talk better. Next step—you train yourself to do so.

For there is no magic formula to transform a mumbler into a spellbinder. No simple wave of the magician's wand, no mumbo jumbo, will do it. You learn speech; you don't inherit it. You've got to work to make it better.

The steps to better speech are well known. They have been trod down the ages by the Demostheneses, the Burkes, the Websters, the Roosevelts, the Churchills, and countless other great speakers.

What are these stepping stones to better speech?

1. Check up on your speech habits now and regularly.

An executive in the business world told me he had taken six speech courses in the last twenty-five years to guard against bad speech habits. He wanted to *continue* to grow as a speaker. Even the greatest opera stars coach after they reach the top. Radio announcers, commentators, and actors practice voice and speech drills daily.

We need to analyze our speech habits from time to time. A speech quiz is a good way to begin. Perhaps after you complete the quiz below, you'll want to let a close friend see your answers to check your judgment. Then you may wish to review the quiz once a month or oftener. You can use it as a refresher.

EXERCISE 1: Self-administered Speech Test

DIRECTIONS: *Below are thirty questions you may use for self-appraisal. They cover various aspects of speech. The higher your score, the better. The average for adults is 250.*

	Yes	No	?
1. Do I suspect at times that I talk in an affected manner?	0	15	5

	Yes	No	?
2. Do I talk with a large amount of saliva in my mouth?	0	15	5
3. Do I use outlandish gestures when I talk with others?	0	15	5
4. Have I ever been accused of using words and gestures inappropriate to my age and sex?	0	15	5
5. Do I discuss private affairs so loudly in public that I am heard by those nearby?	0	15	5
6. Do I speak too rapidly?	0	15	5
7. Do I monopolize the conversation?	0	15	5
8. Do I have a correctible speech defect like a lisp or stutter?	0	15	5
9. Do I clutter up my speech with expressions such as, "D'ya get me?" "Yeah, I'm tellin' ya"?	0	15	5
10. Do I talk a great deal without saying anything worth while?	0	15	5
11. During a conversation do I introduce many topics unrelated to the subject under discussion?	0	15	5
12. Do I look directly at the person with whom I'm talking?	15	0	5
13. Do I have the habit of asking others to repeat?	0	15	5
14. Do I have the *er-er* or *and-er* habit?	0	15	5
15. Do I have the habit of interrupting others in the midst of their sentences?	0	15	5
16. Do I talk with food in my mouth?	0	15	5
17. Do I have the habit of arousing people's curiosity about something and not telling them about it?	0	15	5
18. Do I contribute my share to the general conversation?	15	0	5
19. Do I speak with a shrill or hoarse voice?	0	15	5
20. Do I speak in a nasal twang?	0	15	5
21. Do I ever whisper in the presence of others?	0	15	5
22. Do I take as much care to pronounce word endings or sentence endings as I do word beginnings or sentence beginnings?	15	0	5
23. Do I use big words when simple ones will serve as well?	0	15	5
24. Do I speak in a monotonous tone of voice?	0	15	5

	Yes	No	?
25. Do I talk with a tight jaw so that my words are mumbled and difficult to understand?	0	15	5
26. Do I look up the correct pronunciation of words when in doubt?	15	0	5
27. Do I use good grammar without hesitation or doubt?	15	0	5
28. Do others very often ask me to repeat what I have said to them?	0	15	5
29. Do I speak in a dialect very different from that of the educated people of my community?	0	15	5
30. Do I become husky after talking a good deal?	0	15	5

TOTAL

2. Record your voice.

Voice recording is the best way to study your speech. You can record your voice in a department store, music shop, or studio. It doesn't cost much. Some radio sets now come equipped with voice recorders. Since you can't hear yourself as others hear you, you'll find a reliable voice recording invaluable. This is why.

The sound of our own voices isn't carried to us in the same way as other sounds; that is, by sound waves striking our eardrums. It's conveyed by vibrations of our vocal cords. The bones of the skull conduct these vibrations to the middle and inner ear and thence to the brain. There they are interpreted differently from sounds brought to us from without.

That's why, when we first hear recordings of our own voices, we almost invariably exclaim, "But that doesn't sound like me!"

If you want to get a good sample of your speech, you ought to record yourself reading as well as speaking impromptu. Some speech patterns are unlike in the two activities. You can always tell, for example, when a speaker reads a speech or recites it, without ever looking at him. His flow of words is different.

You may wish to read all or some of the following paragraphs as part of your recording. The added questions are merely suggestions for impromptu speaking. You can speak about something else, if you prefer. You may wish to divide your record about equally between reading and speaking.

EXERCISE 2: Voice Recording

DIRECTIONS: *Preface your reading with "This is (your name), making a speech record on (date)."*

THE FIRST TALKING MACHINE

Did you know that laryngitis is a chief cause of absence from work? Testimony to the fact is the numerous colloquial names for laryngitis, such as "lawyer's croaking," "senator's bane," "clergyman's sore throat," "chalk voice." Like senators, school teachers lose more days from their duties because of laryngitis than from any other cause.

To this list of chronic sufferers should be added salesmen and executives and many others whose job requires a great deal of talking. Commonest cause of laryngitis is improper care and use of the voice. Husky, tired voices are often signs of irritated larynx.

The larynx, or Adam's apple, is a valve at the end of the windpipe. It is composed of seven pairs of delicate muscles and membranes and six sets of cartilages and bones. This piece of "apple" that lodged in Adam's throat catches the breath stream, transforming it into minute pulsations of sound, or *vocalization*. Put to a dozen uses—in the sigh, gasp, yawn, cough, sneeze, hiccup, breathing, guarding the windpipe from foreign matter, lifting, etc. —Adam's apple's most recent evolutionary adaptation is to speech and song. Isn't it startling to think that without Adam's apple we would still be savages, because speech and its later developments—writing and reading— could not have evolved. How difficult it would be to carry on civilization without language!

The seat of our voiced sounds is the larynx. A baby at birth produces a wretched, nasalized cry with the aid of Adam's apple. Unless baby passes breath over the vocal cords, housed in the larynx, he is stillborn. That's why they spank him as soon as delivered—to start him crying.

Vocal cords is a misnomer: they're not cords but little shelves of tissue attached to the walls of the larynx. When separated from each other by pulls and stresses of various muscles and bones, they form a V-shaped chink called the *glottis*. When we speak or sing, the glottis assumes many shapes to accommodate pitch changes.

Pitched at about 435 cycles, baby's cry often reaches the screeching zone of 3,072 cycles. Up to two years of age, he generally uses three tones in babbling and learning to speak. By his sixth birthday, they've increased to a full octave.

Male vocal cords at puberty enlarge to about one-third their previous length within a six-month period. The voice falls about an octave in pitch. During this Penrod time, boys usually get *paraphonia pubetica*. This is a skyscraper term for the cracking, breaking, uncontrollable voice of male adolescents. Girls' voices are not affected to such an extent because the female larynx develops less spectacularly.

In song, the late Nellie Melba produced beautiful tones throughout three octaves. Yet you can't tell by any anatomical means the larynx of a prima donna from that of a woman who had the voice of an old crow. The reason is that voices are controlled and differentiated mainly by hearing; to a lesser extent by anatomical differences of the throat, mouth, nasal cavities, etc.

Adam's apple is a secondary sex characteristic in mankind and some of the animals. The bull moose, whose larynx temporarily increases in size during the mating season, *troats,* or bellows, to attract the opposite sex. In bleaker seasons he is virtually voiceless.

The larynx is higher in woman's throat than in man's and also less protuberant. The average adult male has vocal cords 17 millimeters in length, whereas woman's vocal cords are about two-thirds as long. The size of vocal cords determines to a large extent the pitch of the voice. Large, ruggedly built people ordinarily have heavier, longer cords, therefore lower voices.

Chinese show less sex differences in the larynx than any other race. Largest larynxes are found among the stalwart tribes of the Cameroons. Eunuchs have only slightly larger larynxes than women.

Birds, excepting vultures and condors, have a primitive type of larynx called a *syrynx,* which they use with great efficiency. If the human larynx could produce as much sound per millimeter as a canary's syrynx, a man standing on top of the Empire State Building could project his voice above the Times Square midday din without any difficulty—a distance of ten blocks.

The loudest voiced people are the Tartars, with the Germans a close second. Among the softest spoken are the natives of some South Sea islands. Most powerful individual voices perhaps are developed by the Mohammedan muezzins who brace the larynx by grasping the balustrade of the minaret as they deliver the call to prayer. Coney Island barkers usually "set" the larynx also by holding a cane with both hands against the chest. It helps them get better voice projection.

For strenuous laryngeal gymnastics the *yodel* does as well as any. All you have to do is pass rapidly and alternately from normal to falsetto voices on the same pitch over a short interval. Originally an Alpine call, the Swiss developed it into a kind of singing.

According to the behavior psychologists the vocal cords are always in action during silent reading, counting, reasoning, and other kinds of mental activity. Thought, to them, is *subvocal speech*.

Individuals who lose the larynx by surgical operation may be taught to produce voiced sounds by harnessing the *esophageal belch*. Or, they may be provided with an artificial larynx. A St. Louis policeman some years ago lost his larynx in a gun battle with hoodlums. Fitted with a little metal gadget about the size and shape of an underslung tobacco pipe, held in the corner of his mouth, he learned to speak clearly, although in a monotone.

When we grow old Adam's apple becomes ossified and calcified. Beginning at the top around twenty years and working downward, by sixty years on the average the process is completed. During senility, the loss of elasticity and coordination of the vocal cords results in *paraphonia geratica,* which Jaques in *As You Like It* describes, "pipes and whistles in his sound."

QUESTIONS FOR IMPROVISED SPEAKING

1. How would you describe the larynx?
2. What facts about the larynx did you find most interesting?
3. Why is the larynx so important to modern man?

Probably, as you listen to the recording, you'll find that you're not altogether satisfied with the sound of your voice. Perhaps, as you play the record over and over and try to analyze your dissatisfaction, you'll decide that you hit the same tone too often. Your voice may strike you as monotonous, and since you know that the inevitable effect of a monotone upon the listener is boredom, you may make up your mind that this will never do. In fact, the monotone is a sure cure for insomnia. You may discover other dissatisfactions. Why not fill out the following exercise to check these dissatisfactions?

EXERCISE 3: Voice and Speech Questionnaire

DIRECTIONS: *Listen to your recording at least twice before answering the following questions.*

1. Was my voice too high?_____ Too low?_____ About right?_____
2. Did I speak too rapidly?_____ Too slowly?_____ About right?_____
3. Did my voice sound husky?_____ Twangy?_____ Shrill?_____
4. Did my voice sound too loud?_____ Too soft?_____ About right?_____
5. Did my voice sound monotonous?_____
6. Was my pausing too frequent?_____ Too infrequent?_____ About right?_____
7. Which words did I mumble?_____
8. Which words did I find hard to pronounce?_____
9. Was my impromptu speaking forthright?_____ Hesitant?_____ About right?_____
10. Did I convey the meaning of the passage satisfactorily?_____
11. What did I like about my recording?_____
12. What did I dislike about it?_____

3. Get the most out of your practice.

No one can improve your speech except you yourself. Exercises, voice recordings, teachers can all be of great help. They can show you what to do. But the end product, your speech, like so many other things in this life, is in your own hands. To be specific, your self-appointed job is to build better speaking habits. And that brings up the question: how to build a habit? This is how:

a. **Think it clear.** Get in the right frame of mind. You can establish a habit easily enough, once your attitude is right. Believe that better speech will add to your assurance. Realize it will make you a better companion. Remember it can aid you to gain advancement in your job. Let your dreams help you picture yourself as a first-rate speaker. Then act.

b. **Start with a bang.** When you turn to your exercises, be earnest. Get as much out of them as possible. Talk about your speech-improvement program with friends. Listen to good speakers. Read biographies of famous speakers. In other words, get enthusiastic. It gives you momentum.

c. Perfect it. Many of your present speech habits you established in the first two or three years of your life. Since then, you have had a speaking potential of fifteen or sixteen hours a day—a long time in which to establish your habits. Any changes that occurred since the first years took place by unconscious imitation or by design. If the latter, then you already know how necessary practice is. Remember Harry C. McKenzie's famous motto, "When you stop being better, you stop being good." While practice does not necessarily make perfect, it can make permanent. Half the battle for distinction is to be faithful to details. Don't be bored by them.

So, make time for practice. Space your practice periods at regular intervals to get best results. For example, suppose you're going to give one practice hour a day to speech improvement for fifteen or thirty weeks. How can you spend your daily allotment of sixty minutes best?

If you practice twenty minutes in the morning, twenty in the afternoon, and twenty in the evening, you set your new speech habits quicker than if you practice sixty minutes on end each day. *Spaced practice,* the psychologists call it. That's why one practice period of twenty minutes each evening is a better investment than a whole hour or two just on Sunday.

Go through your routine at the same time in the same way each day. Soon it's easy, becomes automatic.

4. Try never to let an exception occur.

Good habits bog down when we fail to practice them at every turn. Each time you interview someone or answer the telephone or reply to a question, you can have a practice period. That is, if you apply what you've practiced.

When you end an interview or telephone conversation, spend a few seconds recalling how you spoke and what you heard. Good speech habits sometimes grow slowly because we forget to apply what we learn throughout the day. Don't let exceptions occur. Each lapse is a step backward. Every right application strengthens your habit.

5. Have patience.

Many new speech habits require fine muscular coordinations. Take the last three sounds in a word like *wrists*. Many people telescope them into one *s* sound. (This cluster of consonants demands some of the finest coordinations we can make.) Most of us can articulate each of these sounds separately. But when we blend them together we drop the *t*. To say all three in quick, clear succession takes a lot of patient practice. Patience is perhaps the chief virtue in learning to speak better. If your patience is long enough, you can learn to speak like an angel.

6. Develop speech consciousness.

Each time you make a mental note of how someone talks, you develop your own speech consciousness. You sharpen your critical sense. You heighten your hearing. Perhaps you'll want to keep ten or a dozen "measuring sticks" in mind as you listen to your friends and relatives speak. Words like *yes, no, with, idea, because, ask, question, running, come, Mary, student, government* do very nicely as measuring sticks. As you listen to the variant pronunciations, your ear will analyze slurrings, drawls, and dialectal variations. You'll hear *ask* pronounced "ahsk" or "awsk" or "ast" and so on. This will help you guard your own pronunciation.

You can also sharpen your critical sense if you listen to radio speakers. Here you can analyze why you like certain voices, dislike others. Notice how fast or how slow the commentators and announcers speak. Compare your own tempo with theirs. What about the pitch of their voices?

You may wish to study your favorite actors' pronunciation. In one recent movie, *Double Indemnity,* I heard *Los Angeles* pronounced in three different ways. In another, I remember the leading man mispronounced *horizon, percolate,* and *coupon.* When you're alert to the way the stars pronounce and mispronounce you add to your critical sense.

If you attend lectures you may wish to listen for errors of grammar or watch for poorly timed gestures. Awareness of these and other speech do's and don'ts will help you to improve.

7. Practice autosuggestion.

If you were to say to yourself many times each day, "I feel terrible—worse than yesterday, much worse," "My abilities are getting weaker and weaker; the longer I work, the more inefficient I become," "My speech is poorer today than yesterday," before long you and your associates would notice an actual decline in your health, abilities, and speech. For the power of self-direction through suggestion is great and lasting. Our common sense, built up through everyday experiences, makes us realize the truth of "I am, therefore I can, therefore I will." Think what *I am* really means. Then ponder over the big implications of *Therefore I can*. Finally, realize that all worthy desires are possible through *Therefore I will*.

Positive autosuggestion works much better than the negative sort. When the president of a large New England mill was a textile salesman, he used to look into the mirror every morning before going to work and say aloud to himself three times, "John Jones, you're the best textile salesman in America." He'd say it with assurance. He meant every word of it. He spoke *best* louder than the other words. He gestured with his right fist.

He believes that his tone of assurance, his gesture, the determination in his face, and the regularity of his practice helped him no end to get to the top. Now some may smile. They believe this is naive. But aren't they the doubters? Don't doubters need just the kind of help they scoff at? Ordinarily they can't help themselves until they change their attitude, until they embrace positive autosuggestion.

Shortly after World War I, Emile Coué came over from France to lecture on autosuggestion. His formula sentence is still popular, "Every day in every way I'm getting better and better." Why not apply this well-tried sentence to your speech improvement program? Why not say to yourself at least once a day, "I'm speaking better today than yesterday because I'm more speech-conscious tnan before"? Why not repeat many times every day, "I'm speaking more distinctly" or "with greater clarity" or "with a better vocabulary"—or whatever aspect of speech you are improving? Practiced with sincerity, this kind of auto-suggestion helps you to talk better.

These seven recommendations will help you to improve your articulation, voice, and pronunciation. You can adapt them to vocabulary building, public speaking, conversation, etc.

In Caesar's day they personified fortune as an old man with a topknot. "Seize him by the forelock," they said, "for he is bald in the rear." Why not consider each strange word, every opportunity to participate in a discussion, as a chance to increase your ability to talk well? Look up that new word. Use it until it becomes an old friend. Ask questions from the floor. Express your ideas publicly. And you and your associates will notice real growth. Your boss may eye you with new interest. For the man or woman who talks well is easier to admire than the one who doesn't.

Chapter 2: WHY NOT TAKE IT SLOW AND EASY?

JAMES TRUSLOW ADAMS tells a story about a friend of his, a famous explorer. He took some savages on a forced march through the Amazon jungle. The first two days they covered a lot of ground. On the third morning the natives wouldn't budge. They just sat on their haunches. They looked solemn as undertakers. "They're waiting; they cannot move farther," the chief explained, "until their souls catch up with their bodies."

This story reminds me of the fellow who clatters along so dizzily he has to ask what he just said. Too many of us spew out words too fast. We're hard to understand. We say things we don't really mean. Psychologists have a name for it, *logorrhea,* or "running off of the mouth." Yes, haste makes waste, in words as well as other things.

Owen D. Young, as Chairman of the Board of General Electric, said, "Mere fluency is one of the most dangerous qualities a young man in the business world can have. It often misleads the gullible and is under the boss's gravest suspicion. Anyone having it should be trained to control it." The big executives won't buy mere "gift of gab." They want what a wonderful old teacher of mine used to call "good speech with substance behind it." The trouble with gift of gab is it's gone with the wind.

Take it slow and easy is a good rule to follow most of the time. Take it slow enough (a) to say what you want to say, (b) to give your listeners time to hear you, (c) to save yourself energy.

Radio networks are always interested in how fast speakers should talk. One American station in 1928 made the first recommendation. One hundred words a minute is ideal, it said, for announcements. The British Broadcasting Corporation recommends 120 words a minute to its staff announcers. Franklin D. Roosevelt and Thomas E. Dewey averaged 109 and 128 words a minute respectively in their 1944 campaign speeches. President Truman's tempo is faster.

Professor Lawton found radio speeches delivered at 120, 124, and 128 words a minute too slow. He prefers 135 to 140 words a minute. Other authorities recommend 165 to 175 words a minute.

Perhaps a guiding principle is worth more than any number of words per minute. What would you say to this definition? *Speak as fast as you please, so long as you speak well.*

This coverall means that you should shift your tempo from time to time. Shift it to keep your audience awake. Shift it to make what you have to say interesting. But don't shift it into high without a purpose.

The coverall also implies common sense in interpreting thoughts and emotions. For example, you'll probably read Plutarch's letter to his wife upon the death of their child in a slower tempo than a description of a prize fight. The emotional tone is different. We express sadness in a slow tempo. Excitement makes us speak fast.

EXERCISE 4: Reading in a Slow Tempo

DIRECTIONS: *Read the following passage in a noticeably slower tempo than the one you normally use.*

Plutarch to his wife, greeting. The messengers you sent to announce our child's death, apparently missed the road to Athens. I was told about my daughter on reaching Tanagra. Let me hope, that you will maintain both me and yourself within the reasonable limits of grief. What our loss really amounts to, I know and estimate for myself. But should I find your distress excessive, my trouble on your account will be greater than on that of our loss. I am not a "stock or stone," as you, my partner, in the care of our numerous children, every one of whom we have ourselves brought up at home, can testify. And this child, a daughter born to your wishes after four sons, and affording me the opportunity of recording your name, I am well aware was a special object of affection.

DIRECTIONS: *Now read the following poem in the same slower-than-usual tempo:*

KING ARTHUR'S FAREWELL

And slowly answer'd Arthur from the barge:
"The old order changeth, yielding place to new,
And God fulfills himself in many ways,
Lest one good custom should corrupt the world.
Comfort thyself; what comfort is in me?
I have lived my life, and that which I have done
May He within Himself make pure! but thou,
If thou shouldst never see my face again,
Pray for my soul. More things are wrought by prayer
Than this world dreams of. Wherefore, let thy voice
Rise like a fountain for me night and day.
For what are men better than sheep or goats
That nourish a blind life within the brain,
If, knowing God, they lift not hands of prayer
Both for themselves and those who call them friend?
For so the whole round earth is every way
Bound by gold chains about the feet of God.
But now farewell. I am going a long way
With these thou seest—if indeed I go—
For all my mind is clouded with a doubt—
To the island-valley of Avilion;
Where falls not hail, or rain, or any snow,
Nor ever wind blows loudly; but it lies
Deep-meadow'd, happy, fair with orchard lawn
And bowery hollows crowned with summer sea,
Where I will heal me of my grievous wound."
              —*Alfred, Lord Tennyson*—"The Passing of Arthur"

EXERCISE 5: Speaking Slower Than Usual

DIRECTIONS: *Now, as you talk aloud to yourself about some simple subject, carry over that same slower-than-usual tempo. For example:*

1. Reminisce about a departed friend.
2. Speak of a nostalgic experience of your childhood.

EXERCISE 6: Reading at a Medium Tempo

DIRECTIONS: *Ask someone to listen as you read in the tempo that you believe is "medium" for you. If your listener can understand every word you say, if you do not lose your breath after a minute or two of speaking, if you can keep the thoughts in mind, if you can read much faster or much slower—you have four useful criteria to measure your medium tempo. If you wish, use Chapter One of this book as practice material.*

EXERCISE 7: Reading at Your Medium Tempo

DIRECTIONS: *Read the following story in your medium tempo in a good, clear voice.*

"I Sleep Well o' Nights"

Once upon a time there was a man who owned a farm. And this farm was much in the man's mind, for it was his hobby and chief delight. He hired an old fellow to look after the place. Now this hired man was tight-lipped as a hermit. He scarcely ever talked.

The man would drive out to his farm every week end regular as sunset, and he would get much satisfaction in looking over his house and barn, his garden and fields, his animals—all of which were his pride and joy. And he would go to great length to ask how his possessions were doing, all the while plaguing the old fellow with endless questions.

But all the old hired man would ever say was, "I sleep well o' nights," and go about his business. This always made the man hot under the collar, and he would mumble to himself, "Why, the fellow isn't even civil!" and then he would drive back to the city, planning to hire someone else.

And then one night there was an awful storm. The wind blew in terror, and you heard the lightning strike all around you; the rain came down in floods. And the man tossed upon his bed the whole night through, fearing great harm must surely come to his farm.

Early next morning he drove out to see the damage, but he feared to glance upon his house and fields because he had seen destruction all along the way. When he looked with all his eyes—praise the Lord, everything was safe! The chimney was not toppled down; the shutters were sturdy on their hinges; the roof was whole.

Then he hurried to the barn. And his heart beat fast within him, for it was not harmed. Even the haystack was in its place, a covering over it with the ends staked down fast as a tent. And the cows and horses grazed contented, blinking at the diamonds in the dew. Not a bit of destruction did he find anywhere on the place.

As the man watched the old fellow feed the chickens and other fowl, a great warmth welled within him, and his spirit was quickened to see for the first time the meaning of "I sleep well o' nights."

"Surely," said the man to himself, "my hired man knows how to deal with man and God, for he keeps faith with his work and himself. I too shall do likewise, for it is a good thing to be able to say, "I sleep well o' nights."

DIRECTIONS: *Now carry over that same medium tempo into your improvised speaking. Try not to speed it up or slow it down. Give most of your attention to tempo rather than thought content.*

EXERCISE 8: Improvised Speaking at Medium Tempo

DIRECTIONS: *Speak at a medium tempo on*

1. My favorite radio program.
2. What I like about the movies.
3. How I schedule my time throughout the week.
4. What I like about my job.

EXERCISE 9: Reading at a Rapid Tempo

DIRECTIONS: *Read aloud in a good clear voice and in a faster-than-normal tempo the stanza from Browning and then the "sports story." Once you hit your stride, don't slow down or accelerate, but maintain your even, rapid tempo to lend the excitement the selections demand.*

HOW THEY BROUGHT THE GOOD NEWS FROM GHENT TO AIX

I sprang to the stirrup, and Joris, and he;
I galloped, Dirk galloped, we galloped all three;

"Good speed," cried the watch, as the gate-bolt undrew;
"Speed!" echoed the wall to us galloping through;
Behind shut the postern, the lights sank to rest,
And into the midnight we galloped abreast.

GREATEST HORSE OF ALL TIME

If it's heart you're talking about, then we'd like to nominate as the greatest horse of all time Moiffa, champion steeplechaser of New Zealand back in 1903. Standing at 17 hands (average is under 16) he was a big, rawboned, ungainly nag with a set of withers huge as a camel's hump. At first glance, you'd think he was an underfed plug that pulled a dray.

Curious thing about Moiffa's jumping was the way he headed for the highest part of the hurdle—instead of the lowest, as other horses always do. He loved jumping for jumping's sake, and he'd try anything you headed him for. The tougher they came, the better he liked it.

Why not enter him in the greatest of all races, England's *Grand National*? So at the end of the 1903 season, Moiffa was put aboard ship, bound for Liverpool. Less than a day out, the ship ran smack into a terrific storm. The sea apparently swallowed its prey—sail, crew, and Moiffa. For nothing was ever heard of the ship again.

And then reports began to trickle into New Zealand about a giant wild horse. Native fishermen said they saw him grazing on one of the uninhabited volcanic islands.

Once his owner got wind of the rumors, he set out for the isle, and— sure enough—there was Moiffa.

Less than a year after his return from the dead, Moiffa was in England. And, as you've probably guessed by now, brought home the bacon. Because it was Moiffa who won the 1904 Grand National. Moiffa, the horse you couldn't down. The nag with a heart as big as all outdoors. The horse that came back.

EXERCISE 10: Speaking at a Rapid Tempo

DIRECTIONS: *Now carry over that rapid rate into your speaking. You may wish to say a few sentences about a number of topics, such as:*

1. The worst accident I ever saw.
2. The time I took part in an exciting contest.
3. A pep talk to a football team.

EXERCISE 11: Speaking at Various Tempos

DIRECTIONS: *Select some subject you know well and discuss it as you shift your tempo from slow to normal to rapid. Alternate slow tempo with rapid tempo until you are satisfied that you can control your tempo at will.*

These exercises help make you tempo-conscious. You may discover that an average tempo of 120 words a minute suits your personality. Or you may be upset by it. As long as you can vary your tempo, you can impress your listeners with slow, medium, and rapid speaking. That gives you added power to persuade and influence them.

Don't forget that the average person's memory of spoken words is short. When you give directions, orders, or explanations, speak slowly enough to help your listener's memory.

If your sense of tempo is stubborn, why not practice with a metronome? Allow one syllable for each beat; set the metronome at various speeds—very slow at first, then very fast—to teach yourself by contrast. Then set it at a medium speed for your ordinary conversation.

You may wish to read passages of poetry as you "beat out the time." Try Tennyson's:

> Break, break, break,
> On thy cold gray stones, O Sea!
> And I would that my tongue could utter
> The thoughts that arise in me.

> Break, break, break,
> At the foot of thy crags, O Sea!
> But the tender grace of a day that is dead
> Will never come back to me.

Once you can control your tempo you may want to get the most out of the pause. Pauses, well distributed, help you in many ways. They give you time to choose the right words. They allow you to renew your breath at the right time. They break up your thoughts into neat little packages that your listener can handle easily. They help you hold attention. They build up your confidence. They allow you to look up from the printed page to "contact" your audience (when you have to read). They help you build suspense.

Walter Winchell broadcasts at a gallop. His speed lends excitement to what he says. Yet he makes himself understood by pausing well. He dramatizes his pauses with buzzes and bells—to separate his short sentences. These are his signals to the audience to get ready for something new.

Pauses badly placed result in *cluttering*. The Germans call it *word-salad speech*. Your words run together in a mad jumble. If you don't pause at the right time, you're hard to understand. You may give others the impression of being unsure of yourself, breathless, and pretty much of a chowderhead.

Here, for example, we cast a sentence in poor pauses: *As I was / driving to / work this morning I / saw an / automobile going / at about forty-five miles / an hour crash / into a telephone pole./*

Now let's put the pauses in the right places: *As I was driving to work / this morning / I saw an automobile / going about forty-five miles an hour / crash into a telephone pole./*

EXERCISE 12: Pausing

DIRECTIONS: *Read aloud the following boners taken from some sophomores' English papers. Observe the pauses:*

1. The Elizabethan audience / was divided into two parts / those that stood around the proscenium / and those that sat on their balconies./
2. The blond poet Milton / wrote "Paradise Lost" / then his wife died / and he wrote "Paradise Regained."/
3. Sir Launcelot / always rode a black war horse / in French / *hors de combat.*/
4. The three unities / of the classic Greek drama / are love / passion / and love./
5. The seventeenth-century poets / were very romantic / because they always road on bridal paths / macadamized roads / not having been invented / at the time./
6. A division of rhetoric / is *elocutio* / where we get *elocution* / used today in Sing-Sing / and other large prisons./

7. Henry VIII / loved Anne Boleyn the best of all his wives / because she had six fingers on each hand./

8. Shakespeare's plays / are the greatest of all / for they are replete / with diction./

9. Queen Elizabeth / delighted to watch her couriers / dance around Morris chairs./

10. Beowulf / was a vampire / played so well recently / by Bela Lugosi./

You can make a sentence mean opposite things, just by a shift in pauses: *The salesman / said the sales manager / is O.K./ The salesman said / the sales manager is O.K./*

EXERCISE 13: Distributing Pauses

DIRECTIONS: *Read aloud the following passage. Pause as indicated and use your normal tempo.*

WHO'S SMARTER, MALE OR FEMALE?

Darwin's theory of evolution / which was erroneously believed to state that man descended from the apes / (Darwin never said it) / created a lot of controversy,/ as we all know./ But few of us remember that Darwin bequeathed an equally "hot potato" / when he said that the males of the species / not only revealed greater extremes in physical characteristics than the females / but extremes in intelligence too./

The inference is / that males have a corner on the market / when it comes to the best in brains./ Neither Darwin nor anyone else has ever proved it./ But out in California / Dr. Lewis M. Terman,/ famous psychologist of Stanford University,/ found 116 boys of genius level of intelligence to every 100 girls of similar capacity / in the elementary schools,/ 212 gifted boys to 100 gifted girls / in the high schools./

More recently from London / comes a report on an investigation on the subject by Dr. J. A. Fraser Roberts,/ Consultant in Medical Statistics in the British Navy / and Director of the Mental Research Department at Bristol./ His findings should either cause the controversy to flare up again / or put it out once and for all./

Basing his conclusions on a careful study of a large population of children / in all walks of British life,/ Dr. Roberts finds that the number of superintelligent males / far exceeds the number of mentally gifted females./

The boys are no smarter individually;/ there are just so many more of them./

Employing carefully constructed intelligence tests,/ given under scientific conditions,/ he found that the performance of the brightest boy in each group of 1,000 boys / was equalled only by one girl in each group of 2,000 girls./ As in Terman's discovery,/ you don't need a statistician to deduce from this / that the number of boy geniuses is twice that of female mental wizards./

Darwin's old observation / is being corroborated again:/ males are more variable than females./ But in that broad area known as the *extent of average performance,*/ there is virtually no difference between the results of boys and girls./ The norms and standards set for both sexes / are the same./ It's at the genius level / where the males outnumber the females./

Yet,/ the females of our species need not be too concerned,/ for there are compensations at the other end of the scale./ The apparent mental superiority of the male / is exactly negated at the other end of the scale,/ because dull boys / are more numerous than dull girls./ Some authorities / find feeble-mindedness 30 per cent oftener among boys than the opposite sex,/ and there are approximately twice as many idiots among males./ What's more,/ institutions for the feeble-minded have many more male inmates./

If you'll practice these exercises over a long enough period and apply slow, moderate, and rapid tempos throughout the day, you'll notice an increase in the holding power of your speech. For listeners pay attention to speech when it is well paced and well paused. Don't we respect deliberate speakers? And all of us can afford to save energy. So, most of the time, take it slow and easy.

A shoe manufacturer complained he was fagged out at the end of a day. "Do you do much interviewing?" I asked.

"That's all I do," he said.

"Why not try speaking slower?"

Next time we met he said, "You know, it's a funny thing. I'm speaking like molasses in January, but I'm interviewing as many people as I ever did. *And* I don't get so tired."

Like many of us, he finds that *Slow and easy* is a good motto to live by. He is sure that the tongue, being in a wet place, is likely to slip when it goes too fast.

Chapter 3: TONGUE TWISTERS HELP

TRAFFIC COPS sometimes use a tongue twister to find out whether a driver is tipsy. They give him a card. On it is: *Sister Susie sews silk socks, seated serenely on the satin sofa.* Did you know the *s* requires the finest coordinations we can make? That's why it's easily disturbed by alcohol. Result: the poor fellow substitutes *sh* for *s* if he is tight.

Americans like tongue twisters. Middle-aged men and women remember them as exercises in Friday-afternoon elocution classes. Many come from childhood games.

Dr. Francis Potter wrote an article in *The Reader's Digest* about tongue twisters as a part of American folklore. Within a year he got more than thirteen thousand examples from readers.

Tongue twisters sharpen your articulation. They discipline lip and tongue movements. They make you concentrate. They develop precise tongue movements. The theory is, if you can control tough sound combinations in a tongue twister, you can do even better when the sounds are normally distributed. You'll find tongue twisters build speech-consciousness. They also make amusing practice drills.

Do your slips of the tongue ever show? Do they take the form of *spoonerisms?* If so, you transpose sounds from one word to another. The Reverend William A. Spooner, Warden of New College, Oxford University, in chapel one day announced the opening hymn as "The Kinquering Congs Their Titles Take." Another time he approached a female worshipper and asked, "Mardon me, padam, aren't you occupewing the wrong pie?"

To which she tartly replied, "I'm sorry, but what a cheautiful burch this is!"

"Ah, yes," he answered proudly, "many thinkle peep so."

Many other spoonerisms are attributed to their namesake.

You may want to make a collection of your favorite spoonerisms.

Why not also jot down phrases that are hard for you to pronounce, like

1. Inimical Lillian
2. Church steeple
3. Missionary Ridge
4. White vinegar
5. Strange strategic statistics
6. Prurient Prue
7. Ululatory wolves
8. Truly rural
9. Preshrunk shirts
10. Luminous liniment

Which of the ten is hardest for you to say? "Prurient Prue" gives me the most trouble.

Then recite them daily until you master them. Begin slowly and step up your tempo gradually. But don't lose your precision.

EXERCISE 14: Tongue Twisters

DIRECTIONS: *The prescription for lazy lips and sluggish tongue is "Recite tough tongue twisters three times in succession on the double quick!" Since the labial, or lip, sounds are the easiest for most of us to bring under control, you may want to try some b's, p's, f's, and wh's first:*

1. A big black bug bit a big black bear, made a big black bear bleed.
2. Big blue beans in a brown blown bladder.
3. Peter Piper picked a peck of pickled peppers.
   A peck of pickled peppers Peter Piper picked.
   If Peter Piper picked a peck of pickled peppers,
   Where's the peck of pickled peppers Peter Piper picked?
4. Bloom, beauteous blossoms, budding bowers beneath!
   Behold, Boreas' bitter blast by brief
   Bright beams becalmed; balmy breezes breathe,
   Banishing blight, bring bliss beyond belief. . . .
   —*Patrick Fells*
5. Betty Botter bought a bit of butter. "But," she said, "this butter's bitter. If I put it in my batter, it will make my batter bitter. But a bit of better butter will make my batter better." So Betty Botter bought a bit of better butter. and it made her batter better.

6. Fanny Finch fried five floundering fish for Francis Fowler's father.
7. I never felt felt feel flat like that felt felt.
8. What whim led "Whitey" White to whittle, whistle, whisper, and whimper near the wharf where a whale might wheel and whirl?

DIRECTIONS: *Then you may want to move on to t's and d's:*

9. Double bubble gum bubbles double.
10. Thomas Tattertoot took taut twine to tie ten twigs to two tall trees.

DIRECTIONS: *Now, how about a combination of tongue and lip sounds?*

11. When a twiner a-twisting will twist him a twist
    For the twining has twist he three twines doth untwist;
    But if one of the twines of the twist do untwist,
    The twine that untwineth, untwisteth the twist.
    —*Dr. Wallis*
12. Slippery sleds slide smoothly down the sluiceway.

DIRECTIONS: *People who lisp (have trouble with* s, z, sh, *etc.) or who are getting used to artificial dentures should practice these:*

13. Moses supposes his toeses are roses,
    But Moses supposes amiss.
    For Moses he knowses his toeses aren't roses
    As Moses supposes his toeses is.
14. A snifter of snuff is enough snuff for a sniff for the snuff sniffer.
15. Amidst the mists and coldest frosts
    With barest wrists and stoutest boasts
    He thrusts his fists against the posts
    And still insists he sees the ghosts.
16. The sixth sheik's sixth sheep's sick.
17. She sells sea shells by the seashore.
18. The sun shines on shop signs.
19. The seething sea ceaseth, and thus the seething sea recedeth.
20. Shy Sally saw six Swiss wrist watches.
21. Sixty-two sick chicks sat on six slim slick slender saplings.
22. Does this shop stock short socks with spots?
23. Sinful Caesar sipped his soda, seized his snoot, and sneezed.

24. Susan Simpson strolled sedately,
Stifling sobs, suppressing sighs,
Seeing Stephen Slocum, stately
She stopped, showing some surprise.

"Say," said Stephen, "sweetest sigher;
Say, shall Stephen spouseless stay?"
Susan, seeming somewhat shyer,
Showed submissiveness straightway.

Summer's season slowly stretches,
Susan Simpson Slocum she—
So she signed some simple sketches—
Soul sought soul successfully.

Six Septembers Susan swelters;
Six sharp seasons snow supplies;
Susan's satin sofa shelters
Six small Slocums side by side.
                                        —Anonymous

DIRECTIONS: *You will want to try the "tongue protruders" too:*

25. A thatcher of Thatchwood went to Thatchet a-thatching;
Did a thatcher of Thatchwood go to Thatchet a-thatching?
If a thatcher of Thatchwood went to Thatchet a-thatching
Where's that thatching the thatcher of Thatchwood has thatched?
                                        —Anonymous

26. Theophilus Thistle, the thistle sifter, sifted a sieve of unsifted thistles. If Theophilus Thistle, the thistle sifter, sifted a sieve of unsifted thistles, where is the sieve of unsifted thistles Theophilus Thistle, the thistle sifter, sifted?

DIRECTIONS: *Then there are the r's for people who lall:*

27. Around the rugged rock the ragged rascal ran.
28. Three gray geese in the green grass grazing; gray were the geese, and green was the grazing.
29. Bring Bruce some brown bread.

DIRECTIONS: *To sharpen the ear for vowel sounds, try:*

30. A skunk stood on a stump. The stump thunk the skunk stunk, but the skunk thunk the stump stunk.
31. The old scold sold the school a coal scuttle.
32. If a woodchuck could chuck wood, how much wood would a woodchuck chuck if a woodchuck could or would? But if a woodchuck could and would chuck wood, no reason why he should, how much wood would a woodchuck chuck if a woodchuck could and would chuck wood?
33. The rain fell on the plain in Spain.

DIRECTIONS: *Finally, try some twisters containing long words with tricky sound combinations, such as:*

34. She stood on the steps inexplicably mimicking his hiccupping and amicably welcoming him in.
35. Are you copperbottoming 'em, my man? No'm, I'm aluminiuming 'em, Ma'am.
36. Good Morning, this is Gamma Gamma Chapter, Kappa Kappa Gamma, Walla Walla, Washington.

—Your Life

Chapter 4: HOW TO MAKE YOUR VOICE SOUND BETTER

PEOPLE WHO get along well with others usually have persuasive voices. You see, the voice is the dial we use to tune in on other personalities. When your voice is clear and well broadcast, you're easy to listen to. The persuasive voice gets the right kind of results. It quiets frayed nerves. It convinces hesitant minds. It uplifts dejected spirits. It turns away anger. It commands respect. It changes negative attitudes. It increases popularity.

Elbert Hubbard used to prescribe a vocal cure-all. He said the way to get a mild, gentle, and sympathetic voice is to be mild, gentle, and sympathetic. A first-rate prescription, because your voice is the sounding board of your emotions. The way you feel creeps into your voice.

When you're angry, your voice becomes harsh. Self-assurance begets tones of confidence. Great excitement makes the pitch go out of bounds. Unlike inanimate sounds, the human voice is never devoid of feeling; it always reflects our moods.

That's why youngsters whose mothers speak gently are lucky. Boys and girls reared in homes where they hear considerate tones behave better than their less fortunate playmates. School principals report that pleasant-voiced teachers have interested classes. Their pupils are happier. They do better work than those who hear harsh voices all day.

Johnny White was a happy little boy until he went to school. The first week he began to stutter because his teacher frightened him with her yelling. He calmed down and spoke smoothly just as soon as he was given a different teacher.

Lord Byron, the great poet, was a famous judge of feminine beauty. He wrote:

> The devil hath not in all his quiver's choice
> An arrow for the heart like a sweet voice.

This is such a plain truth that you wonder why women don't pay more attention to voice cultivation. Why don't we have more lovely feminine voices—voices like Jennifer Jones's, Ingrid Bergman's, Joan Crawford's, Jinx Falkenburg's, Greer Garson's, and Shirley Temple's? We need more girls like Cordelia, whose old father, King Lear, said, "Her voice was ever soft, gentle, and low—an excellent thing in woman!" Because all of us first learn to speak from our mothers, women have to bear the chief responsibility for how we sound.

Many men and women of good will develop raucous, unpleasant voices. One case in point was a salesman, back from the war. He lost some good accounts because of his loud, irritating voice. He took a hearing test. He could hear all the speech sounds but not his own loudness. He shouted at his customers when he didn't mean to. The point is, his heart was in the right place, but his voice belied it. He had lost the vocal flexibility that persuades customers to buy.

Have you ever gone out of your way to listen to a pleasant voice? Perhaps you did so unconsciously. There are two bakeries in our neighborhood. One is two blocks farther away from home than the other. Whenever the cocker spaniel and I are sent out to get a loaf of bread or some doughnuts, we always go to the farther bakery. Not because the bread is fresher or a better bargain. Nor because the doughnuts have more sugar. But because the counter women speak in gracious, interested voices. You feel they want to wait on you. Their voices are easy on all four of our ears. That's why our six legs gladly travel the four extra blocks!

The most intelligent of seventeen supervisors in a Long Island carbon-paper company had more labor trouble than any of the others. When he gave an order, his men thought he was angry. His voice had a gruff, sarcastic ring he didn't mean at all. Once he heard himself on a phonograph record, he was eager to do something about his voice.

Life today is tense. Noisy subways, trains, and auto exhausts, jangling telephones and loud radios—these things and many more create husky, tired voices, particularly in large cities.

Now a good way to develop "the voice with the smile" is to think of the other fellow. If he always asks you to repeat, then perhaps your voice is throaty or mumbled. If you make him wince, perhaps it's too loud. If your spoken words at home or on the job don't carry enough weight, maybe your voice is to blame. For you may be kind, generous—yes, the best man or woman in the world—yet, if your voice doesn't mirror *you,* you are misjudged. And your row gets longer and harder to hoe.

Here is a case history, taken from Dr. E. J. Kempf's famous study, *The Autonomic System and the Personality:*

An agent, whose business makes it necessary for him to look up data in our office, entered the room. He habitually speaks with a most unusually mushy cast of voice, and upon almost every occasion the workers in the room who did not have to respond to his questions showed unmistakable avertive reactions by the manner in which they twisted in their chairs.

After the man left on this occasion a general series of commentaries verified the fact that the mere sound of his voice aroused wishes that he should leave. This unfortunately poised man probably has suffered intense anxiety to know why his presence causes an aversion for him and has probably never been able to understand the difficulty or change it.

His dreary voice was indeed a handicap—on and off the job. And how readily he could have done something about it!

If you believe you're not as voice-happy as you want to be, why not ask yourself a few questions from time to time? They and their frank answers will help you to be *voice-conscious*.

EXERCISE 15: Build Voice-consciousness

Yes   No

_____ _____ 1. Do I pay attention to how I sound as well as to what I say?

_____ _____ 2. Do I talk loudly enough so that someone with normal hearing 20 feet away in a quiet room can hear me easily?

_____ _____ 3. Do I emphasize important words, make them stand out on pleasant tones, frame them in persuasive inflections?

_____ _____ 4. Or do I utter all words pretty much alike, in a monotone or twang?

_____ _____ 5. Does my voice sound "interested," carry sincere feelings of good will when I say, "Good morning," "How are you?" "May I help you?" etc.

_____ _____ 6. Do I sustain my voice to the end of each sentence?

Some people acquire the persuasive voice without knowing it. Others develop it through study and practice. The best way to begin is really to want a persuasive voice, not just because it creates a good impression on others but also because it builds self-confidence. What is the persuasive voice like?

1. It is appropriate to the sex of the speaker.

This is a matter of vocal pitch, which is controlled by the vocal cords. These are heavier and longer in men than women.

2. It is appropriate to the age of the speaker.

Most of us pass through three vocal ages: immaturity, maturity, and senility. A vigorous grownup should speak like one—not like a child or a very old man or woman. Yet many speakers reach twenty-one and older and still talk in a childish treble. Women have to guard against the babyish voice. Sometimes it is the sign of physical retardation. Oftener it's the result of poor voice habits. Actors mimic babyish voices for comic effects. Most of us can't afford to speak like that.

3. It has appropriate resonance.

All the voiced sounds of American speech are mouthed sounds except *m, n,* and *ng* (as in *king*). These three we emit through the nose. When we direct other sounds through the resonators of the nose, our voices sound *nasal*. The opposite, *denasalized* voice you hear when somebody with a bad head cold talks. His nose is all stuffed up. His *m, n, ng* sounds can't get through. When he says words like *ban, pan, bin, cram,* they sound like "bad," "pad," "bid," "crab." Some people speak as if they have a head cold even when they haven't. Notice how good speakers emphasize *m, n, ng.* But they do not nasalize the other consonants or vowels.

4. It has flexibility.

When you speak with feeling you use a wide range. You probably run the *gamut,* or speaking scale, when you're excited. Notice how good radio announcers and actors, lawyers, preachers, and persuasive salesmen vary their voices. That way they make their words mean more. Words by themselves are poor conveyors of thought. When you couch them in a limber voice, your meaning grows.

We ought to send our voices all the way—from about three notes below our natural pitch to three notes above. Our vocal flexibility may not be extensive enough. Many a good speaker uses a wider range than seven notes, particularly when he telephones and broadcasts, because his listeners can't see his facial expressions and gestures.

5. It has good timbre.

Timbre is the thing that makes each voice distinctive. It's the result of your speech organs, the way you think, where you've lived, what you've heard, and so on. Even like twins speak with a different timbre. It's the voice's personality.

6. It is natural.

You can always tab stilted, precious, or "fawncy" vocal affectations. You know they're insincere. That's why we all like a natural voice. It's a sign of attractive personality. Good speech never divorces naturalness.

Audiences know what they like in a speaker. They list naturalness above all other traits. It's easy to identify. You know it when you hear it.

At Harvard University they studied what radio audiences like. Among the results:

a. People are much more sensitive to affectation in the voices of members of their own sex than of the other sex.
b. Women's voices are more frequently judged to be affected than men's.
c. Male voices are found to be more persuasive.
d. Women's voices are preferred for poetry reading.
e. Men's voices are preferred for political talks, newscasting, weather reports, and announcements.
f. More than 80 per cent of the radio audience attributes definite physical and temperamental traits to the speakers on the basis of voice alone.

7. The right quality is used at the right time.

By *vocal quality* we mean the overtones that feelings impart to the voice. We use oftener than any other vocal qualities *normal, orotund, guttural,* and *whisper.*

Normal quality lacks any deep feeling. We use it when we say, "Please pass the butter," "You have been listening to Station XYZ," "The man cut the grass today, John," "Two and two make four," "What time is it, dear?" We say normal quality is good when it's appropriate to the age and sex of the speaker and when it lacks deep feeling.

Orotund quality is composed of full, rich tones usually delivered at a slow rate. Clergymen employ it in reading the holy scriptures. It results from feelings of holiness, awe, or profound respect. To produce the orotund the speaker exercises his resonating chambers to the full. He stresses the vowel sounds particularly. He ordinarily protrudes his lips to form a natural megaphone. The orotund quality can be extremely effective.

When it is used as a substitute for sincere feeling, it leaves the listener with an impression of bombast and pompousness. Many old-style orators, still heard occasionally at political conventions and elsewhere, make matter-of-fact statements in the orotund quality. "Senator" Claghorn of radio fame gets many laughs by doing just that.

Radio commentators emphasize the seriousness of a remark or stress the deep significance of an event with the orotund. Cornelius W. Van Vorhis, narrator of *The March of Time,* sets the tone of grave importance of his script by using the orotund quality consistently.

A good way to increase your appreciation of the various vocal qualities is to read aloud.

EXERCISE 16: Orotund and Normal Qualities

DIRECTIONS: *Study the passage silently—for mood as well as thought—before reading it aloud. Read in emphatic orotund. Don't be afraid to exaggerate in your first attempts.*

FROM "CHILDE HAROLD'S PILGRIMAGE"

> Roll on, thou deep and dark blue Ocean—roll!
> Ten thousand fleets sweep over thee in vain;
> Man marks the earth with ruin—his control
> Stops with the shore,—upon the watery plain
> The wrecks are all thy deed, nor doth remain
> A shadow of man's ravage, save his own.
> When for a moment, like a drop of rain,
> He sinks into the depths with bubbling groan,
> Without a grave, unknelled, uncoffined and unknown.
> —*Byron*

Here, the poet, carried away by the grandeur of the scene, contrasts it with the puniness of man. The thoughts and feelings are phrased in the high manner. If you understand and feel them, your voice must take on the rich qualities that define the orotund.

Now notice how another author presents the same subject:

DIRECTIONS: *Read the italicized words in the orotund; the remainder in a matter-of-fact normal quality:*

FROM "JURGEN"

This is indeed an inspiring spectacle. . . . *How puny seems the race of man, in contrast with this mighty sea, which now spreads before me like,* as so-and-so has very strikingly observed, a something or other under such and such conditions. . . . Really, now I think of it, though, there is no call for me to be suffused with the traditional emotions. It looks like a great deal of water, and like nothing else in particular. And I cannot but consider the water is behaving rather futilely.

—*James Branch Cabell* *

After recognizing the deep emotions that the sea awakens in most people, the author makes a cold analysis of how it affects him, and that calls forth the normal quality. Try reading this last selection in the orotund—the whole thing—and you'll demonstrate the uses and misuses of two vocal qualities.

Guttural quality is the cramped, harsh, rasping sound that results from constriction of the vocal mechanism. We use it when we speak in rage, hatred, and sometimes fear. The guttural ranges from a slight harshness to profound throatiness. All of us can detect irritability by the change in a speaker's voice; it gets hard and tense. Less frequently we see someone attempt to speak in a temper tantrum. His voice literally explodes in grating sounds. We often confuse hoarse, husky voices with the guttural quality. We interpret them as signposts of negative emotions. That's why husky voices should be corrected—to improve human relations.

EXERCISE 17: Guttural Quality

DIRECTIONS: *Read the passage from Nordhoff and Hall's* Mutiny on the Bounty *as if you were the sadist, Captain Bligh, forcing your mutinous crew to eat pumpkins. Don't be afraid to growl every word of it; it will heighten your appreciation of the guttural quality.*

* James Branch Cabell, *Jurgen*, Robert M. McBride & Company, New York, 1919.

Now let me see who will dare to refuse the pumpkins, or anything else I order to be served. You insolent rascals . . . ! I'll make you eat grass before I've done with you!

Whisper quality has no pure tone; otherwise it has all the character-istics of voice and speech. Used for secretive purposes and by actors to simulate illness or great physical weakness, it has little value in public speaking. Platform speakers occasionally—and actors frequently —use an admixture of pure whisper and normal tone in the license known as *stage whisper*.

By learning to reproduce the various vocal qualities through oral reading or recitation, you heighten your appreciation and understand-ing of other voices and gain increased control over your own. You may wish to do a lot of oral reading. Perhaps you enjoy reading plays aloud to yourself or with friends. It can be profitable fun.

Barring physical disturbances to the speech mechanism, a man's best bet in making his voice pleasant and responsive is to understand and "feel" words as he utters them. He should stress beautiful words, words of positive connotation. For beautiful words should be handled like beautiful women—endearingly.

You may want to practice the ten most beautiful words in the English language as designated by the distinguished lexicographer, Dr. Wilfred Funk: *dawn, hush, lullaby, murmuring, tranquil, mist, lumi-nous, chimes, golden, melody*. Such words, because of the musical ar-rangement of their sounds and their rich meanings, are easy to pro-nounce attractively. When you utter them sincerely, thinking of what they really mean, you can make each one different in vocal quality from all the rest.

In contrast, you may wish to pronounce Fannie Hurst's nominations for the most unpleasant words in our language: *conference, inhibition, depression, wisecrack, swell, reaction, complex, hash, movie, lady, spinach, yellow, prune, whimsical, soup*.

Now put them into sentences—first, sentences indicating your ap-proval of the words; then, sentences expressing negative feelings. If you use the right quality, no listener will doubt how you feel about the thoughts and words you express. A sincere speaker is easy to under-stand and interesting to listen to.

Read a sustained passage, "coloring" each important word with the vocal quality that reveals how you feel about it. Make your voice bobble, ricochet, and twirl your words. Make some of them airy as soap bubbles. Let some of them explode. Let others cascade. Crack the whip over some of them. That way they'll break upon your audience's ears with delightful variety.

Use Alec Phare's list to make your voice sound more interesting. He says:

I like fat, buttery words; such as *ooze, turpitude, glutinous, toady*. I like solemn, angular words; such as *strait-laced, cantankerous, pecunious, valedictory*. I like spurious, gold-plated, black-is-white words; such as *gentlefolk, mortician, free lancer, mistress*. I like suave "V" words; such as *Svengali, svelte, bravura, verve*. I like crunchy, brittle, crackly words; such as *splinter, grapple, justle, crusty*. I like sullen, crabbed, scowling words; such as *skulk, glower, scabby, churl*. I like Oh-heavens, my-gracious, land's-sake words; such as *tricksy, tucker, genteel, horrid*. I like pretty-pretty, flowered, *endimanché* words; such as *elegant, halcyon, elysium, artiste*. I like wormy, squirmy, mealy words; such as *crawl, blubber, squeal, drip*. I like sniggly, chuckling words; such as *cowlick, gurgle, bubble*, and *burp*.

EXERCISE 18: Coloring Important Words

DIRECTIONS: *Read the following selections. Give each of the important words a vocal quality befitting its meaning and "feeling"; try for vocal variety.*

TEN GUIDEPOSTS TO POPULARITY

1. *Sincerity* of your smile.
2. *Warmth* of your handclasp.
3. *Neatness* of your appearance and work.
4. *Tolerance* you have of others' opinions.
5. *Gentleness* of your voice.
6. *Readiness* you display to listen.
7. *Importance* you put on keeping your promises.
8. *Kindliness* in your temperament.
9. *Eagerness* to improve yourself.
10. *Interest* you display in the welfare of others.

PRAYER FOUND IN CHESTER CATHEDRAL (1770)

Give me a good digestion, Lord, and also something to digest.
Give me a healthy body, Lord, with sense to keep it at its best.
Give me a healthy mind, good Lord, to keep the good and pure in sight;
Which seeing sin, is not appalled, but finds a way to set it right.
Give me a mind that is not bored; that does not whimper, whine or sigh.
Don't let me worry overmuch about the fussy thing called I.
Give me a sense of humor, Lord. Give me the grace to see a joke.
To get some happiness from life and pass it on to other folk.

Plan to spend many weeks or even years in improving your voice. Reading a few exercises aloud several times isn't enough. For good voice habits grow slowly, almost imperceptibly. Through sustained practice you can actually change tissue, build new coordinations. Remember how intimately the voice is associated with feelings and moods. Practice the exercises in this chapter and others. Pay critical attention to your own voice throughout the day. These three rules can assure you of a more persuasive voice.

Most important of all, use your reconditioned voice in your daily contacts. Is your "Good morning!" really good? Are your "Congratulations!" enthusiastic? Does your "How are you?" sound interested? Once you make a habit of coloring your words with sincere feelings you'll notice a great uptake in your ability to hold attention. You'll make yourself easily understood, for your voice will sound better that way!

Remember, your voice is you. A man walked into the Oneida County Courthouse and bought a package of cigarettes at the cigar counter on the ground floor. He handed the blind proprietor a five-dollar bill. She delivered the purchase and gave him the correct change. Having finished his business an hour later, the stranger returned to ask why she trusted him when he told her it was a five-dollar bill, for no other persons were about.

"A voice tells me all I need to know," replied the blind girl. "The tone of the voice and the way a person handles words—I can tell whether a person can be trusted. It never fails."

Chapter 5: TIME TO TUNE UP
          YOUR INFLECTIONS

THEY ENTERTAINED the great actress, Modjeska, at a soiree. Her host invited her to give a dramatic reading. She agreed, if she could recite something in her native tongue. Oh, that would be delightful, everybody exclaimed.

The audience was deeply touched by her recitation—some of them to tears—except her husband. Soon after she began, he left the room with handkerchief stuffed in mouth.

Someone followed to protest his bad manners. "Oh, I'm sorry," he said, "but I just couldn't help laughing. You see, my wife was pulling your leg. All she did to make you cry was recite the alphabet in Polish!"

A group of White House correspondents held a round-table discussion one evening just before Franklin D. Roosevelt's third election to the presidency. They enumerated his "winning assets." The most popular of all, they agreed, was "the Roosevelt voice." One public-opinion poll estimated one-fourth of all the people who voted for him did so because they liked the way he expressed himself. His voice radiated friendliness, good will, reassurance.

We influence others by how we say things as much as by what we say. The most profound thinker in the world would not influence a large radio audience with a dreary voice. He would be dialed into silence.

Of course, the ideal speaker conveys good sense and good will by his engaging inflections. When you analyze the most pleasant voice you know, you are struck by its constant, lively play over the *gamut,* or speaking scale. It doesn't bump along in a monotone. It responds to the ever-changing patterns of the speaker's thoughts and feelings.

You call these vocal ups and downs *inflection.* They allow you to evaluate words for your listeners. You emphasize important words with the rise and fall of your voice. You suddenly increase your loudness. Or you quickly diminish it. To hold attention, you may start a new thought at a new pitch.

Although your voice can move in only two directions, you can make all sorts of inflectional patterns. To illustrate, suppose you see a friend about to step in quicksand. You yell, "Look out!" (Try it.) Your voice rises to a shriek. Or imagine a little girl is lost in a forest, and you call frantically, "Oooooooooo Bett-yyyyyyyy." You allow your voice to sing out loud and long. Or mimic a station master calling trains above the station's din. Or talk very quietly to a surgeon in a hospital ward.

Drills like these help sharpen the untrained ear for inflectional changes. Our thoughts and feelings demand vocal variety to make them easy to understand. Vocal variety holds your audience. Just think of the many meanings you can give to a simple word like *well*.

Even your pet dog uses inflections. You know when he is angry by the low pitch of his growl; when happy, by the upswings of his yapping; when sick, by his whimpers.

EXERCISE 19: How to Make One Word Mean Many Things

DIRECTIONS: *Read "well" and change your vocal inflections to give the different meanings:*

1. *Well* in the sense of doubt: "*Well,* I don't know about that."
2. *Well* in the sense of exasperation: "*Well,* how do you like that!"
3. *Well* in the sense of happiness: "*Well,* I'm sure glad to see you."
4. *Well* in the sense of anger: "*Well,* this is the way you behave when my back is turned!"

Sarcasm, irony, contempt, as well as the positive emotions, such as cheerfulness and elation, have typical inflections.

Words inflected one way seem sincere. Another inflection gives them the opposite meaning. The French call this vocal double-dealing *double-entendre,* particularly when the second meaning is off color.

EXERCISE 20: Double-entendre

DIRECTIONS: *Say the following examples, first sincerely and then sarcastically. Listen to your inflections.*

Sincerely	*Sarcastically*
1. Some hair-do!	Some hair-do!
2. I'll give you a hand.	I'll give you a hand.
3. She's beautiful.	She's beautiful.
4. Let me lend you ten dollars.	Let me lend you ten dollars.
5. You don't say so!	You don't say so!
6. He's so nice.	He's so nice.
7. That's some hat!	That's some hat!
8. You've sure lost weight.	You've sure lost weight.
9. I'll tell you the truth.	I'll tell you the truth.
10. Her child is the best behaved.	Her child is the best behaved.

You may recall the chief character in Owen Wister's *The Virginian.* He didn't mind being called ugly names so long as a smile went with them. Notice how your voice reflects your smile. If you are really glad to see a friend, he will know it by the way your voice carries your greeting.

A first step toward better inflections is to find your natural pitch. Your voice may be pitched right already. Or it may be too high or, less likely, too low. Why not find out?

EXERCISE 21: How to Find Your Natural Pitch

DIRECTIONS: *Practice each of the following five steps until you master them.*

1. Hum down the musical scale until you reach your lowest comfortable note. (That means you can prolong the low note loud and clear without any vocal quavers.)
2. Now, produce that low tone several times—call it *do.* Drawl it out as long as your breath supply permits.
3. Begin on that *do* and sing up the musical scale four notes: *do, re, mi, fa.* Prolong the fourth note, *fa.*
4. Begin at your low *do* again and sing up the musical scale five notes, *do, re, mi, fa, sol.* Prolong the fifth note, *sol.*

5. Either *fa* or *sol* is your natural pitch. You will have to decide which of the two is more comfortable after you repeat the exercise many times.

DIRECTIONS: *Once you decide, read aloud in a monotone on your natural pitch. Then speak monotonously on your natural pitch. (This is the note your voice should strike oftenest.) Your natural pitch is the runway from which most of your inflections should take off.*

Our main inflections are *upbend, downbend, sweep,* and *slide.* The *upbend* is a slight upward movement of the voice on a syllable. We express some questions, indecision, or an incomplete thought with the upbend. Its sign is ↗

EXERCISE 22: Inflecting the Upbend

DIRECTIONS: *Questions that demand a yes or no for an answer take the upbend on the last syllable. Read these five questions with the upbend:*

1. Did you go to the movies last night ↗
2. Have you seen our latest product ↗
3. May I show you how it fits ↗
4. Won't you sit down ↗
5. Were you there when it happened ↗

DIRECTIONS: *The upbend is often used by good speakers to inflect all members of a series except the last. Read the following examples with the indicated upbends:*

1. The first four presidents of the U.S. were Washington ↗ Adams ↗ Jefferson ↗ and Madison.
2. Johnny ↗ go to the grocery and buy some matches ↗ apples ↗ potatoes ↗ tomatoes ↗ and bread.
3. The chairman prepared the agenda: meeting called to order ↗ reading of the minutes ↗ treasurer's report ↗ old business ↗ and new business.
4. He checked his tool kit to make sure he had a claw hammer ↗ saw ↗ file ↗ screw driver ↗ and nails.
5. The psychologist inquired when the boy first walked ↗ talked ↗ ate by himself ↗ put his coat on ↗ and took care of his toys.

The *downbend* is a slight downward movement of the voice. We use it to express the end of a thought. The sign of the downbend is ⟋

EXERCISE 23: Inflecting the Downbend

DIRECTIONS: *Read the following words aloud, beginning each of them on your natural pitch and ending with the downbend: no* ⟋ *yes* ⟋ *good* ⟋ *bad* ⟋ *four* ⟋ *end* ⟋ *not* ⟋. *Now apply the downbend to the last word in each of the following:*

1. I said no ⟋
2. Three and three make six ⟋
3. Do it now ⟋
4. Go slow ⟋
5. Accent the positive ⟋
6. It'll rain tomorrow ⟋
7. I'm going next Sunday ⟋
8. January is a cold month ⟋
9. The train was on time ⟋
10. The customer is always right ⟋
11. He deserves a break ⟋

Whenever you use the upbend to end a declarative sentence, you confuse your listeners. You mislead them into expecting something more. Some old-fashioned orators end all their declarative sentences on the upbend. They think their speech is impressive that way. At a recent political convention a senator said something like this: "He is a man of the people ⟋ He came up the hard way ⟋ He will make a great leader for our glorious party ⟋ ." Each of these sentences is a complete statement. Therefore, each should end on the downbend. This is one of the few speech rules you shouldn't break—ever.

DIRECTIONS: *Questions that demand an extended answer we usually ask with a downbend on the last syllable. Read aloud the following examples:*

1. How is it that you came alone ⟋
2. How can you explain your competitor's better price ⟋
3. What road should I take to get there quickly ⟋
4. Will you be kind enough to explain the difference ⟋
5. Where will the boys meet us ⟋

EXERCISE 24: Inflecting the Voice with Upbends and Downbends

DIRECTIONS: *Read the following words aloud three times. First, end all of them with the upbend. Then, end all of them with the downbend. On the third reading, end alternate words with upbend and downbend. Notice how they add flexibility to your voice.*

spring	summer	exercise	machinery
fall	winter	manual	questionable
bank	mother	artichoke	tranquillity
host	villain	pasturage	personable
guest	jonquil	casual	treasonable
ill	viper	heavenly	responsible

DIRECTIONS: *You can indicate the kind of reply you expect by the way you inflect the question. Read the following examples aloud with the indicated upbends and downbends. (The first of each pair demands yes or no for an answer; the second, a longer answer.)*

1. Are you going to Spain ↗ or France ↗
   Are you going to Spain ↗ or France ↙
2. Will you have some oranges ↗ or lemons ↗
   Will you have some oranges ↗ or lemons ↙
3. Do you intend to buy a Buick ↗ or Studebaker ↗
   Do you intend to buy a Buick ↗ or Studebaker ↙
4. Is there a radio ↗ or television set ↗
   Is there a radio ↗ or television set ↙
5. Does the horse walk ↗ trot ↗ canter ↗ or rack ↗
   Does the horse walk ↗ trot ↗ canter ↗ or rack ↙

EXERCISE 25: Applying Upbends and Downbends to Sustained Reading

DIRECTIONS: *Read the following passage with the indicated inflections. (There are other ways of inflecting this passage, but the idea of the exercise is to move your voice in the directions shown.)*

There was an Indiana farmer ↗ whose corn won the blue ribbon at the State Fair ↗ year after year ↙ One day ↗ an enterprising reporter made an interesting discovery ↗ while interviewing the farmer ↙ He found ↗ that the farmer shared his seed corn with his neighbors ↙ "How can you afford to share your best seed corn with your neighbors ↗ when they are entering corn in competition with yours each year" ↗ the reporter asked ↙

"Why sir" ↗ said the farmer ↙ "don't you know ↗ The wind picks up pollen from the ripening corn and swirls it from field to field ↙ If my neighbors grow inferior corn ↗ cross-pollination will steadily degrade the quality of my corn ↙ If I am to grow good corn ↗ I must help my neighbors grow good corn" ↙

The *sweep* is more complex. It's composed of a slight upward and downward movement of the voice during continuous phonation. It's accompanied by increased loudness. It may occur on one word, as in the stressed syllable of *delighted,* or be distributed over a phrase. For example, let's assume you announce a prize fight. You exaggerate the two most important words with vocal sweeps:

The *greatest,* heavyweight of *all* time.

A sweep is distributed throughout a group of words like this:

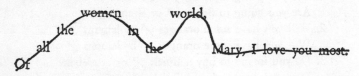

EXERCISE 26: Inflecting the Voice with Sweeps

DIRECTIONS: *Read aloud the following sentences. Let the sweeps come on the italicized words.*

1. All the theories in the *world* bring home no bacon unless they are put into *practice*—and nothing illustrates the power of continued effort so *well* as the fact that a *dime* doubled twenty times is *$104,857.60.*
2. That company expects to do a *million* dollars' worth of business next year.
3. Your failures won't harm you until you begin *blaming* them on the other fellow.
4. "I'd give almost *anything* if these salesmen would eliminate the flattery. That doesn't get 'em *anywhere;* it only makes me *mad."*
5. The ability to speak several languages is an asset, but to hold your *tongue* in one language is priceless.

—*Bill Field*

Sweeps are also used to indicate contrasts and comparisons.

1. A *long* life may not be *good* enough, but a *good* life is *long* enough.
   —*Benjamin Franklin*

2. When you *point* a finger at *someone* else, you point *three* at *yourself.*
   —*Advertiser's Digest*

3. Whenever a farmer sells you a basket of apples, his *reputation* is on the top of the basket; *later* you will discover his *character* somewhere near the bottom.
   —*David T. Armstrong*

4. *Talent* is *power, tact* is *skill; talent* is *weight, tact* is *momentum; talent* knows *what* to do, *tact* knows *how* to do it; *talent* makes a man *respectable, tact* will make him *respected; talent* is *wealth, tact* is ready *money.*
   —*W. P. Sargill*

5. Cannibals say that *woman's* flesh when cooked yields a *bitter* taste, while *man's* flesh in contrast is *sweet* as a capon's breast.
   —*Donald A. Laird*

6. As *woman's* education has become *broader,* her *figure* has grown *narrower.*
   —*Ernest Hooton*

7. In Ancient *Egypt* "wife" meant "the one who clothes her husband," but in *Sparta* wives were the sole property owners.

8. *Gain* all you can. *Save* all you can. *Give* all you can.
   —*John Wesley*

9. A pessimist feels *bad* when he feels *good* for fear he'll feel *worse* when he feels *better.*
   —*Cleveland Plain Dealer*

Less intensive but more regular stress occurs in rhythmic poems and jingles, as in the limericks:

> I'd rather have fingers than *toes;*
> I'd rather have ears than a *nose;*
> And as for my *hair*
> I'm glad it's all *there,*
> I'll be awfully sad when it *goes.*
> —*Gellet Burgess*

> There was a young lady of *Lynn,*
> Who was deep in original *sin;*
> When they said, "Do be *good,*"
> She said, "Would if I *could,*"
> And straightway went at it *agin.*
> —*Anonymous*

A *climactic sweep* is a series of stressed words, each one more intensely emphasized than the last. You use it quite naturally when excited, as in the expression, "We will never surrender—never, *never,* NEVER!"

The radio announcer uses the climactic sweep to awaken suspense. He may say, "And now, ladies and gentlemen, the Mars Oil Company invites you to participate in its nationwide contest. There are hundreds of prizes which you can win. The first prize is more than *one thousand dollars*—yes, more than *two thousand dollars*—it's *five thousand* good American dollars!"

With the *vanishing sweep* you diminish each successive member of the series. When you wish to simulate sound dying out, or express pity, sorrow, and the like, you may find it very useful. In Tennyson's song, for example, the last three words of each stanza indicate vanishing sweep:

> The splendour falls on castle walls
>   And snowy summits old in story;
> The long light shakes across the lakes,
>   And the wild cataract leaps in glory.
> Blow, bugles, blow, set the wild echoes flying,
> Blow, bugle, answer, echoes, DYING, *dying,* dying.

The *slide* is a sustained movement of the voice up or down the gamut. On the uptake it expresses excitement; on the downgrade, depression.

```
                              advance?
                   the                  He
                 stop                     has
             can                             ruined
         you                                      my
      sure                                          life's
    you                                                work.
Are
```

Seasoned speakers use still another inflection, the *pitch shift*. This is a kind of vocal paragraphing. You raise or lower the level of your voice as you take up another division of your speech. Broadcasters often use a check (√) sign to remind them to shift their pitch at least a full note at a certain point. It helps to prevent pitch strain and hold attention. Lowell Thomas and Gabriel Heatter use the pitch shift well. Why not do likewise?

EXERCISE 27: Varieties of Inflection

DIRECTIONS: *Read the following passage and apply the various inflections. Only the sign of the pitch shift is indicated. (You may wish to pencil in the others.)*

THERE IS A RIGHT AND A WRONG WAY TO GRUMBLE

People who get along well with others know the value of grumbling— when and how to do it. It helps relieve the grumbler of tension, even though it causes tension in others at times. It is much better to grumble than to hold a gnawing, silent grudge. "To get it off the chest" is one of the old stand-bys in good human relations. In short, grumbling is a natural thing to do—like being born or breathing or getting the stomach ache. Unless we grumble at least once in a long while, we are suspected of being hypocritical. So, since we must grumble, let's learn to do it right by recalling the rules.

√ The first rule is *Make sure you don't grumble too often.* Novelty is a mighty attractive force in human relations, and the person who grumbles about every little thing is never taken very seriously. His associates soon learn to discount his grumbling. They say, "Oh, don't mind him, he's always grumbling about something or other." Or, "That's just his personality, he doesn't mean it." (If a woman grumbles, they say, "That's how she got her crow's feet." Or, "She's never satisfied. You simply can't please her. Don't let her get you down.") And so the habitual grumbler seldom carries much weight. His is an unhappy existence because he isn't respected.

√ Our second rule goes something like this: *Grumble only when there's something worth grumbling about.* Things have a way of going wrong from time to time, and if we aren't feeling very cheerful, we try to set them aright by grumbling. A workman grumbles because someone "borrows" his tools without asking permission. A truck driver grumbles because of the old truck he must drive. The boss grumbles when his secretary leaves him in the lurch by running away to get married without telling him. How do we know whether something is worth grumbling about?

Two questions give the answer: Does it really matter in the long run? Does it affect other people as well as myself?

√ The third rule is: *Grumble where it will do the most good*. A salesman's wife said not long ago that her husband was always grumbling at home about the reports he had to fill out for his sales manager. Yet she wasn't responsible for the reports, neither could she do anything about them. The man never once grumbled at a meeting of the sales force or complained to the sales manager himself.

There is a reason for most of the things we have to do. If we don't understand why we must do them, we ought to find out. Then if they still seem unreasonable, a good old-fashioned grumble is in order *before the person responsible*—be it husband, wife, foreman, teacher, or big boss. If we aren't brave enough for this, then we should keep our grumbles to ourselves.

√ One of the happiest companies I know has an unwritten law that everybody there learns: *Whenever you have something to grumble about, tell it directly to the person whom you believe to be responsible and ask him if he can't do something about it*. The result is there is little grumbling, no grumbling at all "behind backs," and whatever grumbling there is is wonderfully effective. That is what I call *constructive grumbling*. And that's the only kind men and women of good will tolerate. Because it's the right kind of grumbling, let's call it an American art.

Practice the exercises in this chapter until you make your voice a ready servant to your spoken words. Listen for inflections in the voices you admire most. These two things help you get the kind of inflections you want.

Chapter 6: MAKE YOUR ARTICULATION CLICK

Someone asked a three year old if she knew how to make toast. "Oh, yeth," she said. "Firth you thlithe the bread. Then you put it in the toathter. Then you watch it till it thmoketh. Then you take it to the think and thkwape it."

It's rather easy to forgive poor articulation in a youngster. In fact sometimes, as in this case, it's amusing. But in a grown man or woman it gets you down.

Good speech is a chain of many links. Some of these are articulation, voice, pronunciation, gestures, vocabulary, grammar. Just as a metal chain is no stronger than its weakest link, so speech cannot be good so long as articulation (or any of its other links) is faulty.

We are easy to understand when we articulate clearly. *Articulate*— in Latin—means "to join, or divide into joints." Sounds are the joints of words.

To articulate consonants we bring the lips, teeth, tongue, palate, etc., in contact with each other. All of us are familiar with these so-called *speech organs,* with the possible exception of the *hard* and *soft palates.*

If we press the tip of the tongue against the roof of the mouth, directly behind the teeth, and slowly draw back the tongue, we feel rough cartilage. This rough cartilage is the hard palate. If we retract the tongue farther, the hard cartilage gives way to smooth, pliable membrane. This is the soft palate. It ends in a small wedge-shaped pendulum, the *uvula.* We don't use the uvula to articulate English consonants.

Now, take a hand mirror and open your mouth wide under a good light. (Keep the tongue flat on the floor of the mouth.) Notice the differences between the texture of the hard and soft palates. Better still, feel them with the tip of your index finger. Say *ah* while looking at the soft palate and notice that it retracts to a high position. You need an elastic soft palate to articulate good *k*'s, *g*'s, *ng*'s. It must remain high for clear vowels, too. A lazy or drooping soft palate causes nasality.

You may also want to test your other "articulators."

EXERCISE 28: Lip Test

DIRECTIONS: *Pucker the lips as if to whistle. Then smile broadly with the jaws closed. Use the mirror to see whether you can alternately pucker and smile. If the lips feel taut, strained, or fatigued after three or four continuous repetitions, you may be "lip lazy" and need to practice this and similar exercises over a period of weeks. This strengthens your lip muscles.*

EXERCISE 29: Jaw Test

DIRECTIONS: *Insert two fingers, one on top of the other, between the front teeth. If you feel a strain in the cheek muscles, you may be "jaw bound." That means you talk with a tight jaw, much as a man does while holding a pipe between his teeth. If the strain is uncomfortable when you apply this test, practice it often throughout the day. Use more jaw movement when speaking, even if you have to exaggerate at first. Good speakers can't afford to be "jaw lazy."*

EXERCISE 30: Tongue Test

DIRECTIONS: *Open the jaws to a two-finger width (as described above) and raise the tongue so that the tip touches the center of the upper lip. Slowly move the tongue so that the tip touches the left corner of the opened mouth. Then slowly move the tongue until the tip touches the right corner of the mouth. Don't allow the underside of the tongue to touch the lower lip or teeth.*

We need a free tongue to raise against the hard and soft palates in articulating at least twelve consonants.

EXERCISE 31: Bite Test

DIRECTIONS: *Open the mouth wide. Bring the jaws together slowly, so that the back teeth, or molars, meet. If your upper front teeth now slightly overlap the lower incisors your bite is called "normal."*

Some kinds of lisping are caused by underbiting, gross overbiting, or biting unevenly. If the upper and lower front teeth do not meet and space can be seen between them, the bite is called *open*. The dentist can often correct these *malocclusions,* as he calls them.

EXERCISE 32: Nasal-passage Test

DIRECTIONS: *Hold the left nostril closed. Breathe vigorously in and out through the right nostril. Then hold the right nostril closed and breathe in and out through the left. Are both nostrils about equally free for breath passage?*

We need clear nasal passages for standard resonance of the nasal consonants *m, n,* and *ng* (as in *king*).

General American speech is composed of about forty sounds. Twenty-three of these are consonants. Some consonants are *stopped,* others *continuant.* A stopped sound is one that you cannot prolong. We have six stopped sounds in American speech: *p, b, t, d, k, g* (as in *go*). All the other sounds are continuant; that is, you can prolong them at will.

We need to remember also that some sounds are voiced, others voiceless. The voiceless, or whispered, consonants are *f, h, k, p, s, sh, t, th* (as in *thin*). The voiced sounds are *b, d, g* (as in *go*), *l, m, n, ng* (as in *sing*), *r, th* (as in *thou*), *v, w, y* (as in *young*), *z, zh* (as in *pleasure*).

Cognates are pairs of consonants, articulated alike except for the action of the vocal cords: one of each pair is voiceless; the other, voiced. The cognate consonants are *p-b, t-d, k-g, s-z, sh-zh, f-v, th*(as in *thin*)-*th*(as in *thou*), *ch*(as in *church*)-*j*(as in *judge*).

As you articulate the cognate pairs, pinch your Adam's apple with your thumb and forefinger or tightly cover your ears with your palms. "Feel" the difference between the voiced and voiceless consonants. Some speakers substitute voiceless consonants for their voiced equivalents. Have you ever heard someone say, "I was ma*t* at him" for "I was ma*d* at him"?

Now let's run through the articulation of all the consonant sounds:

EXERCISE 33: Consonants Made with Both Lips: b, p, m, w

DIRECTIONS: *Do the following exercises. Listen to the sounds you make and watch yourself in the mirror as you make them.*

1. Bring both lips together and suddenly release them with voice to pro-
   duce *b*.
   Say: *b*ee, *b*igh, *b*oh, *b*ay
   Say: *b*een, stu*bb*le, *b*i*b*
2. Bring both lips together and suddenly release them with a puff of breath
   to produce *p*.
   Say: *p*oo, *p*igh, *p*ay, *p*oh
   Say: *p*an, shi*pp*er, *p*o*p*
3. Bring both lips together as you hum to produce *m*. Notice that as you
   increase the loudness of the hum you feel the resonance in your nose.
   Notice also that *m* stops as soon as you pinch the nostrils.
   Say: *m*ay, *m*ee, *m*igh, *m*oh, *m*oo
   Say: *m*an, diaphrag*m*, du*m*b, co*m*mentary, hy*mn*
4. Pucker the lips as if to whistle; then blow breath lightly through them
   as they relax, producing *w*.
   Say: *w*ay, *w*ee, *w*igh, *w*oh, *w*oo
   Say: *w*ail, q*u*iet, a*w*ay

EXERCISE 34: Consonants Made with Lower Lip against Upper Teeth: f, v

DIRECTIONS: *Practice each step. Look at it and listen to it.*

1. Bite the lower lip as lightly as possible to allow the breath to escape
   easily as you articulate *f*.
   Say: *f*ay, *f*ee, *f*igh, *f*oh, *f*oo
   Say: *f*ame, *ph*ilosophy, lau*gh*, di*ff*erent, *f*i*f*e
2. Bite the lower lip as lightly as possible to allow vocalization to escape
   easily as you articulate *v*.
   Say: *v*ay, *v*ee, *v*igh, *v*oh, *v*oo
   Say: *v*ale, sa*vv*y, sa*v*e, o*f*, *v*al*v*e

EXERCISE 35: Consonants Made with the Tongue Extended: th (as in thin), th (as in thou)

DIRECTIONS: *Now try these:*

1. Protrude the tip of the tongue slightly between the front teeth and allow
   breath to escape to produce *th* (as in *thin*).
   Say: *th*ay, *th*igh, *th*oh, *th*oo, *th*ill
   Say: *th*ing, brea*th*, my*th*ology, mou*th*

2. Protrude the tip of the tongue slightly between the front teeth and allow vocalization to escape to produce *th* (as in *thou*).
Say: *th*y, *th*ou, *th*o, *th*ere
Say: *th*is, mo*th*er, fa*th*er, brea*th*e

EXERCISE 36: Consonants Made with the Tongue Tip against or Close to the Hard Palate: t, d, n, l, r.

DIRECTIONS: *And these:*

1. Elevate the tongue so the tip touches the hard palate directly above the front teeth. Then release it suddenly with breath to articulate *t*.
Say: *t*ay, *t*ee, *t*igh, *t*oh, *t*oo
Say: *t*ame, walk*ed*, *T*homas, *t*a*t*ter, *t*igh*t*
2. Elevate the tongue so the tip touches the hard palate directly above the front teeth. Then release the tongue suddenly with vocalization to articulate *d*.
Say: *d*ay, *d*ee, *d*igh, *d*oh, *d*oo
Say: *d*o, la*dd*er, ha*d*, *d*a*d*
3. Elevate the tongue and flatten the tip on the hard palate above the front teeth. Then allow vocalization to escape through the nose to produce *n*. Notice that you can't prolong *n* with the nostrils clamped.
Say: *n*ay, *n*ee, *n*igh, *n*oh, *n*oo
Say: *n*o, g*n*u, p*n*eumatic, m*n*emonic, a*nn*ounce, bo*n*e
4. Elevate the tongue, flattening the tip on the hard palate above the front teeth. Then allow vocalization to escape out through the mouth to articulate *l*.
Say: *l*ay, *l*ee, *l*igh, *l*oh, *l*oo
Say: *l*ook, swa*ll*ow, bi*ll*, mi*lli*on, *Lilli*an
5. Raise the *entire* tongue surface as close as possible to the roof of the mouth without touching it. The entire upper surface of the tongue thus closely approximates the roof of the mouth.
Say: *r*ay, *r*ee, *r*igh, *r*oh, *r*oo
Say: *r*ipe, *rh*ubarb, w*r*ote, a*r*ound

EXERCISE 37: Sibilant Consonants Made with the Tongue Grooved to the Hard Palate

DIRECTIONS: *Articulate, look, and listen.*

1. To articulate *s*, raise the grooved tongue and arch it toward the hard

palate, forming a narrow fissure. Force the breath through it with
the teeth together or almost together. As you do this, notice that the
lips are slightly separated and retracted. There is no vocalization.

Say: *say, see, sigh, sew, Sue*

Say: *solemn, psychological, miss, scientific, hasten, certain*

2. Follow the same directions for articulating *z* and add vocalization.

   Say: *zay, zee, zigh, zoh, zoo*

   Say: *zealot, dissolve, his, because, xylophone, gizzard, czar, fuzz, prize, solves, lose, easy, discern*

3. To articulate *sh*, raise the tongue to the hard palate, forming a broader groove in the tongue than for *s* or *z*, and force breath through the groove without any vocalization. Protrude the lips to form a cavity between the lips and teeth and keep the front teeth almost touching.

   Say: *she, shy, show, shoe*

   Say: *sugar, precious, auction, pension, show, ocean, machinery, luscious, surely, session*

4. To articulate *zh*, follow the directions for articulating *sh* and add vocalization.

   Say: *zhay, zhee, zhigh, zhoh, zhoo*

   Say: *azure, brazier, ménage, vision, treasure, negligee, garage*

5. To articulate *ch*, combine *t* and *sh*.

   Say: *chay, chee, chigh, chow, choo*

   Say: *child, nature, match, question, righteous*

6. To articulate *g* as in *George* or *j* as in *joy*, combine *d* and *zh*.

   Say: *jay, jee, jigh, joh, joo*

   Say: *judge, adjourn, soldier, wage, gem*

EXERCISE 38: Aspirate h

DIRECTIONS: *Expire through the opened mouth without any vocalization.*

Say: *hay, hee, high, ho, hoo*

Say: *how, who*

(*H* is prefixed to *w* to form the glide consonant, as in *what, where, why, when.*)

EXERCISE 39: Consonants Made with the Tongue Raised to the Soft Palate: k, g, ng (as in ring)

DIRECTIONS: *Follow these through as before.*

1. Raise the back of the tongue to the soft palate and sharply release breath to produce *k*.

    Say: *k*ay, *k*ee, *k*igh, *k*oh, *k*oo

    Say: *k*ill, *c*urtain, ac*c*use, *ch*iropody, sti*ck*, *q*uietus, lac*q*uer, pi*q*ue, ca*k*e

2. Raise the back of the tongue to the soft palate and sharply release vocal-ization to produce *g* (as in *go*, not as in *George*).

    Say: *g*ay, *g*ee, *g*igh, *g*o, *g*oo

    Say: *g*ale, *gh*ost, rig*g*er, *g*uilt, ro*g*ue, ga*g*

3. Raise the back of the tongue to the soft palate and direct the voice through the nostrils to produce *ng* (as in *king*).

    Say: da*ng*, do*ng*, dee*ng*, di*ng*, de*ng*

    Say: si*ng*, si*ng*er, blan*k*et, si*ng*i*ng*

To enunciate vowels we vary the shape of the mouth. We move the tongue, cheeks, jaw, soft palate—as we produce voice. We provide each vowel with its characteristic resonance-cavity. Since the tongue is the chief agent in molding the vowel chambers, we can classify all the vowels in terms of their tongue positions: front vowels, middle vowels, back vowels.

The five front vowels appear in words like *a*t, *e*nd, *a*te, *i*t, *ee*l. Now enunciate these vowels slowly in the order given, one after the other, as you look into a mirror. Notice that the highest part of the arch of the tongue climbs upward and forward toward the hard palate. Notice how the jaw gradually closes and makes the mouth progressively smaller as the lips retract. Notice also that the tongue tip usually stays behind the lower front teeth and that the soft palate is raised.

There are three middle vowels: the *unaccented,* or *indeterminate,* vowel, as in "lem*o*n," "stud*e*nt," "frig*i*d," etc.; the *closely related* vowel, as in "*u*p"; and the "*r*-vowel," as in "f*u*r," "f*i*r," "h*e*rb," etc. As you say these vowels, notice that the tongue lies rather relaxed on the bottom of the mouth. It is lowered somewhat for *u* as in *up;* raised a bit for sound as in *herb.* Your lips and teeth are close together. You make the mouth opening small. You raise the soft palate.

The five back vowels occur in words like "*a*lms," "*a*we," "*o*ld," "f*u*ll," "f*oo*d." As you utter them in the given order, notice that the tongue arch moves progressively upward toward the soft palate, accompanied by a corresponding closing of the mouth. As the mouth closes you round the lips and increasingly protrude them for each successive vowel. The tongue tip lies on the bottom of the mouth behind the front teeth. As in the production of the other vowels, you raise the soft palate. When it droops, the voice takes on a nasal quality.

Since vowels are the most richly vocalized of all the speech sounds, they carry your voice quality. The eminent voice authority, Dr. Victor A. Fields, author of *Training the Singing Voice,* says, "Your voice is as rich as your vowel."

A single front vowel, as in "*a*te," or a single back vowel, as in "*oa*t," is usually uttered as a diphthong by most Americans, except in the case of some unaccented syllables. A diphthong is composed of two vowels quickly blended, the first of which is louder. Notice when you pronounce *ate* how the tongue shifts upward during enunciation of the vowel; similarly with *oat.*

EXERCISE 40: The Vowels

DIRECTIONS: *Read the words and sentences illustrating the vowels in italics slowly and often. Listen carefully to the sounds as you watch yourself produce them in a mirror. (Notice the various ways in which the vowels are spelled.)*

FRONT VOWELS

Say: *a*t, *a*sk, *a*dd, *A*l, *a*fter, *a*nd, *a*nswer, *a*pt, b*a*d, m*a*d, s*a*d, h*a*d, ch*a*t, f*a*t, l*au*gh, pl*ai*d

*A*l *a*sked S*a*m to *a*nswer the *a*d.

*e*nd, *e*lse, *e*ll, *e*lf, *e*dge, *e*tch, *E*m, *e*bb, b*e*nd, sp*e*ll, s*ai*d, h*ei*fer, fr*ie*nd, l*eo*pard, s*ay*s

*E*llen's g*ue*st went to b*e*d in a t*e*nt.

*a*te, *a*che, *ai*m, *a*le, *ai*d, *A*be, *a*ce, *a*pe, f*ai*l, rel*ay,* g*au*ge, gr*ea*t, th*ey,* h*ei*nous, p*a*ne

J*a*ke's *a*ches and p*ai*ns m*a*de him qu*a*ke.

*i*ll, *i*n, *i*lk, *i*mp, *i*tch, *i*nk, *i*s, *i*d, s*ie*ve, w*o*men, b*u*sy, b*ui*ld, h*y*mn, pr*e*tty, b*ee*n

*I*n *I*pswich l*i*ves a v*i*llainous gr*i*st m*i*ller.

*ee*l, *ea*t, *ea*ch, *E*ve, *e*ke, *ea*st, *ea*se, f*ee*t, rec*ei*ve, bel*ie*ve, p*e*ople, mach*i*ne, k*ey*, qu*ay*

Ph*oe*be bel*ie*ved the Portugu*e*se frequented a sp*ea*k-*ea*sy.

Middle Vowels

DIRECTIONS: *Remember, the indeterminate vowel is never accented.*

Say: lem*o*n, stud*e*nt, mas*o*n, natur*a*l, frig*i*d, *a*bout, tak*e*n, ploughm*a*n
Jas*o*n, th*e* mas*o*n, quarr*e*led with Hel*e*n's gard*e*n*e*r.

*u*p, h*u*t, h*u*ll, m*u*m, *u*gh, *u*nder, *u*ncle, *u*s, n*u*t, m*u*mps, fl*oo*d, d*oe*s, t*ou*ch
The gr*u*mpy *u*mpire c*u*ffed the f*u*nster.

*u*rn, *i*rk, *e*rr, *ea*rnest, *e*rstwhile, *u*rchin, h*e*rb, *I*rma, c*u*rdle, m*u*rmur, l*u*rch
*E*rnest and *I*rma h*ea*rd the b*i*rd ch*i*rp in the b*i*rch.

Back Vowels

Say: *a*lms, *a*mah, *a*rt, *A*rchie, *a*rmy, *a*rctic, *a*rm, *a*rch, f*a*ther, g*u*ardian
The p*a*rson p*a*rted from M*a*ma and P*a*pa at the h*ea*rth.

*a*ll, *a*we, *a*wful, *ou*ght, *a*wl, *a*wkward, *au*ction, t*a*ll, sh*a*wl, t*au*ght, b*ou*ght
P*au*l s*au*ntered along as the squ*aw* c*ou*ghed.

*ow*n, *o*ld, *o*at, *o*ak, *ow*e, *o*de, *o*af, *oa*th, *o*boe, *o*nus, b*eau*, c*oa*l, mistlet*oe*
Alth*ou*gh the b*ow*l broke J*oa*n did not gr*oa*n.

b*oo*k, c*oo*k, f*oo*t, h*oo*d, g*oo*d, t*oo*k, cr*oo*k, sh*oo*k, n*oo*k, sh*ou*ld, b*u*ll, b*o*som.
The w*o*man st*oo*d in the br*oo*k p*u*shing the b*u*ll.

sh*oe*, fl*ue*, ad*o*, c*oo*, m*oo*n, l*oo*n, f*oo*l, br*oo*d, H*oo*ver, lamp*oo*n, gr*oo*m
The l*oo*n s*oo*n sw*oo*ped on the r*oo*ster.

Diphthongs

Say: *out, ow*l, *our, ous*t, hour, *bou*t, round, house, mouse, *now, trou*t, flow*er, plow, sou*th, doubt, *tow*n

The m*ou*se ran ab*ou*t the h*ou*se with*ou*t a sound.

*ic*e, *iv*y, *ir*e, *I*, l*i*e, my, p*i*e, bite, *eye, ai*sle, *is*land, l*igh*t, h*eigh*t, b*uy*, try, g*ui*de

The g*ui*de tr*i*ed to b*uy* a wh*i*te k*i*te.

*oi*l, av*oi*d, t*oy*, b*oy*, s*oy*, j*oy*, v*oi*ce, *oi*ntment, *oy*ster, n*oi*se, point, r*oy*al, empl*oy*, v*oi*ce, c*oi*n, ch*oi*ce

The n*oi*sy b*oy*s p*oi*nted to their t*oy*s.

*ai*r, we*ar*, c*ar*e, b*ar*e, p*ai*r, te*ar*, f*ai*r, st*ar*e, wh*er*e, *e'er*, their, h*ai*r, swe*ar*, b*ar*e, h*ei*r, ch*ai*r

A f*ai*r-h*ai*red be*ar* is f*ai*rly r*ar*e.

Now you may wish to draw up lists of words and pair them with other words, alike save for the vowel sounds. For example: *a*nd-*e*nd; cot-c*augh*t; *a*t-*a*te; p*urr*-p*ear;* b*i*le-b*oi*l; p*oi*se-p*i*es; b*u*ck-b*a*lk; b*a*y-b*uy;* c*oo*k-c*o*ke; *i*ll-*ai*sle; adj*oi*n-adj*ou*rn; b*oo*ty-be*au*ty; b*oa*t-b*ou*ght; *a*ge-*e*dge; phl*e*gm-fl*a*me; m*i*tt-m*ea*t; B*e*n-b*i*n.

Then read the word pairs. Be careful to differentiate the vowels precisely.

Some speakers pronounce words like *ask, past, chance* with a vowel that lies midway between the vowels in "hat" and "*a*lms." (Listen to a Ronald Colman or Greer Garson.) This so-called *intermediate a* is classified as a middle vowel.

The vowel in words like "m*u*te," "*u*nite," "be*au*ty" is a combination of *y* as in "*y*ell" and *oo* as in "*foo*d."

After you practice the various tests and speech sounds in this chapter, turn to the selection below. As you read it, pay close attention to your articulation. With each rereading, strive for greater clarity in the production of your consonants and vowels.

EXERCISE 41: Reading for Clearer Articulation

DIRECTIONS: *Read the following passage slowly enough to articulate all the consonants. Be particularly careful of those at the ends of words. If this means an unusually slow tempo, you'll need to read the passage many times over a period of weeks until you gain facility.*

ON RAISING OUR POPULARITY QUOTIENT

What makes a person popular? We wanted to know the answer to this important question for a long, long time. So, several years ago, we began to ask people to describe the most popular person they knew. Wherever we went, we took our notebook along and jotted down the opinions of the kindhearted men and women we buttonholed. Before long we found that there were about twenty-five items most frequently used in describing the popular man and woman. We then put these items in the form of a printed list.

Next, we asked men and women in all walks of life—machinists and clergymen, stenographers and teachers, lawyers and bricklayers, housewives and foremen, saleswomen and physicians, and many others—to arrange these items in order by numbering them. One represented what in their judgment was the most important ingredient of popularity; and so on down the line, until they came to 25, which was the least important.

Finally, we tabulated the results. Can you guess which item was most often put first? It wasn't attractiveness of appearance nor readiness to mix with others nor even a ready and hearty laugh. These too are important aspects of popularity, but they weren't numbered "1" by the majority of people. Number 1 turned out to be: *The most popular person I know can always be depended upon to do what he (or she) says he will do.*

Rather amazing, isn't it? Yet when we stop to consider, is it? For nothing wears so well in good human relations as dependability. The person whose word is his bond gives us a feeling of security. We can bank on him. We can look to him for help. That is why he is popular.

So, the way to become popular is to increase your dependability. And the way to climb the ladder of dependability is to accept more responsibility in discharging your daily duties well. The wife who gets her husband off to work on time and in a happy frame of mind, the husband and father who takes pride in the welfare of his family, the stenographer whose letters continually improve, the worker who gets his job done on schedule or even before, the boss who doesn't forget to give praise where praise is due—these are the people whose habits lay a solid basis of popularity. By building such habits you are preparing for greater responsibilities. *The world is always looking for men and women who are dependable.*

When we pay our bills on time our credit rating rises. When we establish a reputation as a careful workman rewards are bound to come. When we carry our share of the load our stock goes up. When we keep our word we have the admiration of our fellow workers. These are just a few everyday examples of how people become popular.

And do you know what happens when you steer your course toward greater dependability? Way down deep within you, you have a growing conviction that you are gaining in personal power, that you are influencing people constructively both on and off the job, that you are getting more of the good things out of life. And, most satisfying of all, you have that glorious feeling that you are admired where you work, where you live, and where you play as one who can be counted on to do what he says he will do. *That is the way to increase your popularity.*

Chapter 7: HOW TO CONQUER PRONUNCIATION GREMLINS

WE AMERICANS are rugged individualists when it comes to pronunciation. George Washington pronounced *pumpkin* "PUMP i uhn." Andrew Jackson, they tell us, insisted on saying "di FIK 'l ti" because he liked his old schoolmaster who pronounced *difficulty* that way. Teddy Roosevelt made "DEE light ed" famous. Al Smith used to hold us with his "RADD i oh" speaking. The late Wendell Willkie said "REZ uh voir" instead of "rez uh VWAHR." Such deviations from what educated Americans say represent our dogged right to pronounce words pretty much as we please.

Some of us, though, like to ask questions about pronunciation. Shall we pronounce the first vowel of *economics* as in *eel* or *ell*? (Take your choice.) Should *gibberish* be given a soft or hard *g?* (Either will do.) What about the sound of *e* in *sacrilegious?* (Pronounce it *ee.*) These and many similar questions bother those who want to pronounce words "right."

But as a nation we have never set up government academies to select the one and only pronunciation for each word. Although other countries—France, for example—have for many centuries tried to impose rigid pronunciation standards, America has never done so; and neither has England.

Yet America is very pronunciation-conscious. Year in and year out radio stations and Hollywood studios get more critical letters about mispronounced words than about anything else. There are numerous "letters to the editor" about speech and pronunciation in the better newspapers. Dailies carry interesting columns about words and how to pronounce them. Perhaps you read Frank Colby's "Take My Word for It" in your newspaper; or study Norman Lewis's word quizzes in *Your Life;* or take Dr. Funk's vocabulary tests in *The Reader's Digest.*

In short, Americans have a reputation as pronunciation experts. But Professor John S. Kenyon, pronunciation editor of *Webster's New International Dictionary,* says, "There are few subjects on which educated Americans are so ready to pass judgment and give advice on the basis of so little sound knowledge as pronunciation." Eldridge Peterson, *Printers' Ink*'s distinguished editor, introduced an article on pronunciation in his magazine with these words: "Next to war, there is probably no subject that starts so many arguments as does the pronunciation of words."

The word crank views mispronunciation as a sign of defective character. And word cranks aren't rare birds. Just the other day a man told me why he changed family physicians: "When I heard the doctor say 'SOO per floo uhs' instead of 'soo PER floo uhs,' that was enough for me!" He went on, "Oh, I know a man may be able to write a careful prescription and still mispronounce *superfluous,* but the fact that he does mispronounce a common word makes me downright suspicious of his common sense. He's probably heard it pronounced correctly hundreds of times. Why does he use it if he isn't sure?" In life, as in court, everything we say may be held agin us.

The eighteenth-century poet, Pope, wrote a good pronunciation rule:

> Be not the first by which the new is tried,
> Nor yet the last to lay the old aside.

The way we pronounce words changes—changes so rapidly that by the time a new edition of one of our large unabridged dictionaries is ready for publication (it takes ten or fifteen years at least to get out a new edition), hundreds of its recommended pronunciations are already outmoded. Fifty years ago a "gentleman's gentleman" was a "va LAY"; now "VAL et" is heard instead. The early airplane was supposed to be kept in an "AHNG gar" (hangar) according to the dictionaries; educated Americans from the first kept their airplanes in "HANG erz." A hundred years ago they didn't pronounce *h* in words like *hospital, hotel, humor, humble.* Today educated people pronounce the *h* in these words.

Our best bet is to listen to cultivated speakers and consult good dictionaries. We ought to keep notes on what seem to be unusual pronunciations. These are often the right pronunciations, reminding us that we have pronounced certain words incorrectly for years.

Many of us don't like alternate pronunciations. Americans bent on speech improvement like to learn one correct pronunciation for each difficult word. They want to know whether the "right" pronunciation is long *a* or short *a* for *squalor;* long *i* or short *i* for *isolate.* (You hear educated people say either of them, in both instances.) They want to be told whether the first syllable of *exquisite* "must" be stressed. (Stress the first or the second syllable.)

Now, of course, many words have more than one acceptable pronunciation: *data,* for example. You can find hundreds of others in your dictionary. But in deference to the demand for one correct pronunciation—for each gremlin—we shall use the recommendations of the National Broadcasting Company.

Before going on, however, we ought to discuss the terms *strong forms* and *weak forms.* Almost all of us have more than one standard of pronunciation, depending on the company we keep. When we want to make a good impression we take care to utter our words distinctly— to put them in their best bibs and tuckers. But in ordinary conversation, especially when we mumble along at a fast tempo among our friends and relatives, we drop the *h*'s from words like *his, her, had;* we omit the *t* in combinations such as *must do, sit down, next dozen, wrists sore,* and *slept well,* and the *d* in words like *blandness, kindness,* and the first *t* in *past master* and *postmistress.* The vowels in *that, of, as,* etc., become indeterminant. All these examples are weak forms. Strong forms are more carefully pronounced. You find only strong forms in most dictionaries.

There are three widely used systems of noting English and American pronunciation. Many of us learned the *diacritical markings* in school. A diacritical mark is attached to a letter of the alphabet to distinguish it in sound, for example, ō. Then there is the *International Phonetic Alphabet.* (We'll take it up in a later chapter.)

Perhaps the most popular of all three systems is *respelling.* Respelling is a kind of spelling in accordance with the sounds of words; each sound is represented by a letter or combination of letters. It has the advantages of our ordinary alphabet. Any disadvantages? You can't represent the indeterminate vowel as in lem*o*n, stud*e*nt, etc., unless you use an apostrophe in its place or *uh.* But *uh* also represents the vowel in words like *up* and *cut.* For our purpose the merits of respelling far outweigh its disadvantage. The respelling system we shall use was first proposed by the Board of Geographical Names of the United States Department of the Interior. It is used by newspapers and wire services, such as the United Press, Associated Press, and International News Service.

Capital letters represent primary accent; italics, secondary accent. Thus *advertisement* becomes "*ad* ver TIGHZ m'nt."

KEY

a	as *a* in *hat*
ah	as *a* in *father*
air	as *air* in *fair*
aw	as *aw* in *law*
ay	as *ay* in *day*
ee	as *ee* in *meet*
e	as *e* in *let*

ew ....as *ew* in *few*
ier ....as *ear* in *hear*
igh ....as *igh* in *high*

i ....as *i* in *hit*
oh ....as *o* in *go*
oo ....as *oo* in *foot*
ooː ....as *oo* in *food*
ou ....as *ou* in *house*
oy ....as *oi* in *oil*
uh ....as *u* in *cut*
er ....as *ur* in *fur*
ehr ....as *er* in *ferry*
y ....as *y* in *yet*

ch ....as *ch* in *church*
g ....as *g* in *go*
j ....as *j* in *jam*
k ....as *k* in *kill*
sh ....as *sh* in *shoe*
s ....as *s* in *sit*
z ....as *z* in *zoo*
zh ....as *s* in *measure*
th ....as *th* in *thin*
thː ....as *th* in *this*

Common mispronunciations fall into five groups, illustrated in the following exercises:

EXERCISE 42: Mispronunciations Marked by Omissions

DIRECTIONS: *Read aloud the correct pronunciation of each word and notice also the commonest mispronunciation of each:*

		Don't Say:	Say:
1. arctic		AHR tik	AHRK tik
2. artists		AHR tis	AHR tists
3. Calliope		KAL i ohp	kuh LIGH uh pi
4. candidate		KAN i dayt	KAN di dayt
5. chocolate		CHAW klit	CHAWK uh lit
6. company		KUHMP ni	KUHM puh ni

	Don't Say:	Say:
7. depths	deps	depths
8. diamond	DIGH m'nd	DIGH uh m'nd
9. eleven	LEV 'n	i LEV 'n
10. family	FAM li	FAM i li
11. February	FEB oo: *ehr* i	FEB roo: *ehr* i
12. general	JEN r'l	JEN er 'l
13. government	GUHV er m'nt	GUHV ern m'nt
14. language	LANG wij	LANG gwij
15. only	OHN i	OHN li
16. particular	per TIK uh ler	par TIK yoo: ler
17. really	REEL i	REE 'l i
18. recognize	REK uh nighz	REK uhg nighz
19. temperature	TEMP uh cher	TEMP er uh cher
20. twenty	TWEN i	TWEN ti

EXERCISE 43: Mispronunciations Marked by Additions

DIRECTIONS: *Read aloud the correct pronunciation of each word and notice also the commonest mispronunciation of each:*

	Don't Say:	Say:
1. amateur	AM uh cher	*am* uh TER
2. athlete	ATH uh leet	ATH leet
3. blackguard	BLAK gahrd	BLAG ahrd
4. drowned	DROUN did	dround
5. elm	EL 'm	elm
6. extraordinary	eks truh AWR di *nehr* i	eks TRAWR di *nehr* i
7. film	FIL 'm	film
8. grievous	GREE vi uhs	GREE vuhs
9. hasten	HAYS t'n	HAYS 'n
10. irascible	i RAS kuh b'l	i RAS i b'l
11. mischievous	mis CHEE vi uhs	MIS chi vuhs
12. mnemonic	muh ni MAHN ik	ni MAHN ik
13. often	AWF t'n	AWF 'n
14. ptomaine	puh TOH mayn	TOH mayn

	Don't Say:	*Say:*
15. quay	kway	kee
16. rhythm	RITH: uhm	RITH: 'm
17. schism	SKIZ 'm	SIZ 'm
18. singer	SING ger	SING er
19. subtle	SUHB t'l	SUHT 'l
20. umbrella	uhm buh REL uh	uhm BREL uh

EXERCISE 44: Mispronunciations Marked by Substitutions

DIRECTIONS: *Read aloud the correct pronunciation of each word and notice also the commonest mispronunciation of each:*

	Don't Say:	*Say:*
1. architect	AHR chi tekt	AHR ki tekt
2. archives	AHR chighvz	AHR kighvz
3. cello	SEL oh	CHEL oh
4. charade	chuh RAYD	shuh RAYD
5. chiropodist	chi RAHP uh dist	kigh RAHP uh dist
6. deaf	deef	def
7. diphthong	DIP thahng	DIF thahng
8. draughty	DRAW ti	DRAF ti
9. flaccid	FLAS id	FLAK sid
10. gaol	GAY ohl	jayl
11. gibbet	GIB it	JIB it
12. hearth	herth	hahrth
13. Italian	igh TAL y'n	i TAL y'n
14. orgy	AWR gi	AWR ji
15. percolate	PER kyoo: layt	PER kuh layt
16. radiator	RAD i *ay* ter	RAY di *ay* ter
17. ribald	RIGH bawld	RIB 'ld
18. rinse	rinz	rins
19. this	dis	th:is
20. vaudeville	VAWD uh vil	VOHD vil

EXERCISE 45: Mispronunciations Marked by Misplaced Accents

DIRECTIONS: *Read aloud the correct pronunciation of each word and notice also the commonest mispronunciation of each:*

	Don't Say:	Say:
1. acclimate	AK li mayt	uh KLIGH mit
2. adult	AD uhlt	uh DUHLT
3. alias	uh LIGH uhs	AY li uhs
4. backgammon	*bak* GAM 'n	BAK gam 'n
5. Broadway	brawd WAY	BRAWD way
6. condolence	KAHN duh l'ns	k'n DOHL 'ns
7. defeat	DEE feet	di FEET
8. exquisite	eks KWIZ it	EKS kwi zit
9. finances (n)	fi NAN siz	FIGH nans iz
10. formidable	fawr MID uh b'l	FAWR mi duh b'l
11. ignominy	ig nuh MIN i	IG nuh min i
12. impious	im PIGH uhs	IM pi uhs
13. inquiry	IN kwi ri	in KWIGHR i
14. irrevocable	i ri VOHK uh b'l	i REV uh kuh b'l
15. lamentable	luh MEN tuh b'l	LAM 'n tuh b'l
16. mausoleum	maw SOHL i 'm	maw suh LEE 'm
17. municipal	myoo: ni SIP 'l	myoo: NIS i p'l
18. remonstrate	REM 'n strayt	ri MAHN strayt
19. resource	REE sawrs	ri SAWRS
20. superfluous	*soo:p* er FLOO: uhs	soo: PER floo: uhs

EXERCISE 46: Mispronunciations Marked by Ignorance of Silent Letters, or Aphthongs

DIRECTIONS: *Read aloud the correct pronunciation of each word and notice also the commonest mispronunciation of each:*

	Don't Say:	Say:
1. antique	AN ti kyoo:	an TEEK
2. apropos	*ap* ruh POHZ	*ap* ruh POH
3. asthma	AZTH: muh	AZ muh
4. butte	BUHT ee	byoo:t
5. chasm	CHAZ 'm	KAZ 'm
6. corps	kawrps	kawr
7. debris	day BREES	day BREE
8. gnome	guh NOH mee	nohm
9. listen	LIS t'n	LIS 'n
10. palm	PAHL 'm	pahm

	Don't Say:	*Say:*
11. forehead	FAWR hed	FAHR id
12. hautboy	HOHT boy	HOH boy
13. indict	in DIKT	in DIGHT
14. phlegm	FLEG 'm	flem
15. proboscis	proh BAHS kis	proh BAHS is
16. psalter	puh SAWL ter	SAWL ter
17. pshaw	puh SHAW	shaw
18. Thames	thaymz	temz
19. thyme	thighm	tighm
20. viscount	VIGHS kount	VIGH kount

EXERCISE 47: Words Commonly Mispronounced

DIRECTIONS: *Read the words aloud three times each.*

aborigines	*ab* uh RIJ uh neez
absolutely	AB suh loo:t li
abyss	uh BIS
acceded	ak SEED id
acerb	uh SERB
acumen	uh KYOO: m'n
addressed	uh DREST
adept (a)	uh DEPT
ad infinitum	ad *in* fi NIGH t'm
adjutant	AJ oo t'nt
ad libitum	ad LIB uh t'm
admirable	AD mi ruh b'l
admiralty	AD mi r'l ti
after	AF ter
ague	AY gyoo:
alas	uh LAS
albumen	al BYOO: m'n
allied	uh LIGHD
allopathy	uh LAHP uh thi
ancient	AYN sh'nt
anesthetist	an ES thuh tist
anesthetize	an ES thuh tighz
anti	AN ti

antipodes	an TIP uh deez
Apache	uh PACH ee
apothegms	AP uh themz
applicable	AP li kuh b'l
arbiter	AHR bi ter
archipelago	*ahr* ki PEL uh goh
armistice	AHR mi stis
ascetic	uh SET ik
assigned	uh SIGHND
assuage	uh SWAYJ
athenaeum	ath uh NEE 'm
athletics	ath LET iks
august (a)	aw GUHST
aural	AW r'l
austere	aws TIER
authoritative	aw THAW ri *tay* tiv
auxiliary	awg ZIL yuh ri
aviation	ay vi AY sh'n
aviator	AY vi *ay* ter
aviatrix	*ay* vi AY triks
awry	uh RIGH
bade	bad
beatific	*bee* uh TIF ik
beauteous	BYOO: ti uhs
beckoned	BEK 'nd
beneficent	bi NEF i s'nt
bestow	bi STOH
blatant	BLAY t'nt
blue	bloo:
bravado	bruh VAH doh
breadths	bredths
breaths	breths
brigand	BRIG 'nd
broadcasting	BRAWD *kast* ing
bromidic	broh MID ik
bulwarks	BOOL werks
caballero	kah bahl YAIR oh

caprice	kuh PREES
caramels	KAR uh melz
catastrophic	*kat* uh STRAHF ik
cerebral	SEHR uh br'l
chaise	shayz
chamois (leather)	SHAM i
champion	CHAM pi 'n
chaotic	kay AHT ik
chastisement	CHAS tiz m'nt
chateau	sha TOH
chevalier	*shev* uh LIER
chives	chighvz
choleric	KAHL er ik
cigarette	*sig* uh RET
circuitous	ser KYOO: i tuhs
clematis	KLEM uh tis
clichés	klee SHAYZ
clique	kleek
clothes	klohth:z
cloths	klawths
coalesce	*koh* uh LES
cogitating	KAHJ i tayt ing
comely	KUHM li
commands	kuh MANDZ
comment (n, v)	KAHM ent
commune (n)	KAHM yoo:n
commune (v)	kuh MYOO:N
comparable	KAHM puh ruh b'l
compass	KUHM puhs
concentrate	KAHN s'n trayt
confine (v)	k'n FIGHN
congeries	kahn JIER i eez
congratulate	k'n GRA choo layt
consort (n)	KAHN sawrt
contemplate	KAHN t'm playt
controversy	KAHN truh *ver* si
contumely	KAHN too: mi li

conversant	KAHN ver s'nt
couldn't	KOOD 'nt
counterfeit	KOUN ter fit
coupon	KOO: pahn
covet	KUHV it
crises	KRIGH seez
criterion	krigh TIER i 'n
critique	kri TEEK
cruel	KROO: 'l
cuisine	kwi ZEEN
cupboard	KUHB erd
deafen	DEF 'n
debauch	di BAWCH
deficit	DEF i sit
deluge	DEL yoo:j
demands	di MANDZ
demoniac	di MOH ni ak
demoniacal	*dee* moh NIGH uh k'l
demonstrate	DEM 'n strayt
denizen	DEN i z'n
deprivation	*dep* ri VAY sh'n
design	di ZIGHN
despicable	DES pi kuh b'l
destined	DES tind
digit	DIJ it
diphthongal	dif THAWNG g'l
dirigible	DIR i ji b'l
discretion	dis KRESH 'n
dishevel	di SHEV 'l
disingenuous	*dis* in JEN yoo: uhs
disown	dis OHN
divers	DIGH verz
donkey	DAHNG ki
dotard	DOH terd
doth	duhth
doughty	DOU ti
dour	doo:r

dramatis personae	DRAM uh tis per SOH ner
draught	draft
drought	drout
dysphonically	dis FAHN i k'l i
effulgences	i FUHL j'n siz
eighths	aytths
elevenths	i LEV 'nths
elite	ay LEET
embassy	EM buh si
emeritus	i MEHR i tuhs
encyclopedia	en *sigh* kluh PEE di uh
enervate	EN er vayt
English	ING glish
ennui	AHN wee
ensign (banner)	EN sighn
ensign (officer)	EN sin
entree	AHN tray
epistle	i PIS 'l
epitome	i PIT uh mi
equipage	EK wi pij
erasure	i RAY zher
err	er
esoteric	*es* uh TEHR ik
espousal	es POUZ 'l
ethereal	i THIER i 'l
evening	EEV ning
exigency	EK si j'n si
explicable	EKS pli kuh b'l
exponent	eks POH n'nt
extempore	eks TEM puh ri
extravagancies	eks TRAV uh g'n seez
facts	fakts
faiths	fayths
fantastically	fan TAS ti k'l i
fastidious	fas TID i uhs
felon	FEL 'n

fete	fayt
fiend	feend
fifths	fifths
filth	filth
finesse	fi NES
finger	FING ger
flute	floo:t
forbade	fer BAD
forfeit	FAWR fit
forfeiture	FAWR fi cher
formidably	FAWR mi duh b'l i
fourteenth	*fawr* TEENTH
fourths	fawrths
fracas	FRAY kuhs
fragile	FRAJ 'l
fragmentary	FRAG m'n *tehr* i
franchise	FRAN chighz
from	frahm
gallant	GAL 'nt
garrulity	guh ROO: li ti
gaseous	GAS i uhs
gauge	gayj
generally	JEN er 'l i
genuine	JEN yoo: in
gesture	JES cher
gherkins	GER kinz
ghoul	goo:l
giant	JIGH 'nt
gingham	GING 'm
gist	jist
glacial	GLAY sh'l
goal	gohl
Goliath	goh LIGH uhth
gondola	GAHN duh luh
grimace	gri MAYS
grisly	GRIZ li
growths	grohths

gunwale	GUHN 'l
Guy	gigh
gyrate	JIGH rayt
gyves	jighvz
hadn't	HAD 'nt
hadst	hadst
Hampshire	HAMP sher
haply	HAP li
Hawaii	hah WIGH ee
hearths	hahrths
heifer	HEF er
heinous	HAY nuhs
heir	air
Helena	HEL i nuh
helicopter	*hel* i KAHP ter
helm	helm
hero	HIER oh
heroism	HEHR oh iz 'm
hiatus	high AY tuhs
hiccough	HIK uhp
hideous	HID i uhs
hieroglyphics	high er oh GLIF iks
history	HIS tuh ri
Hohenzollern	HOH en *tsawl* ern
horizon	huh RIGH z'n
hosiery	HOH zher i
hospitable	HAHS pi tuh b'l
housewife	HOUS *wighf*
human	HYOO: m'n
hundredths	HUHN druhdths
hussar	hoo ZAHR
hymeneal	*high* muh NEE 'l
hyperbole	high PER buh li
hypocrite	HIP uh krit
hypocritically	*hip* uh KRIT i k'l i
hyssop	HIS uhp
hysteria	his TIER i uh

ice cream	IGHS KREEM
ignominious	*ig* nuh MIN i uhs
ignorance	IG nuh r'ns
imperturbability	*im* per *ter* buh BIL i ti
impotence	IM puh t'ns
inane	in AYN
inclement	in KLEM 'nt
incognito	in KAHG ni toh
incomparable	in KAHM puh ruh b'l
incongruous	in KAHNG groo uhs
incorporeal	*in* kawr POH ri 'l
indefatigable	*in* di FAT i guh b'l
indefatigability	*in* di *fat* i guh BIL i ti
indicatory	IN di kuh *tawr* i
indictment	in DIGHT m'nt
indiscretion	*in* dis KRESH 'n
indisputability	in *dis* pyooː tuh BIL i ti
indissolubility	in *di* sahl yooː BIL i ti
industry	IN duhs tri
inestimable	in ES ti muh b'l
inevitable	in EV i tuh b'l
inexplicable	in EKS pli kuh b'l
infamous	IN fuh muhs
infantile	IN f'n tighl
infantine	IN f'n tighn
influence	IN flooː 'ns
ingenious	in JEEN yuhs
ingénue	an zhay NOOː
ingenuous	in JEN yoo uhs
ingots	ING guhts
inhospitable	in HAHS pi tuh b'l
insensate	in SEN sayt
insidious	in SID i uhs
integral	IN ti gr'l
interpolate	in TER puh layt
intricacies	IN tri kuh siz

invasion	in VAY zh'n
iron	IGH ern
irreconcilability	i *rek* 'n *sighl* uh BIL i ti
irremediability	i ri *mee* di uh BIL i ti
irreparability	i *rep* uh ruh BIL i ti
irrevocability	i *rev* uh kuh BIL i ti
janissary	JAN i *sehr* i
jocose	joh KOHS
judiciary	joo: DISH i *ehr* i
klieg	kleeg
labyrinth	LAB i rinth
lapel	luh PEL
larynx	LAR ingks
latent	LAY t'nt
lather	LATH: er
lathes	layth:z
leathern	LETH: ern
Leicester	LES ter
length	length
lengths	lengths
lethargic	li THAHR jik
lethargy	LETH er ji
Levant	li VANT
levy	LEV i
licentious	ligh SEN shuhs
Limoges	*lee* MOHZH
limousine	*lim* uh ZEEN
lingually	LING gwuh li
locale	loh KAL
logy	LOH gi
longevity	lahn JEV uh ti
long-lived	LAWNG LIGHVD
lush	luhsh
lyceum	ligh SEE 'm
machination	*mak* i NAY sh'n
Madeira	muh DIER uh
magnanimity	*mag* nuh NIM i ti

maharajah	*mah* huh RAH juh
martyr	MAHR ter
Mary	MAIR i
Maryland	MEHR i l'nd
mayoralty	MAY er 'l ti
meditatively	MED i *tay* tiv li
meerschaum	MIER sh'm
mellifluous	muh LIF loo uhs
memorable	MEM uh ruh b'l
merely	MIER li
Mesopotamia	*mes* uh puh TAY mi uh
microphone	MIGH kruh fohn
mien	meen
mirage	mi RAHZH
modern	MAHD ern
monarchic	muh NAHR kik
monger	MUHNG ger
monosyllabic	*mahn* uh si LAB ik
monseigneur	*mahn* say NYER
monsieur	muh SYER
months	muhnths
moral	MAWR 'l
morass	muh RAS
Morpheus	MAWR fyooːs
mountain	MOUN t'n
mouths	mouthːz
mused	myooːzd
museum	myooː ZEE 'm
musicale	myooː zi KAL
naive	nah EEV
naiveté	nah *eev* TAY
nemesis	NEM i sis
niche	nich
nineteenths	*nighn* TEENTHS
nonce	nahns
nonchalant	NAHN shuh l'nt
nourished	NER isht

nuptial	NUHP sh'l
nymphs	nimfs
oaths	ohth:z
obdurate	AHB doo rit
occasion	uh KAY zh'n
opined	oh PIGHND
oral	OH r'l
orangery	AHR enj ri
orchid	AWR kid
organization	*awr* g'n i ZAY sh'n
Orion	oh RIGH 'n
ornate	awr NAYT
otiose	OH shi ohs
overseer	OH ver *see* er
overt	OH vert
pageant	PAJ 'nt
palfrey	PAWL fri
palimpsest	PAL imp sest
palsied	PAWL zeed
pandiculated	pan DIK yoo: lay t'd
panjandrum	pan JAN dr'm
pantomime	PAN tuh mighm
parachute	PAR uh shoo:t
paramour	PAR uh moo:r
parentheses	puh REN thi seez
parenthetically	*par* 'n THET i k'l i
pariah	puh RIGH uh
parliament	PAHR li m'nt
parliamentary	*pahr* li MEN tuh ri
paths	path:z
patois	PAT wah
patronymic	*pat* ruh NIM ik
pattern	PAT ern
penal	PEE n'l
perambulating	per AM byoo layt ing
percale	per KAYL

perpetuity	*per* pi TYOO: i ti
philology	fi LAHL uh ji
phonetically	fuh NET i k'l i
physique	fi ZEEK
piquant	PEE k'nt
placard (n)	PLAK ahrd
plaid	plad
plethora	PLETH uh ruh
policeman	puh LEES m'n
policemen	puh LEES men
portend	pawr TEND
portentously	pawr TEN tuhs li
positively	PAHZ i tiv li
postern	POHS tern
postprandial	pohst PRAN di 'l
potion	POH sh'n
precedence	pri SEED 'ns
precedent (n)	PRES i d'nt
precincts	PREE singkts
preface	PREF is
preferment	pri FER m'nt
prelate	PREL it
presentiment	pri ZEN ti m'nt
presumptuous	pri ZUHMP choo uhs
pretexts	PREE teksts
proboscis	proh BAHS is
process	PRAHS es
program	PROH gram
progress (n)	PRAHG res
protégé	PROH tuh zhay
protestation	praht es TAY sh'n
pulpit	POOL pit
pumice	PUHM is
pumpkin	PUHMP kin
purloin	per LOYN
purport (n)	PER pawrt
pyramidal	pi RAM i d'l

qualitatively	KWAHL i *tay* tiv li
quandary	KWAHN duh ri
quantitatively	KWAHN ti *tay* tiv li
quarantine	KWAHR 'n teen
quay	kee
query	KWIER i
queue	kyoo:
quiescent	kwigh ES 'nt
quietus	kwigh EE tuhs
radio	RAY di oh
rapine	RAP in
raspberry	RAZ *behr* i
rather	RATH: er
reality	ri AL i ti
realty	REE 'l ti
recipe	RES i pee
recluse	ri KLOO:S
recognize	REK uhg nighz
refuse (v)	ri FYOO:Z
regimen	REJ i men
remonstrate	ri MAHN strayt
renascence	ri NAS 'ns
reparable	REP uh ruh b'l
repartee	*rep* er TEE
repast	ri PAST
requisite	REK wi zit
resound	ri ZOUND
respite	RES pit
retail	REE tayl
reverberation	ri *ver* ber AY sh'n
revocable	REV uh kuh b'l
riband	RIB 'nd
righteous	RIGH chuhs
rived	righvd
robust	roh BUHST
robustious	roh BUHS chuhs
roof	roo:f

Roosevelt	ROH zuh velt
root	roo:t
roué	roo: AY
rouge	roo:zh
route	roo:t
routine	roo: TEEN
rudimentary	*roo:* di MEN tuh ri
ruin	ROO: in
ruinous	ROO: i nuhs
ruthless	ROO:TH lis
saith	seth
salient	SAY li 'nt
savagery	SAV ij ri
scabies	SKAY bi eez
scathed	skayth:d
scimitar	SIM i ter
scintillate	SIN ti layt
scion	SIGH 'n
scourge	skerj
scythes	sighth:z
sects	sekts
sedan	si DAN
seethed	seeth:d
sepulchral	si POOL kr'l
sepulcher	SEP 'l ker
sepulture	SEP 'l cher
serum	SIER 'm
seventeenths	*sev* 'n TEENTHS
sevenths	SEV 'nths
seventieths	SEV 'n ti uhths
sheathes	sheeth:z
sheaths	sheeth:z
shibboleth	SHIB uh leth
sieved	sivd
sine qua non	SIGH nee kway NAHN
singularly	SING gyoo ler li
Sioux	soo:

sirloins	SER loynz
sixteenths	*siks* TEENTHS
sixths	siksths
sixtieths	SIKS ti uhths
skein	skayn
sleight	slight
slough (v)	sluhf
slovenly	SLUHV 'n li
soldiers	SOHL jerz
solitaire	*sahl* i TAIR
somber	SAHM ber
soothed	soo:th:d
spectacularly	spek TAK yoo ler li
spiritual	SPIR i choo: 'l
sponsors	SPAHN serz
spouse	spouz
squalid	SKWAHL id
squalor	SKWAHL er
staff	staf
statistical	stuh TIS ti k'l
statistician	*stat* is TISH 'n
statistics	stuh TIS tiks
status	STAY tuhs
stealth	stelth
Stephen	STEE v'n
stertoring	STER ter ing
stipend	STIGH pend
strengthens	STRENG th'nz
strengths	strengths
strewn	stroo:n
Stygian	STIJ i 'n
Styx	stiks
sulfuric	suhl FYOO:R ik
sumptuous	SUHMP choo: uhs
superfluity	*soo*: per FLOO: i ti
superfluous	soo: PER floo: uhs
supine	soo: PIGHN
suppliant	SUHP li 'nt

suppose	suh POHZ
swathes	swaythːz
systematize	SIS t'm uh tighz
tact	takt
temperament	TEM per uh m'nt
temperance	TEM per 'ns
tempestuous	tem PES chooː uhs
tentatively	TEN tuh tiv li
texts	teksts
theaters	THEE uh terz
theory	THEE uh ri
thither	THːITHː er
thousandths	THOU z'ndths
thyme	tighm
timbre	TIM ber
tithe	tighthː
tracts	trakts
transient	TRAN sh'nt
traverse	TRAV ers
tremendous	tri MEN duhs
trespassing	TRES puhs ing
tribune	TRIB yooːn
triumphal	trigh UHM f'l
triumphs	TRIGH uhmfs
tumultuous	tooː MUHL chooː uhs
turmoil	TER moyl
tympanist	TIM puh nist
ubiquitous	yooː BIK wi tuhs
ultimatum	*uhl* ti MAY t'm
unintelligibility	*uhn* in *tel* i juh BIL i ti
unprecedented	uhn PRES i *den* tid
unraveled	uhn RAV 'ld
usurpation	*yoo*ː zer PAY sh'n
valiant	VAL y'nt
variable	VAIR i uh b'l
variant	VAIR i 'nt

various	VAIR i uhs
vehement	VEE i m'nt
vehicular	vi HIK yooː ler
verbiage	VER bi ij
verbose	ver BOHS
veritably	VEHR i tuh bli
vertices	VER ti seez
via	VIGH uh
vicar	VIK er
victuals	VIT 'lz
vineyard	VIN yerd
virus	VIGH ruhs
viscount	VIGH *kount*
vise	vighs
voluptuous	vuh LUHP chooː uhs
wan	wahn
wand	wahnd
what	hwaht
when	hwen
where	hwair
which	hwich
whoop	hooːp
wondrous	WUHN druhs
wouldn't	WOOD 'nt
wouldst	woodst
wreathed	reethːd
wreaths	reethːz
wriggled	RIG 'ld
writhed	righthːd
yeasts	yeests
yeomanry	YOH m'n **ri**
yonder	YAHN der
zealots	ZEL uhts
zealous	ZEL uhs
zoological	*zoh* uh LAHJ i k'l
zoology	zoh AHL uh ji

Chapter 8: DON'T LET FOREIGN WORDS GET YOU DOWN

HOLLYWOOD STAR names on Istanbul marquees, travelers from Turkey tell us, don't gibe with American spellings, although Klok Geybl, Weeta Eyvurt, Surli Templ, Spensr Tresi, Gheri Kupr, Rozlund Rusl, Jinja Rojaz are just as popular over there as here. The reason for the creative orthography—logical enough if you speak Turkish—is the world-wide conundrum: How shall we pronounce foreign words?

When we pay close attention to radio, screen, and forum speakers, we hear foreign words pronounced in various ways. Our friends across the sea have the same experience. Even in France, where they have an official *académie* to dictate "right" pronunciation, you hear variants.

After World War I, the Parisians named a street for President Woodrow Wilson. They pronounced it somewhat like "VOOD roh VEEL s'n"—contrary to their Forty Immortals' advice.

You sometimes meet a fellow who expects consistency. He shakes his head. He wonders whether radio announcers and actors live in the Tower of Babel. He hears one announcer call the French general "duh GOHL." Another on the same station says "duh GAWL." He frets about American place names of foreign origin, says we speak with a forked tongue.

Some actors pronounce *Los Angeles* with a soft g. Others use a hard g right in the same movie. Most Midwesterners Americanize only the first part of *St. Louis;* Southerners, only the last syllable of *Louisville.*

Our friend, who wants to be sure he pronounces foreign words right, asks, "Shall I pronounce the Red dictator's name 'STAH leen,' 'stah LEEN,' 'STAH lin,' 'stah LIN,' 'STAW leen,' etc.? Whose word should I take?"

Sooner or later he hears two points of view. The one says, "Keep foreign words in their native sounds." Thus Mr. Mikeruhfone and Miss Cyclorammer, you mustn't say, "ber LIN" but "bair LEEN" when you refer to the capital of Germany. And in the Philippines our boys took "bah tah AHN" (*Bataan*), not "buh TAN." Why? Because the natives pronounce it that way. Since you're a paid purveyor of phonemes, Mr. M. and Miss C., you ought to pronounce the world's words with polylingual validity. Well, anyway, those of the Western world and maybe Chinese and Japanese.

The other extreme view is easier to live with: "Americanize the pronunciation of all foreign names." Do what the Marines did to "kah lah KAH nah" (*Guadalcanal*); keep the situation well in hand with "gwad 'l kuh NAL." Let your boat touch "pawrt SED," not, as the Egyptians say it, "PORT sah EED." And don't forget to change English names either. England's great democratic leader becomes "CHURCH hill," even though he pronounces it "CHURCH il." The Thames River in Connecticut is "thaymz," and the champions of this view would change its English namesake ("temz") to the same pronunciation.

Between these poles you have a middle course laid out by two simple rules:

1. Unless there are compelling reasons to the contrary, preserve native pronunciations as far as your speech sounds permit.

Thus the Chinese leader's name is "jyahng jyeh-shuh" (*Chiang Kai-shek*); the Rumanian oil center *Ploești,* "plaw YEHST"; the Scotch parish *Wemss,* "weemz." By the same rule *Paraguay* becomes "pah rah GWAH ee"; *Jerez,* the Spanish sherry center, "hay RAYTH"; the *Ubangi* tribe in the Congo, "oo BAHNG gee," not "yoo BANG ji."

The trouble with the rule is that too many educated Americans pronounce strange words as spelled—even though they don't always pronounce their own native words the way they look. That explains why we hear Chiang Kai-shek's name pronounced "chi AHNG KIGH SHEK," etc.

2. If our speech doesn't include certain foreign sounds, then use the closest approximations.

In German the umlauted vowels as in *Göring, Führer* don't occur in American speech. So why not pronounce these names "GER ing," "FYOOR er"?

We don't blend in the final *n* with a preceding nasalized vowel as the French do in words like *Gobelin*. That's why we hear "GOH buh lan" in America. BBC has its announcers say "righsh" for the German word *Reich;* NBC prefers "righk." Neither English nor General American has the German sound *ch,* made by scraping the throat.

Each one of us must make his own choice. But before making yours, you may want to recall that the two billion, one hundred seventeen million people of the world speak upwards of fifteen hundred languages. Each one of us learns to speak one language better than any other. Did you know that no one can speak a foreign language as well as his native language? After he's grown-up, that is.

Some of our forty speech sounds don't occur in other languages. The *th* sounds, as in *thin* and *thou,* and *a* as in *at* don't appear in Italian, for instance. Most Americans would be hard put to it to produce some Hottentot sounds—those made by striking the fingers against the cheek. Foreign speech sounds take long and faithful practice to master. Even then you fall short of perfection. This leads to the common-sense conclusion: a spurious accent is much worse than Americanized pronunciation of foreign words.

It seems to me we need more tolerance of variant pronunciations. We also need much more faith in the common man's guardianship of pronunciation.

Given time enough, he is the best authority in the long run. We seldom argue about the pronunciation of names like *Plato, Caesar, Charlemagne, Galileo, Dante, Michelangelo, Napoleon.* Why? Because we standardized them through long, common usage. Give the man on the street—and his eventual and reluctant disciples, the dictionary makers—time enough, and words like *Suojarvi, Bahol Bolabayuha Sena, Zaporozhe* will be no problem at all—provided he uses them often enough. Until he has had time to do just that, though, perhaps we ought to follow the recommendations of authorities.

EXERCISE 48: Pronouncing Foreign Names

DIRECTIONS: *Pronounce each of these foreign words three times. (This list is made up of foreign words from home and abroad. It's only a sampling of the many we hear pronounced in various ways.)*

Abou ben Adhem   (AH boo: ben AHD hem)
   Poem by Leigh Hunt; also its chief character.

Addis Ababa   (AHD is AH bah bah)
   Capital of Abyssinia.

Aeneid   (i NEE id)
   Latin epic by Virgil, recounting the wanderings of Aeneas after the fall of Troy.

Aeschylus   (ES kuh luhs)
   Greek tragic poet.

Aesop   (EE sahp)
   Greek fabulist.

Aïda   (ah EE duh)
   Opera by Verdi; also its heroine.

Alabama   (*al* uh BAM uh)
   Southern state and river of the United States.

Amazon   (AM uh zahn)
   South American river, the largest in the world.

Amherst   (AM erst)
   English and American family and geographical name.

Amundsen, Roald   (AH muhn s'n)
   Norwegian polar explorer.

Ankara   (AHNG kuh ruh)
   Turkish city.

Anna Karenina   (AH nah kah REN yi nuh)
   Novel by Tolstoy; also its heroine.

Antietam   (an TEE t'm)
  Creek in Pennsylvania and Maryland; battle in Maryland, 1862.

Apache   (uh PACH ee)
  One of a tribe of American Indians of New Mexico and Arizona.
  (uh PASH)
  The French "apache," a Parisian gangster.

Apennines   (AP uh nighnz)
  Italian mountain chain.

Aphrodite   (*af* roh DIGH ti)
  Greek goddess of love and beauty.

Appalachian   (*ap* uh LAY chi 'n)
  Designating a mountain system of eastern North America.

Appomattox   (*ap* uh MAT uhks)
  County and river in Virginia; where Lee surrendered to Grant, 1865.

Argentina   (*ahr* j'n TEE nuh)
  South American federal republic; called also *Argentine* (AHR j'n teen)
  Republic.

Aroostook   (uh ROO:S took)
  River and county in Maine.

Asia   (AY zhuh)
  The largest continent.

Asunción   (ah *soo:n* SYOHN)
  Capital of Paraguay.

Ave Maria   (AH vay mah REE uh)
  Hail Mary.

Azores   (uh ZAWRZ)
  Portuguese islands in the North Atlantic.

Bahamas   (buh HAY muhz)
  The Bahama Islands, archipelago in the British West Indies.

Bahía Blanca   (bah HEE ah BLAHNG kah)
  Seaport in Argentina.

Balaklava   (*bah* lah KLAH vah)
  Russian seaport in Crimea; battle, 1854.

Balearic Islands (*bal* i AR ik)
  Island group in the Mediterranean; a province of Spain.

Baluchistan (buh *loo*: chi STAHN)
  Native state in northwest India.

Banff (bamf)
  Town in Alberta, Canada.

Baton Rouge (*bat* 'n ROO:ZH)
  Capital of Louisiana.

Beethoven (BAY toh v'n)
  German composer.

Benares (be NAH riz)
  Sacred Hindu city, India.

Bengal (ben GAWL)
  Province in India.

Betelgeuse (BEE t'l joo:z)
  A star in Orion.

Bismarck (BIS mahrk)
  German statesman.

B'nai B'rith (buh NAY buh REETH)
  Jewish fraternal society.

Bogotá (*boh* goh TAH)
  Capital of Colombia.

Boise (BOI si)
  Capital of Idaho.

Bolivar (boh LEE vahr)
  South American place name; South American liberator (1783-1830).

Bolivia (boh LIV i uh)
  South American republic.

Bowdoin (BOH din)
  College in Maine.

Brazil   (bruh ZIL; Portuguese: brah ZEEL)
    Federal republic, South America.

Bremen   (BREM 'n; German: BRAY m'n)
    City in Germany.

Bruges   (broo:zh)
    City in Belgium.

Brussels   (BRUHS 'lz; French: Bruxelles, broo: SEL)
    Capital of Belgium.

Bucharest   (*boo*: kuh REST)
    Capital of Rumania.

Buenos Aires   (BWAY nohs IGH rays)
    Province and capital, Argentina.

Cadogan   (kuh DUHG 'n)
    English family name.

Calliope   (kuh LIGH oh pi)
    Chief of the nine Muses.
      (KAL i ohp)
    A circus organ.

Cavalleria Rusticana   (*kah* vahl ay REE ah *roo:s* ti KAH nah)
    Opera by Mascagni.

Cebu   (say BOO:)
    Island and town, Philippine Islands.

Cecil   (American: SEE sil; British: SES il)
    Masculine personal name.

Celt   (selt) or (kelt)
    Member of a race akin to the ancient Gauls and Britons, including
    the Gaels, Irish, Welsh, and Bretons.

Ceylon   (see LAHN)
    British island colony, south of India.

Cheops   (KEE ahps)
    Egyptian king, builder of the Great Pyramid.

Cheviot Hills (CHEV i uht)
    Range between England and Scotland.

Chiang Kai-shek (chi AHNG KIGH SHEK)
    Generalissimo, head of Chinese government.

Chicago (shi KAW goh)
    City in Illinois.

Chihuahua (chi WAH wah)
    State and city, Mexico.

Churchill, Winston (CHERCH il)
    English statesman.

Cleopatra (*klee* oh PAY truh)
    Queen of Egypt.

Clio (KLIGH oh)
    The muse of history.

Cóbh (kohv)
    Seaport in the Irish Free State.

Coimbra (KWEEM brah)
    City and university in Portugal.

Costa Rica (KAHS tuh REE kuh)
    Republic of Central America.

Dáil Éireann (dawl AIR uhn)
    Irish Chamber of Deputies.

Dairen (DIGH REN)
    Seaport in Southern Manchuria.

Dalai Lama (dah LIGH LAH muh)
    Chief Tibetan Lama.

Delhi (DEL ee)
    Capital of India.

Descartes (*day* KAHRT)
    French philosopher.

Des Moines (di MOYN)
    River, county, and city, Iowa.

de Valera, Eamon   (AY m'n day vuh LAY ruh)
   Statesman, Irish Free State.

Devonshire   (DEV 'n shir)
   County in southwest England.

Don Quixote   (dahn KWIK suht)
   Spanish satirical romance by Cervantes; also its hero.

Dostoevski (or Dostoyevsky)   (*daws* toh YEF ski)
   Russian novelist.

Elizabethan   (i *liz* uh BEE th'n)
   Referring to Queen Elizabeth's time.

Elysium   (i LIZH i 'm)
   Abode of the blessed after death; a paradise of Greek mythology.

Euripides   (yoo RIP i deez)
   Classic Greek dramatist.

Fahrenheit, Gabriel   (FAHR 'n hight)
   German physicist; thermometer.

Faneuil, Peter   (FAN 'l)
   Boston merchant, builder of Faneuil Hall, "the Cradle of Liberty."

Fiume   (FYOO: may)
   Seaport in northeast Italy.

Galápagos   (gah LAH pah gohs)
   Islands belonging to Ecuador.

Gandhi, Mohandas K.   (moh HAHN duhs GAHN di)
   Assassinated Hindu leader.

Genghis Khan   (JEN gis KAHN)
   Mongol conqueror.

Götterdämmerung   (*gert* er DEM uh roong)
   In Norse mythology, the "twilight of the gods"; opera by Wagner.

Greenwich Village   (GREN ich)
   Part of Manhattan, New York City.

Gruyère   (groo: YAIR)
   District in Switzerland; cheese.

Guinea   (GIN i)
    Coast region in West Africa.

Haakon   (HAW kahn)
    Name of several kings of Norway.

Haile Selassie   (HIGH li se LAHS ee)
    Emperor of Ethiopia.

Haiti   (HAY ti)
    Island and republic in West Indies.

Heifetz, Jascha   (YAH shah HIGH fets)
    Famous violinist.

Helsinki   (HEL sin ki)
    Capital of Finland.

Himalayas   (hi MAH luh yuhz)
    Literally "snow abode"; mountain system forming northern boundary
    of India.

Hiroshima   (HEE roh SHEE mah)
    City in Honshu, Japan.

Hyderabad   (HIGHD er ah bahd)
    Native state and city, in the Deccan, India.

Ibn Saud   (IB 'n sah OO:D)
    King of Saudi Arabia.

Idaho   (IGH duh hoh)
    State in northwest United States.

Il Trovatore   (eel *troh* vah TOH ray)
    Opera by Verdi.

Iran   (i RAHN)
    Persian name of Persia.

Iraq   (i RAHK)
    Kingdom in southwest Asia: official name of Mesopotamia.

Istanbul   (*ee* stahn BOO:L)
    Turkish city.

Iturbi, José (hoh SAY ee TOOR bee)
    American pianist of Spanish origin.

Keynes, John Maynard (kaynz)
    English economist.

Khyber (KIGH ber)
    Pass between Afghanistan and India.

Leif Ericsson (layf EHR ik s'n)
    Norse explorer.

Leipzig (LIGHP sik)
    City in Germany.

Leverhulme (LEE ver hyoo:m)
    English viscount.

Lhasa (LAH sah)
    City in Tibet.

Linlithgow (lin LITH goh)
    Scottish name.

Linnaeus (li NEE uhs)
    Swedish botanist.

Los Angeles (laws AN ;'l uhs)
    City in California.

Magdalene (MAWD lin)
    College of Cambridge University.

Marie Antoinette (*mah* REE *ahn twah* NET)
    Wife of Louis XVI.

Maugham, Somerset (SUHM er suht MAWM)
    English author.

Modjeska (muh JES kuh)
    Polish actress.

Mona Lisa (MOH nuh LEE zuh)
    Portrait by da Vinci.

Monongahela (muh *nahng* guh HEE luh)
    River running from West Virginia to the Ohio River at Pittsburgh,
    Pennsylvania.

Mozart, Wolfgang Amadeus (WOOLF gahng *am* uh DEE uhs MOH
    tsahrt)
    Austrian composer.

Oahu (oh AH hooː)
    Chief Hawaiian island.

Pestalozzi (*pes* tuh LAHT si)
    Swiss educational reformer.

Ptolemy (TAHL i mi)
    Name of several kings of Egypt.

Reykjavik (RAY kyuh *veek*)
    Capital of Iceland.

Roosevelt (ROH zuh velt)
    Theodore, twenty-sixth President of the United States; Franklin
    Delano, thirty-second President of the United States.

Scheherazade (shuh *hair* uh ZAH duh)
    Queen, fictitious teller of the stories in the *Arabian Nights.*

Sibelius (si BAY lyoos)
    Finnish composer.

Sousa, John Philip (SOOː zuh)
    American bandmaster and composer.

Spokane (spoh KAN)
    County and city in Washington.

Stalin (STAH lin)
    Russian political leader.

Taj Mahal (tahj muh HAHL)
    Famous mausoleum at Agra, India.

Tannhäuser (TAHN hoy zer)
    German minnesinger, identified with a legendary knight; subject of
    opera by Wagner.

Taoism (TOU iz 'm)
    A religion of China.

Tibet (ti BET)
  Chinese dependency.

Tientsin (TYEN TSIN)
  City in Hopei province, China.

Tschaikowsky (chigh KAWF ski)
  Russian composer.

Uruguay (YOO:R oo gway)
  River and republic in South America.

Venezuela (*ven* i ZWEE luh)
  South American republic.

Wilkes-Barre (WILKS *bar* i)
  City in Pennsylvania.

Willamette (wi LAM et)
  River in Oregon.

Yom Kippur (yahm KIP er)
  Jewish Day of Atonement.

Ypsilanti (*ip* si LAN ti)
  City in Michigan.

Zoroaster (*zoh* roh AS ter)
  Founder of Persian religion.

Zuñi (ZOO: nyi)
  Indian of New Mexico.

Chapter 9: PRONUNCIATION QUIZZES FOR THE BRAVE

Mᴇᴍʙᴇʀs ᴏꜰ the Ancient and Honorable Order of Quiz Masters and Mistresses fall into two classes: some like them easy; some like them tough. One of the quizzes below is for the first, the other for the second, class.

The first quiz grew out of a list of words the New York Board of Examiners of the Department of Education used to measure the pronunciation of teacher candidates. The second one I prepared for a radio station to give to aspiring announcers.

If you studied the chapter on pronunciation gremlins, you won't find the quizzes too difficult. After you take the quizzes, you may want to refer to the recommended pronunciations on pages 69-84.

You may find the quizzes fun to read to friends. You may want to use them as a game at a party. Please remember that friends can be "severest critics" when scoring your pronunciation.

A good way to take the quizzes is to read them aloud in your best voice. Take the jawbreakers in your stride. Be nonchalant. Read them as if you used the words every day. Don't get flustered if you stumble. All of us pull pronunciation boners from time to time. Some of the words have alternate pronunciations. The scoring is based on the recommendations of the National Broadcasting Company. You'll find the lines numbered for ready reference.

Let's take the easy quiz first.

EXERCISE 49: A Teacher's Pronunciation List

DIRECTIONS: *Put a check before the preferred pronunciation. Answers are printed upside down below. If you miss no more than 7, you're good.*

1. alias	**a.** AY li uhs	**b.** uh LIGH uhs
2. almanac	**a.** AL muh nak	**b.** AWL muh nak
3. incognito	**a.** in KAHG ni toh	**b.** in kahg NEE toh
4. infamous	**a.** in FAY muhs	**b.** IN fuh muhs
5. irrefutable	**a.** i ree FYOO: tuh b'l	**b.** i REF yoo tuh b'l
6. languish	**a.** LANG gwish	**b.** LANG wish
7. leniency	**a.** LEE ni 'n si	**b.** LEN i 'n si
8. mausoleum	**a.** maw suh LEE 'm	**b.** maw SOH li 'm
9. morass	**a.** muh RAS	**b.** MAW ruhs
10. palaver	**a.** PAL uh ver	**b.** puh LAV er

11. pariah	a. pair IGH uh	b. puh RIGH uh
12. percolate	a. PER kyoo: layt	b. PER kuh layt
13. persist	a. per SIST	b. per ZIST
14. philatelist	a. fi LAT uh list	b. fi luh TEL ist
15. pianist	a. PEE uh nist	b. pi AN ist
16. portentous	a. pawr TEN tuhs	b. pawr TEN shuhs
17. pyramidal	a. pi ruh MID 'l	b. pi RAM i d'l
18. syndrome	a. SIN droh mi	b. SIN drohm
19. via	a. VIGH uh	b. VEE uh
20. xylophone	a. ZIL uh fohn	b. ZIGHL uh fohn

1-a; 2-b; 3-a; 4-b; 5-b; 6-a; 7-a; 8-a; 9-a; 10-b; 11-b; 12-b; 13-a; 14-a; 15-b; 16-a; 17-b; 18-a; 19-a; 20-b.

EXERCISE 50: Pronunciation Quiz for Radio Announcers

DIRECTIONS: *Even though radio announcers—like the rest of us—pull pro-nunciation boners from time to time, they are pretty good on the whole. They have to be—to get jobs on the large stations where they are given stiff pronunciation and voice tests before they are hired.*

Below is a test composed of pronunciation demons and prepared for one large station. All you have to do to measure your verbal strength against your favorite announcer's is to read the passage at first sight at your usual rate. Give the sentences as much vocal inflection as you can. The test words are in italics and numbered for ready reference.

IF YOU WERE A RADIO ANNOUNCER

Under the *klieg* (1) lights the *harassed* (2) *radio* (3) announcer *corrugated* (4) his *forehead* (5), *cogitating* (6) on the *vagaries* (7) of *English* (8) *orthoepy* (9) and *phonemic* (10) *extravagancies* (11). He feared *ignominy* (12). "*Ugh!*" (13) he *opined* (14) *sotto voce* (15), "only an *ancient* (16) *curator* (17) of some *otiose* (18) and *sacrilegious* (19) *athenaeum* (20) or perhaps a *perambulating* (21) *encyclopedia* (22) could make *progress* (23) with this *heinous* (24) *palimpsest* (25).

"How I wish I might have been *either* (26) a *dour* (27) *ignoramus* (28) with *aquiline* (29) *proboscis* (30) in some *effete* (31) *romance* (32) or an *impious* (33) *caballero* (34) watching a *robustious* (35) *melee!* (36) Better even a *flaccid* (37) *tympanist* (38) in the *harem* (39) of some *esoteric* (40) *maharajah* (41) or *recondite* (42) *blackguard* (43) *nourished* (44) on *rationed* (45) *oleomargarine* (46) than to be *concocting* (47) *bromidic* (48) *clichés* (49) at the *inane* (50) *commands* (51) of *yonder* (52) *grisly* (53) *panjandrum!*" (54)

Again (55) he *mused* (56), "These *laryngeal* (57) *effulgences* (58), I *suppose* (59), are the *sine qua non* (60) of *ethereal* (61) *broadcasting* (62). But I'd much *rather* (63) speak *ad libitum* (64)." *Alas* (65), his *postprandial* (66) *garrulities* (67)—*unraveled* (68) *ad infinitum* (69)—were *superfluous* (70). *After* (71) all, he was a well-paid *staff* (72) *janissary* (73), *assigned* (74) to an *aesthetic* (75) *program* (76). As the *director's* (77) *aged* (78), *ascetic* (79) finger *beckoned* (80), our *hero* (81) *acceded* (82) to the *demands* (83) of the *occasion* (84) and *luxuriated* (85) in the *lush* (86) *verbiage* (87) of *apothegms* (88), with a *machination* (89) here and a *pronunciamento* (90) there, *sieved* (91) *from* (92) the *sponsor's* (93) *long-lived* (94) *brochure* (95).

Hours later *when* (96) the *microphone* (97) was *quiescent* (98), he *addressed* (99) an *inquiry* (100) to his *lingually* (101) *acerb* (102) *spouse* (103)—who, by the way, was wearing a *fuchsia* (104) *blouse* (105) *décolleté* (106)—in *sepulchral* (107) *orotundities* (108), "I *ask* (109) you, O *Mellifluous* (110) One, did I *err* (111) *phonetically* (112) this *evening?*" (113) *To which* (114) she replied *dysphonically* (115), "No, my *hirsute* (116) *wight* (117)," *pandiculated* (118), and fell into the arms of *Morpheus* (119). Later when *Leslie* (120)—that was the *uxorious* (121) announcer's *patronymic* (122)—dreamed of an *ubiquitous* (123), *monosyllabic* (124) *patois* (125), a *beatific* (126) smile *hovered* (127) over his *wizened* (128) *physiognomy* (129), and he *wriggled* (130) closer to his wife, *Calliope* (131). Thus, *stertoring* (132), he was found, long after Old *Sol* (133) had crossed the *horizon* (134).

KEY TO PRONUNCIATION

(1) kleeg
(2) HAR uhst
(3) RAY di oh
(4) KAHR uh *gayt* id
(5) FAHR id
(6) KAHJ i tayt ing
(7) vuh GAIR eez
(8) ING glish
(9) awr THOH uh pi
(10) foh NEEM ik

(11) eks TRAV uh g'n siz
(12) IG nuh min i
(13) uh
(14) oh PIGHND
(15) SAHT oh VOH chay
(16) AYN sh'nt
(17) kyoo: RAY ter
(18) OH shi ohs
(19) sak ri LEE juhs
(20) ath uh NEE 'm

(21) per AM byoo layt ing

(22) en *sigh* kluh PEE di uh

(23) PRAH gres

(24) HAY nuhs

(25) PAL imp sest

(26) EE th:er

(27) doo:r

(28) ig nuh RAY muhs

(29) AK wi lighn

(30) proh BAHS is

(31) e FEET

(32) roh MANS

(33) IM pi uhs

(34) kah bahl YAIR oh

(35) roh BUHS chuhs

(36) may LAY

(37) FLAK sid

(38) TIM puh nist

(39) HAIR em

(40) es uh TEHR ik

(41) *mah* uh RAH juh

(42) REK 'n dight

(43) BLAG ahrd

(44) NER isht

(45) RAY sh'nd

(46) oh li oh MAHR juh reen

(47) kahn KAHK ting

(48) broh MID ik

(49) klee SHAYZ

(50) in AYN

(51) kuh MANDZ

(52) YAHND er

(53) GRIZ li

(54) pan JAN dr'm

(55) uh GEN

(56) myoo:zd

(57) luh RIN ji 'l

(58) i FUHL j'n siz

(59) suh POHZ

(60) SIGH nee kway NAHN

(61) i THIER i 'l

(62) BRAWD kast ing

(63) RATH: er

(64) ad LIB uh t'm

(65) uh LAS

(66) pohst PRAN di'l

(67) guh ROO: li tiz

(68) un RAV 'ld

(69) ad *in* fi NIGH t'm

(70) soo: PER floo: uhs

(71) AF ter

(72) staf

(73) JAN i sehr i

(74) uh SIGHND

(75) es THET ik

(76) PROH gram

(77) di REK terz

(78) AY jid

(79) uh SET ik

(80) BEK 'nd

(81) HIER oh

(82) ak SEED id

(83) di MANDZ

(84) uh KAYZH 'n

(85) luk SHOOR i ayt id

(86) luhsh

(87) VERB i ij

(88) AP uh themz

(89) *mak* i NAY sh'n

(90) proh *nuhn* si uh MEN toh

(91) sivd

(92) fruhm

(93) SPAHNS erz

(94) LAWNG LIGHVD

(95) broh SHOOR
(96) hwen
(97) MIGHK ruh fohn
(98) kwigh ES 'nt
(99) uh DREST
(100) in KWIGHR i

(101) LING gwuh li
(102) uh SERB
(103) spouz
(104) FYOO: shuh
(105) blous
(106) day kahl TAY
(107) suh POOL kr'l
(108) oh ruh TUHND i tiz
(109) ask
(110) muh LIF loo: uhs

(111) er
(112) foh NET i k'l i
(113) EEV ning
(114) hwich

(115) dis FAHN i k'l i
(116) HER soo:t
(117) wight
(118) pan DIK yoo: layt id
(119) MAWR fyoo:s
(120) LES li

(121) uhks OH ri uhs
(122) *pat* roh NIM ik
(123) yoo: BIK wi tuhs
(124) *mahn* uh si LAB ik
(125) PAT wah
(126) *bee* uh TIF ik
(127) HUHV erd
(128) WIZ 'nd
(129) *fiz* i AHG nuh mi
(130) RIG 'ld

(131) kuh LIGH oh pi
(132) STER ter ing
(133) sawl
(134) huh RIGH z'n

Put a check before each word you missed. Then determine your total by allowing 1 point for each error. The lower the score, the better. If your score is 40, you're good; 25, excellent; and anything below 12 puts you among the more careful announcers, who average 10 on this test.

Chapter 10: WHICH AMERICAN DIALECT IS BEST—FOR YOU?

Most of us don't realize we speak a dialect. We ordinarily link the word with jokes or vaudeville. But there is no such thing as speech without the earmarks of dialect.

You may have a "Down East" nasal twang. Or drawl as they do
in parts of the South. Or emphasize the *r* sound like a Midwesterner.
If you pronounce *oyster* "erster," *idea,* "idee-r," *Greenpoint,* "Green-
pernt," you may be a native of a certain section of Brooklyn. In each
case you speak a dialect of the great American language.

Which dialect is the best?

Let's try to answer that question. There are of course a great many
American and English dialects. We usually think of our native accents
in three groups. These are: (*a*) *Eastern,* (*b*) *Midwestern,* or *General
American,* and (*c*) *Southern.* The three are families; they have subdivisions—no one knows exactly how many.

The Southern family includes *Virginian Tidewater, General Low-
land,* and *Southern Hill.* Listen to men like Harry S. Byrd of Virginia,
Randolph Scott, Tom Connally of Texas, James S. Byrnes of South
Carolina, and Kay Kyser as examples. Southern also includes the less
populous *Cajun, Creole, Bayou,* and others. How many in all? At least
a baker's dozen is a fair guess.

In 1620 the first boatload of slaves arrived in Jamestown, Virginia,
to work the large plantations laid out before the Pilgrims landed in
New England. The Negroes and their children soon felt at home in
the South.

Southern culture of the time was indebted to France as much as to
England. (You will recall that the Louisiana Territory still belonged
to France in 1800.) You heard French almost as often as English. In
1736, Charleston had two theaters, one of them French. Half the population spoke *la belle langue.* Many early records of Virginia and Maryland were written in French. This was the language of the cultivated
homes and the great plantations.

Charles II, the Merry Monarch, and his court also influenced the
tastes of the South. This king, after a long exile in France, introduced
won't as a contraction for *will not, wan't* for *was not* and *were not.*
Charles set the style of using *ain't* for *amn't* and *aren't.* But only the
illiterates said *ain't* instead of *is not, has not,* or *have not.*

The slaves learned an English dialect with a heavy French savor.
They dropped consonants at the ends of words. They brought to their
new language deep and throaty voices—the result of large resonating

chambers. The Negroes spoke and sang in languorous tempo. The slave women looked after the planters' children and thus became the mothers of the dialects we now call *Southern*.

Southern dialects today strike your ear with characteristic intonation patterns. A Southerner breaks up, or "fractures," his vowels so that each one becomes two vowels, or a diphthong. He says "ya-es" for *yes*. He often drops word endings, especially consonants, as "chile" for *child*. In some sections of the South, they pronounce words like *thing,* "theng." In the same regions *penny* becomes "pinny," etc. About twenty-two million Americans speak Southern dialects.

The Eastern, or New England, dialect has ten or more subdivisions. These are harder to describe than the Southern dialects. A group of speech experts, under the American Council of Learned Societies, prepared more than seven hundred dialectal maps of certain sections of New England. The dialect of Boston's famous Back Bay is the best known. Henry Cabot Lodge, Jr., of Massachusetts, speaks it. So do Bette Davis and Ray Milland of Hollywood.

You will remember also that the Pilgrims landed on Plymouth Rock in 1620. They brought with them several dialects. The educated Pilgrims used the standard speech of seventeenth-century England. They carried it into the pulpit and schoolroom and spoke it in their homes. This dialect resembled today's Midwestern, or General American. It is the kind you hear Douglas Browning (ABC), Lowell Thomas (CBS), George F. Putnam (MBS), Ken Banghart (NBC), and many other nationwide announcers and commentators use.

In both dialects the *r* is pronounced wherever spelled. Words like *staff, dance, fancy* have the same vowel sound as *am* and *cat*. (The English did not pronounce words like *past* and *fast* with an *ah* sound until the late eighteenth century. In the beginning this was an affectation, introduced by the great actor, David Garrick.) In both seventeenth-century standard English and General American, *h* is sounded before *w* in words like *where, what, when*. Then, as now, they gave secondary stress to the third syllable of *cemetery, stationary, military,* etc. They never telescoped their words. They never said "cemetry," etc. The vowel in *fob, shot, clock* in both dialects sounds like the one in *alms, calm*. Until the 1750's, educated Londoners and Bostonians and Philadelphians all spoke pretty much alike.

Englishmen who went to Ohio a century later scolded us for the "barbarity" of our speech. Pronunciations had changed. Strange idioms had crept into the frontier dialects. But another reason for the differences between English and American speech was the change in England's standard dialect.

Around 1800 London and her surrounding country forsook the dialect used elsewhere in England. She established a different standard speech. The new standard became known as the *Oxford Accent*.

The Oxford Accent was originally the local dialect of Oxfordshire. In the old days each county had its local speech forms. The Oxford Accent spread fast when the sons of the growing upper-middle classes went to the great "public" schools of Eton and Harrow and the old universities, Oxford and Cambridge. Here they lost their local accents. They learned to talk like their tutors, trained at Oxford University. Then, as now, if you were an Englishman, you were known as a public-school man by the dialect you spoke.

The Oxford Accent has wide intonations. If you speak it, you drop the *r* except before a vowel. You pronounce *farther, sister, mother,* "fahthuh," "sistuh," "mothuh." Your vowel in *calf, staff,* etc., is the same as that in *alms*. Your vowel in *fob, clock, shot,* etc., is almost like the one in *chalk*. You don't stress the third syllable of *cemetery, military, dictionary, strawberry,* etc. You pronounce them "cemetry," "militry," "dictionry," "strawbry." You drop the *h* from words like *what* and *when*. Winston Churchill and Anthony Eden, both public-school men, speak the Oxford Accent, as does Ronald Colman.

BBC is the new name for the Oxford Accent, because it is the standard the staff announcers of the British Broadcasting Corporation must use.

Some few Americans want all our announcers, actors, and teachers to speak the Oxford Accent—"to hasten the day when all English-speaking people will pronounce alike." They want most educated Americans, who use General American, to learn to speak all over again. This seems to me a rigid point of view.

The following exercise points out some contrasts in fairly common

words. The first column shows British Broadcasting Corporation recommendations; the second column, National Broadcasting Company's.

EXERCISE 51: English and American Pronunciations Contrasted

DIRECTIONS: *Pronounce each of the words in the two indicated pronunciations. Study the differences of stress and sound.*

		BBC	*NBC*
1.	again	uh GAYN	uh GEN
2.	asthma	AS muh	AZ muh
3.	ate	et	ayt
4.	barrage	BA rahzh	buh RAHZH
5.	Berkeley	BAHK li	BERK li
6.	Caribbean	ka RIB i 'n	*kar* i BEE 'n
7.	castle	KAHS 'l	KAS 'l
8.	casualty	KA zuh wuhl ti	KAZH yoo: 'l ti
9.	centenary	sen TEEN uh ri	SEN tuh *ner* i
10.	clerk	klahk	klerk
11.	congratulatory	k'n GRAT yoo *lay* tri	k'n GRAT yoo: luh *tawr* i
12.	Derby	DAHB i	DER bi
13.	docile	DOH sighl	DAHS il
14.	doctrinal	dawk TRIGHN 'l	DAHK tri n'l
15.	futile	FYOO: tighl	FYOO: t'l
16.	geyser	GEEZ uh	GIGH zer
17.	Himalaya	him uh LAY uh	hi MAH luh yuh
18.	idyll	ID il	IGH d'l
19.	immanent	im AY n'nt	IM uh n'nt
20.	intestinal	in tes TIGHN 'l	in TES ti n'l
21.	issue	IS yoo:	ISH oo:
22.	kimono	KI muhn oh	ki MOH nuh
23.	laboratory	luh BAW ruh tri	LAB uh ruh *tawr* i
24.	lieutenant	lef TEN int	loo: TEN 'nt
25.	medicine	MED sin	MED uh s'n
26.	midwifery	MID wif ri	MID *wighf* er i
27.	missile	MIS ighl	MIS 'l
28.	omniscience	awm NIS i ens	ahm NISH 'ns

		BBC	*NBC*
29.	premature	PREM uh tyuh	*pree* muh TYOO:R
30.	project (n)	PROH jekt	PRAHJ ekt
31.	quandary	kwahn DAIR i	KWAHN duh ri
32.	Ralph	rayf	ralf
33.	Reich	righsh	righk
34.	reveille	ri VAL i	REV i li
35.	reverberatory	ri VUHB uh *ray* tri	ri VER ber uh *tawr* i
36.	schedule	SHED yoo:l	SKED yoo:l
37.	sheik	shayk	sheek
38.	strafing	STRAHF ing	STRAYF ing
39.	threnody	THREE noh di	THREN uh di
40.	tryst	trighst	trist
41.	zodiac	ZOH dyak	ZOH di ak

Another reason for the difference between English and American accents was the trek of New Englanders westward as the country grew. They called Ohio, before she was admitted into the Union in 1803, *New Connecticut*. The Connecticut Yankee took his dialect along with his family when he settled on the Ohio.

Professor J. P. Fruit recalled in 1890 the dialect he heard as a boy back in the 1830's in the Ohio Valley. They pronounced words like *stone, coat,* and *bone* in the old Connecticut style, using the vowel sound *aw*. They rhymed *put* with *but*. They gave *hoarse* and *course* the same vowel as *horse* and *corse*. They called a *chair*, "cheer." They said "sut" for *soot*, "quishion" (with three syllables) for *cushion*. They rhymed *bury* with *fury*. They called a *snake*, "sneck."

Those who remained in New England gradually took on new dialectal ways. The relatively dry climate, as compared with English fogs, and the greater variation in temperature probably produced actual thickening of the membranes and caused the *Down East Twang*. The rigorous winters encouraged you to talk with pinched nostrils and a tight jaw—to keep the cold air out. In that way your speech sounds came through the nose easier than the mouth. You found the vowel sound in *am* simpler to pronounce than *ah* and *r*. And thus you changed "fahrmyahrd" (farmyard) to "famyad," etc. Other characteristics which grew up are: the distinctive sound in words like *fur fir, err;* the dropping of the final *r* in words like *sister, brother* unless a vowel follows; the intrusion of the *r* between words that end and begin with vowels, such as "Canad-er-is growing."

The Oxford Accent not only gained a dominant position in the mother country but established itself in the universities here. It influenced the cultural centers of Boston and New York. They were in closer cultural contact with London than with the Midwestern parts of the United States.

The late Franklin D. Roosevelt's pronunciation was heavily flavored with influences of the Oxford Accent, although it was generally classified as Eastern.

Of the three large families of American dialects, the Eastern is spoken by fewest people, scarcely eleven millions. It is rapidly declining in influence.

Which dialect is the best? If you live outside the General American belt, you are wise to speak like your educated neighbors. For good speech doesn't attract attention to itself. It's like protective coloration. You don't stand out when you speak like your associates. Using the standard speech of your community helps you socially and in business. It helps you to belong.

General American is recommended especially for nationwide broadcasting and travel. General American covers most of the land. It extends west of the Connecticut River down through the middle Atlantic states—except the lower eastern shore of Maryland and lower Delaware. It spreads west of the Texas and Arkansas cotton lands. It goes north up through central Missouri. It blankets the Midwestern, Western, Northwestern, and Mountain states. Most of Canada is under its influence.

Of course, many of us would like all our quaint dialects to continue. But we are probably doomed to disappointment. You can't travel very far these days by auto, plane, or train without hearing General American. You hear it in the movies and on the air. In World War II millions of Southerners and New Englanders moved into the manufacturing centers where General American reigns. All these influences are killing off the less vigorous dialects.

There are at least eight strong reasons why General American will continue to grow:

1. It is now our most representative dialect. Almost a hundred million of us speak it. It is the major dialect of English-speaking Canadians, too.
2. Its influence spreads while that of the other American dialects gradually dies out. It prevails in the area where isolated "dialectal islands" are virtually nonexistent, unlike Southern and Eastern.
3. It's crowding Oxford Accent off the Broadway boards. Our leading actors now favor General American unabashedly. Up to ten years ago they thought they had to mimic their English cousins.
4. The National Broadcasting Company and other big networks prefer General American for their nationwide announcers. The most popular announcers, such as Harry Von Zell and Don Wilson, speak General American.
5. It is the most popular dialect of the movies. More than 50 per cent of all Oscars have gone to actors and actresses who speak General American. Joan Crawford, Bing Crosby, Jennifer Jones, James Cagney, Gary Cooper, Ginger Rogers, and James Stewart are among them. The others speak Eastern or use a foreign accent.
6. The great majority of teachers of speech enrolled in the American Speech and Hearing Association and the Speech Association of America speak General American. They teach it as a model.
7. It is the easiest of our dialects for Europeans to understand. Professor J. R. Firth, of the Phonetics Department of the University of London, says that General American heard in the movies is more popular among the British than their own dialects.
8. Because of the economic leadership of the United States, General American bids fair to increase its hold on foreign ears. There is evidence that General American is preferred to Oxford in many foreign countries.

If things continue in the same direction, perhaps by 1996 all educated Americans will speak General American. So, if you are changing your dialect, you may want to consider very seriously the benefits of General American.

A good way to learn General American is to select a model of your own sex. Men may wish to listen to the speech of announcers like Harry Von Zell and Don Wilson; to actors like Fredric March,

Clark Gable, Robert Taylor, Fred MacMurray; to public figures like Harold E. Stassen and Thomas E. Dewey.

Women may wish to select their models from well-known speakers like Jennifer Jones, Clare Boothe Luce, Joan Crawford, Shirley Temple.

Another way is to listen to phonographic courses of General American pronunciation. These you can obtain in music shops and department stores.

A third way is to study dictionaries that record pronunciation in General American. The most comprehensive of these is *A Pronouncing Dictionary of American English,* by John S. Kenyon and Samuel Knott.

A fourth—and the best—way is to study under a speech teacher whose own speech is General American.

Any of these procedures means sustained practice and close listening. For it takes time to absorb a new dialect into your blood stream. Any superficial attempt leads to inconsistency or affectation. And what could be worse?

Chapter 11: A STRAIGHT BACKBONE
DOES THE TRICK

IS IT TRUE that posture affects voice? That it impresses others in definite ways? That it's a sign of emotional control? The answer to all three questions is yes. The latest findings tell us posture is a fair key to a man's whole personality.

The great psychologist, Professor Alfred Adler, who first described the *inferiority complex,* studied pessimists. He discovered their postures are typical. Even in sleep, the pessimist curls himself up into the smallest possible space. He often draws the covers over his head.

Camptocormia, a neurosis, makes a man stand like a gorilla. Some of our soldiers and sailors had camptocormia in World War II. The *camptocormiac* stands with his body bent forward from the waist. His arms hang ape-style. There is nothing physically wrong with him. But he can't straighten up no matter how hard he tries. His strange posture is a physical acting out of his subconscious conflicts. Camptocormiacs often feel, "I'm the lowest of the low. I'm the doormat of the human species. I'm only fit to be walked on." Usually they hate their fathers and transfer this hatred to their officers.

Camptocormia is rare in peacetime. But we see slumping, kyphotic, or "question-mark," postures everywhere. Perhaps fear of atomic bombs is the burden. Anyway, the psychologists link slovenly postures to unhappy attitudes toward self, work, and those around us.

The old theory of how our emotions get stirred up said, "You see a bear, you become afraid, and then you run." The newer belief changes the order: "You see a bear, you run, and *then* you become afraid."

Have you ever tripped on a step and just caught yourself in time? *After* you caught your balance, your heart thumped, and you broke out in cold perspiration. You didn't experience fear until the danger had passed. Translated, this all means: If you make yourself smile, you actually feel like smiling; when you carry yourself well, you add to your self-assurance. Your moods catch the contagion of your postures.

Friends and relatives may become blind to our slouches. But others judge us by how we stand, sit, and walk. Some personnel managers "snap judge" an applicant for a job. They say to themselves, "He is determined or weak," "buoyant or listless," "quick to act or hesitant," "purposive or irresolute," simply by watching how a man carries himself.

Do you agree that poise and dignity mark good posture? When you carry yourself well, you make a wholesome impression on your audience. If your stance is firm, your sitting posture straight, you look well. Poor posture ruins appearance.

Our posture tells others a whole lot about us. They may be wrong in their judgment sometimes. But the easiest way to convince them that stooped shoulders don't support an empty head is to sit and stand with a straight backbone. The old French philosopher, Bruyère, observed, "A blockhead cannot come in nor go away nor sit nor stand like a man of sense."

So the first step toward good posture is to maintain a happy frame of mind. If we haven't learned how to stop worrying, if we are pessimistic or too often negative, if we don't get along well with others— we need to set our emotions in order. Else our posture may become telltale. Emotional ease frees us from bodily tensions. It allows us to breathe rhythmically. It encourages direct contact with our audience.

EXERCISE 52: Gaining Ease of Body Movement

DIRECTIONS: *Practice the following drills every day until your coordinations come easy. Don't do them too vigorously—as if you were really performing them in their natural settings. They are simply imitations of work and play coordinations, designed to increase easy use of your body.*

1. Stand firm on both feet. Swing a golf club for a long drive down the fairway. Swing a putter to sink a 10-foot putt.
2. Stand on the balls of your feet. Hold the badminton bird in the left hand and swing the racquet in an underhand serve with the right hand.
3. Stand straight and flat-footed, with the left side of the body toward the target. Hold the bow and arrow in position for an aim. Then let the arrow fly.
4. Grasp a bowling ball in the right hand and bowl it.
5. Lift a very heavy sledge and drop it with all your might.
6. Lift an ax over your right shoulder and swing it in a downward arc across the body. Swing it up and let it drop of its own weight.
7. Hold a scythe by its handles and cut a swath through a hayfield.
8. Hold a lantern out of the side of a car and swing it as if you were signaling the engineer.
9. Hold a 10-pound shot in the right hand, shoulder-high. Then put the shot without moving from a standing position.
10. Crouch as if you were ready to take off on a 100-yard dash. Go at the sound of the gun.

Good posture helps public speakers breathe and speak easily. The movements of the neck, shoulders, spine, ribs, and chest must be free and flexible. There must be no constriction of the windpipe, larynx, and organs of articulation.

We bring most of the 639 muscles of the human body—and its 222 bones—into play, directly or indirectly, when we take various postures. "The whole man speaketh." Yet we concentrate on the larger muscles when checking up on posture. We can control those of the back, chest, and throat quite easily.

The neck and throat muscles that surround the windpipe protect it against injury. They help hold it in an upright position for easy breathing. A web of muscles holds the larynx normally against the fifth vertical vertebra of the spine. The muscles that connect the Adam's apple with the breastbone, shoulders, skull, etc., permit the larynx free movement when we swallow, gasp, and the like.

Bad posture swings the cradled larynx out of line. It brings on vocal strain. Listen to your voice while you stoop to lift a stack of books from the floor. It sounds different from your usual voice, doesn't it?

Don't you see that a flat chest and drooping shoulders strain the throat and neck muscles? When we overstrain the neck and throat muscles, the voice suffers.

Speakers who tilt their chins upward and heads backward while shouting jerk the voice box out of place so that it can't work well. Result is lots of coughing or throat-clearing, hoarseness, and unpleasant tones. The right kind of posture prevents such embarrassments.

Good posture also promotes the right kind of muscular tonus. It's not true that good speakers are relaxed. No one ever completely relaxes his muscles—not even in profound sleep or under hypnotism. Why? There is a red nucleus in the brain. It controls muscular tonus. Your muscles "firm up" with rest. A sagging face, drooping posture, and flabby movements all point to the tired man or woman. Well-rested muscles respond quickly because they have good tonus.

Those who warn us to relax completely really mean something else. They mean we ought to use only as much tension as we need to obtain the best effects. Whether we lie down, stand up, or gesture, we shouldn't use any excess effort. For excess effort wastes our strength, prevents good results. That's why trained speakers get rid of the fidgets. The fidgets eat up energy.

Our problem then is to develop good posture for good speech, for good health. Why not make it part of your personality? Why not begin by giving yourself a postural analysis?

EXERCISE 53: Posture Analysis

DIRECTIONS: *Do the following drill:*

1. Stand before a large mirror and take a good look at your posture, both front and side views.
2. Back up against the wall, your heels slightly separated 2 inches from the floor board.
3. Feel the wall with your buttocks, shoulder blades, and the back of your head.
4. Stand tall, trying to reach the ceiling with the top of your head. Do not tilt the head.
5. Take a deep breath so that your chest (but not your shoulders!) heaves high; try to make your breastbone reach your chin but be careful not to move your chin downward. Draw in your abdomen.
6. Now walk over to the mirror and look at yourself again. Study the difference.

Retain the "feel" of your new carriage and wear it throughout the day. Every now and then you may need a check up. Repeat the drill. You can give yourself a check up almost anywhere without attracting attention. When you step into an elevator why not stand straight against the back wall?

At first your new posture may seem strained because of previous slouching. Remember that you can maintain this new posture comfortably, assuming that your muscles and skeleton are in fair condition. Good posture is not military. The shoulders aren't bent back or out of line. They aren't hunched up. You don't hold your arms stiffly at your sides. If you feel uncomfortable when performing the posture analysis, perhaps you haven't followed directions exactly.

If you aren't in "the pink" you may wish to take some push ups on arising. Why not take a swim once a week? Use the breast stroke to develop the muscles at your armpits and shoulders—the *pectoralis major*. These support the chest and hold it high. Why not walk more in the fresh air with your attention centered posture-wise? Notice how you cover the ground easily when you keep a straight backbone. Hold the torso in the new posture at table, desk, or workbench.

The rewards, of course, are many. Good posture aids circulation and digestion. It encourages deep breathing, upon which good speech depends. It makes for *euphoria,* the sense of well-being that convinces you now is the best time of life.

There are other benefits, too. Many of us have to fight against "middle-aged spread." This is the time of life when "bay windows," "corporations," "pot bellies," and "fallen chests" develop. Good posture is a devastating weapon in the Battle of the Bulge.

Good posture is responsible for the right kind of gait. Actresses spend hours walking up and down stairs with books on their heads to develop body control. They want to avoid the bouncy, clumsy shuffle of adolescents. Too many women don't walk gracefully. Yet almost every woman could if she practiced. It would add to her beauty, hold the male eye.

Dynamic public speakers influence their audiences in the right way with well-coordinated movements. They walk across the platform, rise, sit down, and execute gestures with ease. They take care to sit in dignity. They don't drape themselves over a podium or sink their hands into pockets. They don't stand with their arms rigidly behind them. (It makes the "kewpie line" stand out.) For they know that good speech is a matter of sight as well as sound.

You may wish to add the following drill to your daily practice.

EXERCISE 54: Posture Drill

DIRECTIONS: *Do these exercises several times over:*

1. Stand before a mirror as you raise your arms above your head. Try to touch the ceiling but keep your feet flat on the floor. Look straight into the mirror, not upward. Notice that the breast bone comes close to your chin.
2. Now let your arms drop slowly to a loose hanging position. Retain the high chest position.
3. Walk around the room several times. Keep the chest high between repetitions of the drill.

Poor postures sometimes result from chronic fatigue. Until recently, we were advised to combat tiredness with rest. But that is no longer blanket advice. Hard workers are ordinarily hard players. The efficiency expert, Dr. Lillian Gilbreth, recently announced the results of an important discovery: stenographers and secretaries who go dancing after eight hours of sustained work feel more refreshed the following day—and do better work—than their friends who go early to bed. What has all this to do with good posture?

Simply this: if you want to carry yourself well, don't get too tired. Stretch, yawn, close your eyes for a few minutes throughout the day. Swallow often and slowly. Spell work with play and stay refreshed. Such suggestions, when you make them habits, can result in improved posture. This is a necessary part of our program to talk better.

John B. Kress, Instructor in the Office of Physical Education at the United States Military Academy, gives his classes six rules for good posture. Why not use them as a daily check list until all the ease and poise that mark good posture are yours?

Six Guide Rules

1. Stand tall, walk tall, sit tall.

Children and adults alike have a tendency to sag or slump. This tendency develops into habit, and it then becomes difficult to reestablish good posture patterns.

2. Maintain good body balance.

The weight should be balanced evenly between the heels and balls of the feet. The head, shoulders, hips, knees, and ankles should be in line. When one part of the body gets out of line, the body balance is disturbed and strain is thrown upon the muscles and joints.

3. Flatten the abdomen by drawing it upward.

Roll the hips under. The stomach wall should be fairly taut. If the low abdominal musculature is drawn upward toward the chest cavity, the chest will be moderately elevated, and the shoulders will be square. Do not raise the shoulders or force them backward.

4. Point the feet straight ahead.

Support the weight of the body on the outer edges of the foot, not on the long arch. Use the toes for support in standing and walking. Do not walk from the inner border of the foot.

5. Keep the back fairly flat.

The normal spine has three curves: forward at the neck, backward at the shoulders, and forward at the low back. These curves should be mild and flow smoothly one into the other. They should not be exaggerated.

6. Use your head.

Think good posture. Look the world straight in the face. Do not tilt the head forward, backward, or sideward. Remember the six rules of good posture.

Chapter 12: GET THE MOST OUT OF YOUR LUNGS

A WINDBAG IS a fellow who wastes his breath. There are two kinds of windbags. The one bores you with yards of empty words. Like the young lawyer. At the end of his three-hour plea, the jury felt like convicting him instead of his client. The D.A. got up and said, "Your Honor, I will follow the example of my young opponent and submit the case without argument."

The other kind of windbag wheezes. His ideas may be all right. He may be worth listening to. But he's always out of breath. You feel he needs *your* breath to keep *him* going. He really ought to learn to get the most out of his lungs. For once he knows how to save his breath he can speak in long phrases when he has to—and do a good job of it.

We use up a lot of energy pumping our lungs, especially in public speaking. Here they do double duty: supply air for life needs, breath for vigorous speech. So why overwork them when the right way is the easy way?

John Doe's full breath supply of about 4,000 cubic centimeters is his *vital capacity*. It's just double that of his wife, Jane. Of course it varies with body build, health, breath habits, and the like. Joe Louis's vital capacity is greater than Santa Claus's.

John Doe inhales, exhales about 500 cubic centimeters with each breath as he dozes in his armchair. He unconsciously saves some *residual air* for emergencies. He takes a little longer to breathe in than out. Let him run for the bus, and he uses 1,500 cubic centimeters of *complemental air* on each quick intake. A lovesick man expels the same amount on a deep sigh. A good healthy snorer—going full blast—uses a little more.

Now the platform speaker needs complemental air to reach the back rows, sustain long sentences and good inflections. By trial and success (or training) he learns to breathe deep. He makes each cubic centimeter work. How does he do it? He learns *central breathing*. And that needs explanation.

His chest cavity, or *thorax,* is a bird-cage. It houses his lungs and heart. It's supported by the rings of twelve paired ribs and cartilages attached to his spine and breastbone, or *sternum.* He raises and lowers the ribs with his *intercostal,* or in-between-the-ribs, *muscles.* His lungs are elastic, nonmuscle tissue. They hang inertly until atmospheric pressure expands or contracts them. The action of the ribs and *diaphragm* governs the atmospheric pressure upon the lungs.

The diaphragm is an apron of muscle. It separates the chest cavity from the abdomen. It connects with the lower ribs, breastbone, and spine. The abdomen contains many vital organs: liver on the right, stomach and spleen on the left, intestines everywhere, and so on.

Strong muscles run up and down and sidewise over the front wall of the abdomen. These create powerful compression during breathing and other activities. When we pull these muscles in, the diaphragm moves up. When we breathe deep, the diaphragm moves down and pushes the *viscera,* or vital organs, outward.

Of course posture affects breath supply. Drooping postures lower the diaphragm. When you stand erect you raise the diaphragm and increase its activity. Deep breathing increases circulation and intestinal movements. It aids your general health.

Breathing is a reflex touched off at birth. The cold air strikes the lungs. It stimulates the respiratory center of the brain. The breath supplies oxygen to the body and carries off carbon dioxide.

We can't stop our breathing, but we can modify it in four main ways:

Clavicular breathing refers to the *clavicle,* or collarbone. You move the top of the chest and shoulders in clavicular breathing. Speakers who hunch up their shoulders when they take a deep breath are almost always clavicular breathers. Their breath supply is shallow because they don't use their entire capacity. These are the gaspers, almost always short of wind.

Costal breathing refers to the ribs. It centers around the activity of the upper and lower ribs. Back in 1893, Dr. Thomas J. May recorded women's breathing habits on a smoked drum. He found women were rib breathers. Their breath rhythms were without exception different from men's. He put down costal breathing as a sex characteristic of women. But ever since the corset disappeared, women have breathed more like men.

Diaphragmatic breathing refers to the diaphragm. It's better than the other two types because it accommodates more breath.

Central breathing combines costal and diaphragmatic breathing. It's the best of all. Speakers and singers who use it have more breath and better voices. To get a good idea of how central breathing works:

1. Stand with a straight backbone before a large mirror (preferably in your birthday clothes).
2. Take a deep breath through the mouth. What happens to your breathing apparatus? Lung volume increases in three dimensions: vertically by the downward movement of the diaphragm; from rear to front, by the raising of the ribs which causes the breastbone to move up and forward; from side to side, by the outward and upward movement of the fifth and seventh ribs.
3. Now puff out the breath in a long, slow expiration. Notice: The chest contracts. The diaphragm relaxes (it returns to its natural domelike shape). The ribs and sternum also contract by relaxation. The lower ribs drop because of relaxation and the pull of the abdominal muscles.

EXERCISE 55: How to Develop Central Breathing

DIRECTIONS: *Perform the following drill daily:*

1. Lie on your back, stretched out, left arm at your side, right hand on the region of the diaphragm. Now cough and feel the diaphragmatic movement.

2. Now breathe deep with your eyes closed, as if you were falling off to sleep. Feel the rise and fall of the diaphragm; feel your chest expand. (Did you know that you can't fall asleep until you breathe deep?)

3. Now breathe deep as you stand up straight.

4. Take a deep central breath and hum for as long as your breath supply lasts. (Notice how you have to take three or four deep breaths to renew your residual supply.)

5. Stand straight and then bend forward from the waist. Allow the arms to drop limply. Now pant vigorously for about ten seconds. Notice how the intercostal muscles and those of the lower part of the back respond. Stand straight and breathe deep to activate these "panting muscles."

It may take you several months—even a year—to develop into a good central breather if you practice daily. The time you take depends upon your posture, health, and speech habits. You'll know when you've reached your objective. You can observe yourself between two mirrors.

In central breathing your shoulder blades spread apart. Your neck muscles are quite active. Your ribs stretch farther apart. The back muscles near the lower spine and around the lowest ribs work hard. The diaphragm moves like a bellows.

It's fun to measure your growth as a central breather. From time to time you may wish to measure the circumference of your chest and abdomen. Watch the tape as you take a deep breath. You may even want to get a wet spirometer to gauge your breath capacity. Once you plot the results of your periodic check ups you'll try to break your own records.

EXERCISE 56: Applying Central Breathing to Speech

DIRECTIONS: *Practice the following drill:*

1. Take a deep central breath and prolong the vowel sound *ah* as in *alms* in a good resonant voice for as long as you can. (Once your voice quavers or gets breathy you know that your complemental air is exhausted.)

2. Repeat many times until you are satisfied with the strength and resonance of your voice.

3. Now prolong each of the following vowels slowly and clearly: *ay, ee, igh, oh, oo.* (Repeat them as a sequence for as long as your breath lasts.)

4. Now take a deep breath and count slowly in a clear, loud voice. (Each day try to add one more number until you can count to 15 or more on one breath. Be sure to make the last number as loud as the first.)

5. On a deep central breath read the following sentences. (Pay attention to your breathing and voice rather than the thought. You may wish to begin to read in a monotone. Renew your breath at every period and comma.)

  1. He didn't marry for beauty. He didn't marry for wealth. He didn't marry for companionship. He didn't marry for the sake of a home. He didn't marry for love. He didn't marry.

  2. When a girl stands with her intended at the altar, you know she is about to draw her beau into a knot.

  3. Husbands should be frank and tell their wives everything, and wives should be generous and believe it.

  —The Woman

  4. The fickleness of women I love, is only equaled by the infernal constancy of the women who love me.

  —George Bernard Shaw

  5. Suicides occur more often among married men and women than single persons, among the educated more than the uneducated classes, in urban more than in rural districts, between five and seven in the morning more than any other two-hour period, on Sundays more than on any other day, in May more than in any other month, between the ages of fifty and fifty-five years more than in any other five-year span, and in time of peace more than in times of war.

  —True

6. Take a deep breath and talk about what you see in the room. (Keep your voice clear and resonant, just as you did in the reading exercises.)

Hold on to your new breathing habits as you talk throughout the day. You'll notice your vigor and vocal persuasiveness increase. With central breathing as a habit, you can make yourself heard by a sizable audience. For your new breath control guarantees more resonance. That's the way to get the most out of your lungs.

Chapter 13: HOW TO ADD TO YOUR WORD POWER

Every one of us," said William Randolph Hearst's great editor, Arthur Brisbane, "is trying to transfer an idea from his own head into some other brain. And *that* is done with words." The words we choose to convey our ideas make for success or failure in our human relations.

J. F. MacGrail, well-known business educator, says that word power is to an executive what cutting and polishing are to a rough diamond. When you cut and polish a diamond, you don't add anything to the diamond. You bring out its wealth. Many a man gets in a rut because he lacks enough word power—or the right kind. Each one of us reveals a full or shallow mind, a narrow or broad one, by the words we know.

At Stevens Institute of Technology, Johnson O'Connor ran experiments on winning personality traits. He came to a remarkable conclusion: "An exact knowledge of the meanings of English words accompanies success in the business world more often than any other single aspect of personality we have uncovered."

The National Institute for Human Relations gives four vocabulary tests in its courses for business and professional people. The results tell us something about the cash value of word power. The best score on these tests is 100. Now see how the average scores of various groups line up:

Advertising-account executives 85
Bakery-route salesmen 46
Business executives (who earn $25,000 and up a year) 88
Certified public accountants 65
Credit men 60
Dentists 72
Department-store buyers 58

Not only does word power go hand in hand with earning ability; word power also reveals how high your intelligence is. That doesn't mean a large vocabulary belongs only to the college graduate.

One of the three largest grocery chains recently tested its executives. They took thirteen aptitude tests. All the executives scored far above the average on the vocabulary tests. But the highest man never went beyond elementary school! (The low scorer—still far above average, mind you—was a college graduate.) Yet the top scorer didn't want to take the vocabulary tests at first. He feared his formal education wasn't enough to let him do justice to the tests.

Psychologists test intelligence by giving you things to do—follow directions, solve problems, interpret patterns, and the like. But of all tests of intelligence those based on vocabulary are the best. Why? Because thoughts spring only from words. Man would still be a kind of ape if he hadn't learned to talk. He is without equal in the animal kingdom simply because of his word power. The behavior psychologists tell us that "when we read silently or think, our speech organs make imperceptible movements." They call all thinking *subvocal speech*.

Words must take credit for each and every advance mankind makes. Behind his every victory or invention, in back of all his organizations, are plans. Everybody makes and carries through his plans with words.

Whether you take out tonsils for a living, sell automobiles, build bridges, raise funds for the community chest, boss an office force, make atomic energy—you think in words. There's no other way. That's why your word power measures your intelligence.

Can you raise intelligence through word study? Yes. Dr. George S. Stoddard, President of the University of Illinois, proved when he was a professor of psychology that the *intelligence quotient* can grow.

Since words are the tools of the intelligence, what better way is there to improve yourself than to develop more word power?

How much word power do John and Jane Doe have? Book critic Sterling North started a controversial answer to the question recently. He quoted H. L. Mencken, author of that great book, *The American Language,* as saying, "Noncollege men and women, provided they read a few books, have a vocabulary of 25,000 to 30,000 words." On the other side of the mat, S. Stephenson Smith, who wrote *How to Double Your Vocabulary,* holds that the average American has a mere 10,000 words.

Smith's figures add up like this: The average American adult has 8.4 years of education to his credit. He has to read forty-five full-length books to meet just once his thirty thousandth word! In *People and Books,* published by Book Manufacturers Institute in 1947, they tell us the average American with an eighth-grade education reads three and a half books a year.

Newsweek uses only 250 words over the 10,000 commonest in an average issue of 50,000 words. *Time's* score is 350 over the 10,000 level. Even those who know 30,000 or more words usually prefer the comfort of a simple vocabulary.

Both Mencken and Smith agree that the average American knows many more words than most people credit him with. When we hear editors of pulp magazines say that John Doe uses only 1,000 different words in his daily human relations, we can be sure he knows many more.

We sometimes forget that we have a number of different vocabularies. The one we use most, of course, is our *speaking vocabulary.* Our daily responsibilities are much alike. Being common, we express them readily in about 1,000 words. *Basic English* gets along nicely with only 800 words, all of which can be printed on one side of a business letterhead.

Sometimes we spruce up our speaking vocabulary by giving it a bookish flavor. We throw in an unusual word. Perhaps we wish to impress someone. Instead of saying, "Bad day today," we may try, "What inclement weather." When called upon to address a formal audience we may also add some unusual words. But by and large

1,000 different words serve us pretty well to talk with others in passing.

Then there is our *reading vocabulary*. This one is larger than the speaking vocabulary. Many of the unusual words we read make sense simply because of the context in which they appear. If we see them alone—in a word list, for example—we can't always define them. You may know the intent of words like *hackneyed, trite, effete, banal, rococo*—when they turn up in a paragraph. To differentiate each one is something else again.

Our *hearing vocabulary* is also larger than our speaking vocabulary. Strange words take on meaning as soon as the speaker accompanies them with vocal inflections, gestures, and facial expression. These aids, along with context, define the words for us.

Maybe we learn as much as 90 per cent of our huge vocabularies by way of context. Certainly most of us don't look up word origins very often. If we did we would find that *aggravate* really means "add weight to"; *docile*, "teachable"; *splendid*, "shining." We use such words broadly. Most of us use *aggravate, docile*, and *splendid* as synonyms for *irritate, meek* (or *gentle*), and *excellent* respectively. But because almost everybody else uses them in a broad way, we get by.

If we want to increase our exact knowledge of words, we ought to turn oftener to the dictionary. Wasn't it Buffon who said, "When you read the dictionary, you read all the books ever written"? Every word, like every man or woman, has a fascinating life history. A good dictionary is nothing more nor less than a collection of biographies— of words. It gives their genealogy and pedigree, tells how their meanings have changed.

Let's look at a few word histories:

browse. This word originally meant the food cattle grazed on when grass was scarce. It comes from the French *broust, brout*, meaning "bud." The cattle had to feed on young shoots in the early spring. The earlier word *brough* may have been related to *bragh*, "break"; they also broke off the buds and twigs. A *browser* was a fellow that fed his noble master's deer in the wintertime. When you browse in a library you chew a bit of this book, a bit of that one.

husband. In Anglo Saxon *hūs* meant "house"; *bōnda*, "freeholder." A husband was the master of the house. Later on it meant he had a wife.

Later on also, *husband* referred to one who tills the soil; now he is a *husbandman.*

mugwump. The Algonquin Indian *mugguamp* means "chief." James G. Blaine in 1884 used the word to describe those who left the party and refused to support him for the presidency. Dr. Joseph K. Shipley, in *Biography of Word Origins,* recently defined a mugwump as "a fellow who sits on a political fence, his *mug* on one side, his *wump* on the other."

tuxedo. If you wear a tuxedo you are a wolf. For *tuxedo* comes from *p'tuksit,* another Algonquin word. The Algonquins used it in a scornful sense to describe the Wolf Tribe of the Delaware Indians. They also lent their name to Tuxedo Park and Tuxedo Lake, where in the 1880's a wealthy pleasure resort was established. Here the tailless dinner jacket, the Tuxedo, was first worn.

vernacular. The old Romans called a slave born in one's house *verna.* A domestic was later *vernaculus.* Hence *vernacular* came to mean our everyday language or a language used by the people of a certain country or place.

cunning. When Shakespeare refers to the villain, Iago, as a *"cunning* fellow," Shakespeare means a crafty, artful fellow—sly in circumvention. How different from the meaning we hear today in an expression like, "My, what a *cunning* baby you have!"

A good dictionary is of course indispensable. My favorite desk dictionary is *Webster's Collegiate Dictionary, Fifth Edition.* I like it because it's handy. It doesn't take up too much space. It's authoritative. It gives a good cross section of the six hundred thousand words in *Webster's New International Dictionary.* I like its typography. I'm used to its symbols and abbreviations. I use it every day.

You will find other good desk-size dictionaries, such as Funk and Wagnalls' *College Standard Dictionary,* the *Winston Simplified Dictionary,* Grosset & Dunlap's *Words,* or Random House's *The American College Dictionary.* The point is, the dictionary is your powerhouse. For you can't build the right kind of word power without a good dictionary.

Now the way to get the most out of your dictionary is to use it well. Let's look up *abrupt,* for example. My *Webster's* says:

ab·rupt' (ăb·rŭpt'), *adj.* [L. *abruptus,* past part. of *abrumpere,* fr. *ab-* + *rumpere* to break.] 1. Broken off; very steep, or craggy, as promontories. 2. Sudden; hasty;

unceremonious. **3.** Having sudden transitions from one subject to another; unconnected; as, an *abrupt* style. **4.** *Bot.* Suddenly terminating, as if cut off.—ab·rupt′ly, *adv.*—ab·rupt′ness, *n.* **Syn.** Unexpected, quick; headlong, impetuous, precipitate; rough, curt, brusque, blunt; disconnected; sheer, perpendicular, vertical, sharp.— **Abrupt, steep, precipitous.** Abrupt applies to a surface (as an acclivity or declivity) which rises or descends at a sharp pitch or angle. **Steep** implies such an angle as renders ascent, less frequently descent, difficult. **Precipitous** suggests steepness like that of a precipice.—**Ant.** Gradual; deliberate; gentle, smooth, suave.

The dot after *ab* shows how the word is divided into syllables. Next comes the pronunciation, noted in parentheses. The symbols for indicating pronunciation are given at the bottom of each dictionary page. (You will also want to study "A Guide to Pronunciation" in the introductory matter.)

If you're interested in grammar you will want to pay attention to the italicized abbreviations: *adj.* means, of course, that *abrupt* is an adjective. Later on in the definition, *adv.* and *n.* refer to the adverb and noun forms of *abrupt*. Other symbols for parts of speech, such as *v.i.* (intransitive verb) and *v.t.* (transitive verb) are given in the fore-part of the dictionary.

The entry in brackets tells us about the etymology of *abrupt*. It came from the Latin (L.) *abruptus,* past participle of the Latin verb *abrumpere. Abrumpere* is then analyzed: the prefix *ab-* and the root *rumpere,* meaning "to break." (If you wish to know the meaning of the prefix, look it up under *ab-*.)

English is a gold mine because it has borrowed freely from all sorts of languages: German (*Ger.*), Greek (*Gr.*), Irish (*Ir.*), French (*F.*), Old French (*OF.*), Anglo-Saxon (*AS.*), Middle English (*ME.*). When you see an entry like "*It.* fr. *L.* fr. *Gr.,*" you know the word referred to came into English by way of Italian, which borrowed it from Latin, which in turn borrowed it from Greek. Abbreviations for all the lending languages appear in the prefatory material of the dictionary.

Remember the four definitions of *abrupt?* The first definition refers to the physical characteristics of an object, like a hill. The second defines *abrupt* in its relations to manners or human actions. The third definition pertains to thought and speech. The fourth indicates the technical use of the word in botany.

My dictionary says that a *synonym* (**Syn.**) is "one of two or more words of the same language having the same or nearly the same essential meaning." The opposite of synonym is of course *antonym* (**Ant.**). Fourteen synonyms are listed for *abrupt*. Notice how they are grouped by semicolons to show closeness of meaning. For example, the three members of the second group all convey the idea of rashness. My dictionary also lists five antonyms for *abrupt*.

You may become so interested in certain words you will want to look them up in an unabridged dictionary. There you can learn more about their history—when they were first used in our language and so on. If you follow these ten steps in tracing the meaning of a word you can do a very thorough job. Here they are:

1. Look up every new word that comes your way.
2. Write the word down in a notebook kept for the purpose of increasing your word power.
3. Write down the language from which it was borrowed and the meaning of the foreign-language root word.
4. Write down its meaning or meanings at present.
5. Pronounce it aloud three or four times—oftener if need be. Look at it as you pronounce it so your eye will aid your ear and vice versa.
6. Write it in a sentence and read the sentence aloud.
7. Write down any synonyms you find listed.
8. Write down any antonyms you find listed.
9. Speak it and write it when communicating with educated people (unless of course it is too unusual).
10. Turn to your notebook in spare moments to review your increasing horde of new words.

EXERCISE 57: Two Dozen Words for You to Look Up

DIRECTIONS: *Here are twenty-four fascinating words to test your ability to use the dictionary. Why not apply the ten steps described above to make the words your own.*

amazon	carnival	pecuniary	advertise
tawdry	banker	belfry	wiseacre
pernicious	nice	mountebank	psychology
docile	callow	steward	hypocrite
conspire	sinister	focus	hector
tragedy	scene	educate	ejaculate

As you get the dictionary habit you learn a large number of *roots, prefixes,* and *suffixes.* These help you to recognize the meaning of other new words. The root of a word gives its basic meaning. The prefix gives a particular twist to the root meaning and is put before the root. The suffix comes after the root and usually shows the grammatical classification of a word.

Let's take *retracting* as an example. The root is *tract-.* It comes from the Latin *trahere, tractus,* and means "to draw." The prefix is Latin *re-.* It means "again" or "back." The suffix is *-ing.* It shows the word is a participle, or gerund. Sometimes a suffix like *-able* does double duty: in *manageable,* for instance, it means "able to be managed" and also shows the word is an adjective.

While all words have roots, not all have prefixes and suffixes. Here is a common root word: *come.* A prefix changes it to *be-come.* A suffix makes it *com-ing.* Both prefix and suffix give us *be-com-ing.* Many words, of course, are made of more than one root, such as *manufacture.* It comes from two Latin roots, *manus,* "hand" and *facere,* "to make."

EXERCISE 58: Some Twenty-five-dollar Words to Test Your Etymology

DIRECTIONS: *Psychologists and physicians often describe common ailments in a sort of twenty-five-dollar tripletalk. It sounds to laymen like some of the words below—for instance, numbers 1, 10, 14, or a combination of all three. A first glance at these sixteen polysyllabic vocables—sorry, it's catching—sixteen long words may give you acute spasmophemia (see number 12). But have another look.*

Most of them come from familiar Latin and Greek roots. You may recognize some of them from your high-school days. You'll be surprised how many of the numbered words you can match up with the lettered definitions by a little deduction and guessing. Answers are printed upside down below. A score of 8 to 11 is good; 11 to 14, excellent. Better than that makes you an old orismologist.

1. Monauralism

2. Labioschisis

3. Melotherapy

a. A bodily state marked by unusual activity.

b. Abnormal smallness of the tongue.

c. Reading disability marked by reversal of letters.

4. Logorrhea   d. Speech disorder marked by nasality.
5. Strephosymbolia   e. Foreign accent, outlandish dialect.
6. Pododynia   f. Lisping.
7. Rhinolalia   g. Harsh, breaking voice of boys during
                                    adolescence.
8. Parasigmatism   h. Hearing through one ear only.
9. Microglossia   i. Harelip.
10. Dysphonia Puberium   j. Existence of supernumerary fingers or
                                    toes.
11. Barbarolalia   k. Adam's apple.
12. Spasmophemia   l. Carefree tendency of extroverts.
13. Pomum Adami   m. Pain in the foot.
14. Polydactylism   n. Excessive loquacity, "running off of the
                                    mouth."
15. Rhathymia   o. System of cure in which music is used.
16. Hyperkinesis   p. Stuttering.

1-h; 2-i; 3-o; 4-n; 5-c; 6-m; 7-d; 8-f; 9-b; 10-g; 11-e; 12-p; 13-k; 14-j; 15-l; 16-a.

The science of the meaning of words is *semantics*. My friend, Professor Wendell Johnson of the University of Iowa, shows in his book, *People in Quandaries,* how word meanings affect our mental health. When you and I know multiple meanings of words—how people of different backgrounds use them—we are tolerant and relaxed.

As you grow in word power you feel a new confidence. You are a better, a more discerning listener. You doubtless find your sense of humor on the upswing. You become more quick-witted. You may even improve upon the dictionary, as for example:

argument. Discussion in which a husband is permitted to have next to the last word.
                                                    —*David McNeil*
bachelor. A man who thinks before he leaps and then doesn't leap.
                                                    —*John Newton Baker*
conceit. A form of I-strain that doctors can't cure.
                                                    —*Horace MacMahon*
dime. A dollar with all the taxes taken out.
fib. A lie that has not cut its teeth.
                                                    —*Ambrose Bierce*
income. The amount of money that, no matter how large it is, you spend more than.

inflation. Instead of not having the money you haven't, you'd have twice as much, but it would be worth only half of what you haven't got!

relatives. People who wonder how you manage to be so well off.

But seriously, this business of building word power is never ending. We who respect what Dorothy Thompson calls, "that glorious and imperial mongrel, the English language," work day in and day out to gain mastery over its words. It isn't easy. It takes a long time. But it's worth it.

Chapter 14: THE SEVEN-DAY DIET— OF VOCABULARY TESTS

Now LET's take some vocabulary tests. They help us to know ourselves better. We can see how our scores compare with the averages. If our scores are high, then we have every right to lift our heads. If below average, then we should mend our word ways.

You may want to take one test a day for seven days. By the last day you can set the habit of looking up new words daily. For if you want to get the most out of this chapter, you'll turn to study the dictionary after you score each test. Why not look up each new word you find? In that way you learn the word's history and a whole raft of synonyms and antonyms.

You may also fall under the spell of crossword puzzles. My favorites (they're double-deckers and deucedly difficult) are in *The New York Times Magazine.* Crossword puzzles are first-rate aids to vocabulary growth. They teach us new words, make us remember others quickly. They help eat up dreary days, lonely nights, and weary miles.

The seven tests below are by no means easy. Occasionally you may guess your way to a higher score on one of them than you really deserve. But don't let that stop you from guessing—as long as you eventually go to the dictionary to make sure.

EXERCISE 59: First Day's Vocabulary Test

DIRECTIONS: *Below are twenty-one rather unusual words referring to men and their activities. Select the best definition of each. If you get 11 right, you're good; 17, excellent; and anything higher is something to shout about.*

1. He is a *precentor* because he
   a. leads a virtuous life.
   b. conducts a choir.
   c. heads a gang.
2. He is a *gaucho* because he
   a. is left-handed.
   b. dances in an underground cafe.
   c. herds cattle in South America.
3. He is a *navvy* because he
   a. labors on a railroad or canal.
   b. is enlisted in the King's Navy.
   c. flirts with girls at every chance.
4. He is a *nawab* because he
   a. keeps a harem.
   b. swabs the decks of yachts.
   c. is a wealthy Hindu.
5. He is a *raconteur* because he
   a. tells anecdotes well.
   b. strolls on the boulevards.
   c. sings in musical productions.
6. He is an *apiarist* because he
   a. keeps live birds in a huge cage.
   b. makes a living from bees.
   c. teaches phonetics.
7. He is a *prestidigitator* because he
   a. sucks his thumb.
   b. performs sleight-of-hand tricks.
   c. speaks in sign language.
8. He is an *apothecary* because he
   a. utters wise sayings at the right time.
   b. mixes drugs for a living.
   c. rides to work on a bicycle.

9. He is a *cosmopolite* because he
   a. likes the bright lights.
   b. lives in the city.
   c. feels at home throughout the world.

10. He is a *mullah* because he
    a. loans money at high rates of interest.
    b. mulls over his worries at all times.
    c. is learned in the Mohammedan law and teaches it.

11. He is a *calligrapher* because he
    a. writes well-shaped letters.
    b. takes exercise regularly.
    c. tumbles and juggles.

12. He is a *seismographer* because he
    a. measures the movements of earthquakes.
    b. studies the stars through a telescope.
    c. photographs deep-sea life in a bathosphere.

13. He is a *docent* because he works as a
    a. preacher.
    b. teacher.
    c. poacher.

14. He is a *penologist* because he
    a. pitches ball left-handed.
    b. grows peanuts for vitamin-B content.
    c. is interested in prisoners and prisons.

15. He is a *provost* because he is a
    a. guard.
    b. superintendent.
    c. monk.

16. He is a *funambulist* because he
    a. drinks with a funnel.
    b. bathes on Saturday nights only.
    c. walks a tightrope.

17. He is a *pomologist* because he raises
    a. fruit in orchards.
    b. dogs in kennels.
    c. flowers in greenhouses.

18. He is an *orthodontist* because he
    a. repairs broken limbs.
    b. straightens teeth.
    c. treats aching spines.

19. He is a *flautist* because he
  a. plays a flute.
  b. flouts society.
  c. delves into old books.
20. He is a *prolocutor* because he
  a. asks questions in a minstrel show.
  b. presides at a formal meeting.
  c. always votes for the losing candidate.
21. He is a *peripatetic* because he is
  a. always walking about.
  b. always talking to himself.
  c. always grumbling to other people.

1-b; 2-c; 3-a; 4-c; 5-a; 6-b; 7-b; 8-b; 9-c; 10-c; 11-a; 12-a; 13-b; 14-c; 15-b; 16-c; 17-a; 18-b; 19-a; 20-b; 21-a.

EXERCISE 60: Second Day's Vocabulary Test

DIRECTIONS: *Here is an easier test than the preceding one. All you have to do is put S if one of the four words following the colon means the same or nearly the same as the word before the colon. Put O if one of the four means the opposite. If you get 13 of them right, your score is average; 16, good; anything above 22, excellent.*

1. happy:	last	ghastly	gay	wild
2. brave:	cowardly	buoyant	boyish	callous
3. lowly:	exalted	excited	exact	plump
4. evident:	lavish	manifest	incessant	manifold
5. innocent:	guilty	pungent	crumpled	garish
6. torrid:	frigid	urbane	fictile	fierce
7. lustrous:	hilarious	glossy	famous	lustful
8. coeval:	recent	ancient	indecent	contemporary
9. complex:	caustic	intricate	tepid	intrinsic
10. rigid:	valiant	flexible	rural	forlorn
11. tyrannical:	dolorous	domineering	tympanic	divine
12. transparent:	pretty	opaque	thin	light
13. similar:	same	analogous	harden	simile
14. judicious:	jolly	sorrowful	bearded	irresponsible
15. ungainly:	poor	graceful	sacrilegious	rich
16. fictitious:	true	delicious	romantic	fractious
17. acute:	academic	obtuse	frugal	pertinent
18. irrational:	orient	ocular	logical	saltatory
19. effect:	afferent	aspect	cause	hoax
20. stationary:	vagrant	stationery	stale	stalwart

21. supercilious:	draft	arrogant	lecherous	profound
22. sinister:	candid	jaundiced	omnivorous	sudorific
23. timorous:	intrepid	craven	cantankerous	seraphic
24. indolent:	persistent	obligatory	sanctimonious	cerebral
25. sedentary:	fastidious	exudative	redolent	kinetic

1-S; 2-O; 3-O; 4-S; 5-O; 6-O; 7-S; 8-S; 9-S; 10-O; 11-S; 12-O; 13-S; 14-O; 15-O; 16-O; 17-O; 18-O; 19-O; 20-O; 21-O; 22-O; 23-O; 24-O; 25-O.

EXERCISE 61: Third Day's Vocabulary Test

DIRECTIONS: *This one's the most difficult. You cross out the word in each line that is not related in meaning to the other four. If you get 10 of them right, your score is average; 12, good; 15 or more, excellent.*

1. petty	microscopic	dwarfed	minute	gigantic
2. infamous	intransigent	avaricious	humane	penurious
3. destructive	noxious	baneful	deleterious	ameliorative
4. incarcerate	manumit	immure	immew	confine
5. dormant	tranquil	serene	nostalgic	placid
6. elegiacal	rhapsodic	dolorous	lamentable	doleful
7. amenity	comity	gaudy	urbanity	courtly
8. clavier	clavicle	sternum	tibia	femur
9. overt	opaque	patent	manifest	obvious
10. pervious	permeable	penetrable	piscine	pervasive
11. risibility	relevancy	pertinency	appositeness	patness
12. depilate	obvious	epilate	tonsure	glabrous
13. ascetic	dour	aesthetic	abstinent	austere
14. cacophonous	mellifluous	inharmonious	discordant	dissonant
15. pharynx	carboy	demijohn	flagon	cruet
16. proclivity	dais	penchant	proneness	effete
17. trite	hackneyed	cephalic	rococo	effete
18. necromancy	manito	mystagogy	obiism	fecundity
19. aspersion	noxious	mephitic	pestilential	noisome
20. saffron	gamboge	cerise	henna	stigma
21. truculent	irascible	potent	manic	choleric
22. anthropology	psychology	sociology	geology	ethnology
23. giraffe	sphinx	aardvark	flamingo	shoat
24. mediocre	median	modal	mundane	medium
25. meteorology	cirrus	cumulus	welkin	nadir

The words that should be crossed out are: 1-gigantic; 2-humane; 3-ameliorative; 4-manumit; 5-nostalgic; 6-rhapsodic; 7-gaudy; 8-clavier; 9-opaque; 10-piscine; 11-risibility; 12-obvious; 13-aesthetic; 14-mellifluous; 15-pharynx; 16-dais; 17-cephalic; 18-fecundity; 19-aspersion; 20-stigma; 21-potent; 22-geology; 23-sphinx; 24-mundane; 25-nadir.

EXERCISE 62: Fourth Day's Vocabulary Test

DIRECTIONS: *Underline the word that makes the best sense to complete each sentence. If your score is* 12, *it's average;* 17, *good;* 20 *or above, excellent.*

1. The amount of money earned each year by a savings account is called the: commission, dividend, interest, premium, profit.
2. The colors of the plumage of hummingbirds are: iridescent, opaque, diaphanous, squalid, lugubrious, piebald.
3. The adjective referring to *cat* is: feline, equine, bovine, leonine, porcine.
4. One who swims is called an: agitator, natator, navigator, aviator, fulminator.
5. Animals that kill are said to be: rapacious, herbivorous, docile, tyrranical, posthumous.
6. An instrument used in surgery is called a: pedometer, scalpel, turbine, spirometer, accelerator.
7. A person who studies weather conditions is called a: toxicologist, meteorologist, palmist, philologist, agronomist.
8. Trees that shed their leaves annually are called: omnivorous, deciduous, arboreal, intransigent, tortuous.
9. The person appointed to kill the bull in a bullfight is known as the: toreador, matador, picador, moidore, corridor.
10. Kings were often: mendicants, tyrants, leprechauns, archeologists, octogenarians.
11. Children are ordinarily: vicious, depraved, whimsical, paracides, seraphic.
12. Color blindness is known as: daltonism, strephosymbolia, kaleidoscopy, myopia, dysphonia.
13. Olfactory, Gustatory, Kinesthetic, Aural, Tactile: is the name given to the sense of taste.
14. Savages are often: hostile, urbane, suave, genteel, civilized.
15. Most birds of temperate climates are: stationary, fluvial, migratory, anorexic, polylingual.
16. Comatose, Varicose, Dextrose, Cellulose, Tetrous: veins are often painful.
17. Diplomas are frequently made of: pigskin, parchment, papyrus, materia medica, celluloid.

18. The technical word for cave dweller is: troglodyte, Homo sapiens, monolith, archetype, giant.

19. Effusive people are: laconic, taciturn, loquacious, bellicose, unreliable.

20. Rotatory refers to: revolving, rebellion, rescinding, regurgitation, remand.

21. In states of great anger the human voice is: auroral, guttural, aural, dulcet, enticing.

22. Fat people are always: jubilant, penitential, obese, testy, pragmatic.

23. Sedan refers to a kind of: table, chair, horse, sofa, chaise longue.

24. An adjective that refers to life in the country is: urbane, bucolic, insupportable, procumbent, refulgent.

25. A statement that is not clear is called: inviolable, accretive, ambiguous, palliative, sporadic.

1-interest; 2-iridescent; 3-feline; 4-natator; 5-rapacious; 6-scalpel; 7-meteorologists; 8-deciduous; 9-matador; 10-tyrants; 11-whimsical; 12-daltonism; 13-gustatory; 14-hostile; 15-migratory; 16-varicose; 17-parchment; 18-troglodyte; 19-loquacious; 20-revolving; 21-guttural; 22-obese; 23-chair; 24-bucolic; 25-ambiguous.

EXERCISE 63: Fifth Day's Vocabulary Test

DIRECTIONS: *Supply the best word to complete the statement. A score of 11 is average; 18, good; 21 or better, excellent.*

1. A period of a thousand years is known as a _____.
2. A four-footed animal is known as a _____.
3. An archer carries his arrows in a _____.
4. The study of the derivation of words is known as _____.
5. One who owes money is called a _____.
6. The instrument that is mounted on the end of a rifle for hand-to-hand fighting is known as a _____.
7. An _____ is one who specializes in diseases of the ear.
8. Animals that eat only meat are called _____.
9. The _____ is located where the sky meets the land or sea.
10. Rubber is known for its _____ quality.
11. A payment by the government to the unemployed is called a _____.
12. A _____ is one who advocates extreme, rapid, or sweeping change.
13. A _____ is a concerted action taken to withhold business from a person or group.
14. One who gives money for the alleviation of distress among human beings is called a _____.

15. A person who collects postage stamps is known as a _____.
16. _____ is a disorder of speech marked by hesitancy.
17. One who collects books is known as a _____.
18. The technical name for a horseshoer is _____.
19. A _____ is a book in which a summary of accounts is kept.
20. One who travels to a shrine as a devotee is known as a _____.
21. A professional tramp is a _____.
22. A patois is a kind of _____.
23. The steersman of a racing shell or boat is known as a _____.
24. One who believes that everything in nature is ordered for the best is known as an _____.
25. Animals that sleep during the winter are said to _____.

1-millenium; 2-quadruped; 3-quiver; 4-etymology; 5-debtor; 6-bayonet; 7-otologist; 8-carnivorous; 9-horizon; 10-elastic; 11-dole; 12-radical; 13-boycott; 14-philanthropist; 15-philatelist; 16-stuttering, stammering; 17-bibliophile; 18-farrier; 19-ledger; 20-pilgrim; 21-hobo; 22-dialect, speech; 23-coxswain; 24-optimist; 25-hibernate.

EXERCISE 64: Sixth Day's Vocabulary Test

DIRECTIONS: *There are four legs to this test. All of them refer to words and phrases that have become current in the fields of politics, war, diplomacy, and labor. A fair score is* 10; 14, *good;* 18 *or above, excellent.*

DIRECTIONS: *Underline the word defined:*

1. An about face or abrupt change in diplomatic policy is a: démarche, plebiscite, coup d'état, revolution, putsch.
2. The Chinese motto broadly meaning *All for one and one for all!* and adopted by Carson's Raiders in World War II is: hara-kiri, gung ho, wai-wai, jai alai, hubba hubba.
3. Spreading jobs by limiting work or output with the purpose of preventing unemployment is: featherbedding, kickbacking, wildcatting, bargaineering, rubber stretching.
4. Extermination of racial and national groups is: paracide, omnicide, genocide, hecatomb, pyre.
5. One who tries to apply an abstract political theory with little or no regard for practical considerations is a: demagogue, doctrinaire, démenti, diatriber, malcontent.

DIRECTIONS: *Four out of each set of five words below are related. Which one is not?*

1. Bushido, kamikaze, baka, banzai, amah.
2. evzone, sapper, sniper, Maquis, jeep.
3. radar, isotope, transpondor, walkie-talkie, coaxial cable.
4. Esperanto, Babel, Ilo, Novial, Volapük.
5. Blitzkrieg, Herrenvolk, Generalissimo, Panzer, Fuehrer.

DIRECTIONS: *Match the appropriate letters and numbers:*

1. Yellow dog
2. Pairing
3. Pakistan

4. Zaibatsu
5. Issei

a. Moslem nation in India.
b. Refers to a contract excluding the hiring of union members.
c. An agreement between two members of a legislative body on opposite sides of an issue that in case of the absence of one the other will refrain from voting.
d. Big business clans of Japan.
e. Japanese who immigrated to the United States before World War II.

DIRECTIONS: *Supply the best word to complete the statement:*

1. A _____ is a concerted action taken to withhold business from a person or group.
2. An _____ curtain implies strict censorship and limitation of travel.
3. _____ is the term applied to the official ways of diplomatic courtesy and deportment.
4. A _____ session of a peace conference is one attended by all those representatives entitled to be present.
5. A government report on any subject, especially a publication by the British Foreign Office, is known as a _____.

1-boycott; 2-iron; 3-protocol; 4-plenary; 5-White Paper.

1-b; 2-c; 3-a; 4-d; 5-e.

1-They are all Japanese words except *amah*; 2-They are all warriors except *jeep*; 3-They all refer to radio except *isotope*; 4-They are all artificial languages except *Babel*; 5-They all refer to Nazi Germany except *Generalissimo*.

1-démarche; 2-gung ho; 3-featherbedding; 4-genocide; 5-doctrinaire.

EXERCISE 65: Seventh Day's Vocabulary Test

DIRECTIONS: *In this test there are more definitions than adjectives to be defined. Select the appropriate definition for each word in the first column. If you get a score of 14, your knowledge of unusual adjectives is average; 17, good; 18 or above, excellent.*

1. Arid
2. Somatic

3. Recreant
4. Glabrous

5. Protean
6. Laggard
7. Libidinous
8. Omniscient
9. Perfidious

10. Hedonistic
11. Contumacious
12. Truculent

13. Occult
14. Loquacious
15. Congruous
16. Obsolescent
17. Insensate
18. Friable
19. Strident
20. Integral

a. Lewd, "full of passion"
b. Exceedingly changeable, taking on different shapes
c. Dry, barren
d. Pertaining to the body (as opposed to the mind)
e. Deep, bottomless
f. Smooth, bald
g. Cowardly, unfaithful to duty
h. Beautiful, pretty
i. Harmoniously related, appropriate, suitable, fitting
j. Slow, loitering, lazy
k. Diamond-shaped
l. Having universal knowledge, infinitely wise
m. Easily pulverized
n. Living for pleasure
o. Savage, cruel, scathing
p. Treacherous, deliberately false to a trust
q. Talkative, garrulous
r. Bereft of reason, brutal
s. Pertaining to magic, mysterious
t. Going out of use, outworn
u. Necessary to complete the whole
v. Stubbornly disobedient, resisting authority
w. Harsh-sounding, shrill

1-c; 2-d; 3-g; 4-f; 5-b; 6-j; 7-a; 8-l; 9-p; 10-n; 11-v; 12-o; 13-s; 14-q; 15-i; 16-t; 17-r; 18-m; 19-w; 20-u.

You may want to continue your word study after you complete this book. Why not get Roget's *Thesaurus,* a standard collection of synonyms and antonyms; also Clarence Stratton's *Improving Your Vocabulary* or some other complete vocabulary builder? These books are good friends in any man's library.

Chapter 15: WHEN AND WHEN NOT TO USE GOBBLEDEGOOK

Gobbledegook," says Maury Maverick, "means not only big, foolish words," but it is also "talk or writing which is long, pompous, vague, involved, usually with Latinized words." The former congressman from Texas invented the word when he remembered how turkey gobblers—empty-headed critters—squawk. He makes a strong plea for simple words. He blasts the users of ten-gallon words and all ornate verbiage.

Does that mean we should never use gobbledegook? Probably not. Like most things in heaven and on earth, there's some reason for gobbledegook. Plain words don't *always* work with plain people.

Some years ago a psychologist went horseback-riding with a group of youngsters. The smallest was a moppet of five. He was in the sadistic period known as the *Questioning Age.* "What's that?" he said, as he pointed a finger at a telephone pole.

"Why, you know what that is; it's a telephone pole."

"Why's it a telephone pole?"—not letting well enough alone.

"Well, it holds up the wires, so we won't get tangled up in them as we ride along."

"What are the wires for?" he asked with a determined gleam in his eye.

"To talk to people. Don't you ever talk with your daddy when he telephones from the office?"

"Oh, yes. But why do I talk with him?"

In final desperation, the psychologist said, "To stimulate acoustically the tympanum of your pater's auricle so he can cerebrate."

"Ugh," grunted the tiny diehard, whipped up his nag, and kept the peace for a spell.

The psychologist learned a valuable lesson: *Gobbledegook is a godsend during the Questioning Age.*

Gobbledegook is magic in the ears of many oldsters, too. A mother of little education brought her son, Tommy, to the speech clinic. He talked as if his nostrils were closed. His schoolteacher said something had to be done about Tommy's speech. The therapist looked down Tommy's throat and found huge tonsils. They blocked the passages from the throat to the nose, where much of the resonance in normal speech takes place.

He told the mother in simple language—told her to take Tommy to a surgeon as the first step in the speech improvement program. But the mother said no. After all, didn't Tommy's nine brothers and sisters have tonsils? And weren't they making out all right?

The next week she returned with the boy for a speech lesson. The therapist again looked into Tommy's throat. He was very grave this time, shook his head dubiously.

"What's wrong? What do you see?" she asked in excitement.

"Tommy has malign hypertrophy of the nares and pharynx. He's got *paraphonia clausa.*"

"Oh, my! Oh, my!" she screamed and took off to the surgeon's, Tommy treading the air. *Gobbledegook is very valuable in certain human relations.*

They tell the story of the Hollywood executive. He advertised for an assistant with a Harvard degree. When the candidate for the job appeared, the executive asked, "Where's your diploma?" The young man said he was sorry, he didn't carry it with him. Then the high-powered tycoon, favorably impressed with the young fellow, said, "Well then, prove you're a Harvard grad—just say a big *woid.*" The young man delivered *antidisestablishmentarianism* and got the job. *Gobbledegook sometimes pays good dividends.*

Every experienced psychiatrist knows the healing powers of gobbledegook. One famous one, Dr. Morton Prince, reports a typical case:

I was consulted by a neurotic patient of mine for a very sharp pain in the foot. . . . On examination I found the tissue decidedly puffy and exquisitely tender to the touch. She walked with considerable pain and limped badly. . . . From the puffiness and tenderness, I was inclined to the belief that there was a local injury of some kind but was much in doubt. However, I assured her in a confident tone that the case was plain and that the trouble was *pododynia*.

The word evidently struck her imagination, and she was contented. Presently she said, "What is *pododynia?*" I laughed and said, *"Pododynia* is pain in the foot." Upon this she laughed heartily and said, "Never mind. I feel much better already. It is a great comfort to know what it is," and then she added, "If you doctors would always tell us what is the matter, we should not suffer half so much and would get well much quicker."

In the course of a few hours or so she was walking about without limping and free from pain.

Gobbledegook had once again come to the rescue in a humane cause. Do you ever listen to *Candid Microphone?* It's one of my favorite radio programs. As you probably know, "Candid Mike," Allen A. Funt, is a deliberate eavesdropper. He maneuvers unsuspecting people into peculiar situations. Then he takes down their words on a recording machine. The edited result is the program.

"Candid Mike" sometimes uses big words to test out people's reactions. Once he used *superfluous* as if it was a synonym for *superb, great, wonderful*. He asked a woman who was the most superfluous man she knew. "Oh, my husband, of course. He's very superfluous!"

Another time he used *equestrian:* "Don't you think a bill should be passed to keep equestrians from entering the country?"

"Certainly, I do," said a strong-minded woman. "They're lazy, they're selfish, and they won't work."

Funt called to a man, "Don't go into that store. It's *retroactive."*

"Oh, they all have labor trouble," was the rejoinder.

All of which proves that you can get some fun out of gobbledegook. Gobbledegook refreshes the spirit. Many of us would like to join a movement to translate a thousand and one hackneyed expressions into robustious gobbledegook. For example:

Go to hell!	Avaunt to the infernal purlieus!
You give me a pain in the neck!	Thou leavest me with torticollis!
Burning the midnight oil	Combusting oleaginous materia à la lucubration
Square meals	Rectangular collations
Clocklike precision	Horologic meticulosity
Drunkard's grave	Dypsomaniac's sepulcher
Tower of Babel	Edifice of polylingualism
Shifty-eyed jerk	Nystagmatous wight
Deep study	Umbilical contemplation
Flowery words	Floriated verbiage

Does your cerebral cortex absorb the semantic intent of the transmutations? At any rate, thanks are in order for the new word, *gobbledegook*.

Such uses of gobbledegook—and there may be others—don't excuse us from its misuses. Gobbledegook used indiscriminately spells trouble. One day the boy, Benjamin Franklin, said to his father, "I have just swallowed *acephalous molluscus.*" Terrified, the old man dragged his son into the kitchen for a dose of bitter emetic. Catching his breath, Ben yelled, "But, Father, I only meant to tell you I just ate an oyster." Ben has plenty of company to testify that *Gobbledegook can be dangerous.*

Perhaps the bottom reason why we ought to know many big words is to understand the fools who use them. Do you know these five *word types?*

1. Sir Empty Head.

He prefers resonant mouth-filling words. He reveals mental pomposity. His motto is: *Never use a simple word when you can find a big one.* He chooses, for example, *hirsute* instead of *hairy, bovine* instead of *cowlike*. He gives you *penurious* for *stingy, obese* for *fat, oleaginous* for *oily*. He favors Latin and Greek derivatives instead of the good, old, terse Anglo-Saxon that everybody knows.

2. Professor Pedant.

Technical jargon is his oyster. His mind is narrowly educated. He's an intellectual snob. His human relations suffer because ordinary people can't understand him. He makes a poor conversationalist: his audience feels inferior; they don't know what his technical words mean. His high-priced vocabulary may be a defense against inferiority feelings. He fears ready exchange of ideas.

Technical words are of course necessary, especially in a discussion of scientific problems. A scientist needs to know them when he speaks with other scientists—or instructs intelligent laymen. But some of our greatest scientists discuss their subject in simple words. Do you remember Huxley's famous lecture on geology? He called it "A Piece of Chalk." He told all about the earth's complex formation using simple words and homely illustrations.

3. Mrs. Malaprop.

This old lady lived long before her birth about two hundred years ago. In Sheridan's *The Rivals,* one of the characters said, "She decks her dull chat with hard words which she don't understand." Mrs. Malaprop rolled 'em in the aisles with her imperious disregard for word meanings, still does. She demands that her niece forget her lover. "Illiterate him from your memory," she warns Lydia Languish, or "you forfeit my malevolence forever." She wants to get Lydia married to someone else and says, "I shall be glad to get her from under my intuition." She admits that she was "never a progeny of learning," but certain things give her "hydrostatics" (hysterics). She compliments Captain Absolute by calling him "the very pineapple of politeness."

"Candid Mike" proves that the old lady still lives—in both sexes— and is going strong. Ever meet her?

4. General Linguistic.

He prefers general words to particular words. He's often inexact, hazy, or mentally timid. Watch out for him, for he may be deliberately vague and deceptive. As you listen to him, you note he prefers words in the first column to those in the second:

Generalized Words	Specific Words
jewelry	ring
criminal	thief
book	novel
terrain	prairie
scientist	botanist
conveyance	bus
receptacle	wastebasket
card game	pinochle
athlete	pole vaulter
room	parlor
coin	quarter
floor covering	carpet
quadruped	horse
timepiece	watch

Notice how much more interesting specific words make a sentence than generalities:

a. The man read the book in the room.
John Smith read the novel in the parlor.

b. The athlete bought the timepiece from the criminal for a coin.
The pole vaulter bought the watch from the thief for a quarter.

c. It was summertime when the odors of New York are unpleasant and when one doesn't need an artificial light to see the things on the table.
It was August when New York smells like a drugstore and the housewife doesn't need electricity to show her the spoons and dishes at dinner.

5. Herr Cliché.

He likes worn-out clichés, mixed metaphors, trite expressions. Frank Sullivan, in *The New Yorker,** did a good job of describing a *Herr Cliché*. He called him Mr. Arbuthnot:

Question—Mr. Arbuthnot, you are an expert in the use of the cliché, are you not?
Answer—Yes, sir, I am a certified public cliché expert.

* Reprinted by permission of the author. Copyright, 1934, *The New Yorker.*

Q.—In that case would you be good enough to answer a few questions on the use and application of the cliché in ordinary speech and writing?

A.—I should be only too glad to do so.

Q.—Your occupation?

A.—Well, after burning the midnight oil at an institution of higher learning, I was for a time a tiller of the soil. Then I went down to the sea in ships for a while, and later, at various times, I have been a guardian of the law, a gentleman of the Fourth Estate, a poet at heart, a bon vivant and raconteur, a prominent clubman and man about town, an eminent . . .

Q.—Just what is your occupation at the moment, Mr. Arbuthnot?

A.—At the moment I am an unidentified man of about forty, shabbily clad.

Q.—How do you cliché experts reveal yourselves, Mr. Arbuthnot?

A.—In our true colors, of course.

Q.—And you expect to live to . . .

A.—A ripe old age.

Q.—What do you shuffle off?

A.—This mortal coil.

Q.—What do you thank?

A.—My lucky stars.

Q.—What kind of retreats do you like?

A.—Hasty retreats.

Q.—What do you do to hasty retreats?

A.—I beat them.

Q.—Regarding dogs, what kind of dog are you?

A.—A gay dog.

Q.—And how do you work?

A.—Like a dog.

Q.—And you lead?

A.—A dog's life.

Q.—So much for dogs. Now, Mr. Arbuthnot, when you are naked, you are . . .

A.—Stark naked.

Q.—In what kind of daylight?

A.—Broad daylight.

Q.—What kind of outsider are you?

A.—I'm a rank outsider.

Q.—How right are you?

A.—I am dead right.

Q.—What kind of meals do you like?

A.—Square meals.

Q.—What do you do to them?

A.—Ample justice.

Q.—What is it you do to your way?

A.—I wend my way.

Q.—And your horizon?

A.—I broaden my horizon.

Q.—When you buy things, you buy them for . . .

A.—A song.

Q.—You are as sober as . . .

A.—A judge.

Q.—And when you are drunk?

A.—I have lots of leeway there. I can be as drunk as a coot or a lord or an owl or a fool . . .

Q.—Very good, Mr. Arbuthnot. Now, how about the fate of Europe?

A.—It is hanging in the balance, of course.

Q.—What kind of precision are you cliché users partial to?

A.—Clocklike precision.

Q.—And what kind of order?

A.—Apple-pie order.

Q.—When you watch a parade, you watch it from . . .

A.—A point of vantage.

Q.—And you shroud things . . .

A.—In the mists of antiquity.

Q.—What kind of threats do you make?

A.—Veiled threats.

Q.—And what kind of secrets do you betray?

A.—Dark secrets.

Q.—How about ignorance?

A.—Ignorance is always abysmal.

Q.—When you travel, what do you combine?

A.—I combine business with pleasure.

Q.—And you are destined . . .

A.—To go far.

Q.—Thank you, Mr. Arbuthnot. What time is it?

A.—It is high time.

Q.—How do you point?

A.—I point with pride, I view with alarm, and I yield to no man

Q.—What do you pursue?

A.—The even tenor of my way.

Q.—Ever pursue the odd tenor of your way?

A.—Oh, no. I would lose my standing as a cliché expert if I did that.

Q.—As for information, you are . . .

A.—A mine of information.

Q.—What kind of mine?

A.—A veritable mine.

Q.—What do you throw?

A.—I throw caution.

Q.—Where?

A.—To the winds.

Q.—As a cliché user, have you any pets?

A.—Yes, I have pet aversions.

Q.—What kind of cunning do you affect, Mr. Arbuthnot?

A.—Low, animal cunning.

Q.—I see. Well, Mr. Arbuthnot, I think that covers the ground for the time being. I'm sure we're all very grateful to you for your cooperation and your splendid answers, and I think that everyone who has listened to you here today will be a better cliché user for having heard you. Thank you very, very much.

A.—Thank *you*, Mr. Steuer. It's been a pleasure, I assure you, and I was only too glad to oblige.

Dr. Rudolph Flesch has done more perhaps than any other single man alive to make gobbledegook unpopular. He preaches the good sense of stating things simply. He'll take a sentence from a newspaper like, "University of Washington scientists reported today experiments have shown that microplankton organisms act as radioactivity 'carriers' in Bikini waters, keeping the waters radioactive." Then he'll change it into readable style for the layman: "Discovery of the missing links that will spread dangerous atomic bomb atoms to human beings was reported today at the University of Washington."

What he says to writers can help public speakers as well. Why are some speakers hard to listen to? Too many long sentences and too many Latin and Greek words. Flesch comes up with these important conclusions about sentence length:

AVERAGE SENTENCE LENGTH IN WORDS

Very easy .... 1 to 8
Easy 11
Fairly easy 14
Standard 17
Fairly difficult 21
Difficult 25
Very difficult 29

Not long ago the president of a company asked me to look over the manuscript of a speech. He was going to give it before an assembly of factory employees. It averaged twenty-seven words in sentence length. Some of the sentences were as long as sixty-three words! Is it any wonder there are so many labor misunderstandings today? How are employees going to understand their employers if they don't talk plain? At a recent meeting of the American Management Association the delegates voted that "communication" is the biggest problem facing management today.

Flesch defines "standard writing" as "what the average American will read with ease and interest." No sentence should therefore contain more than nineteen words. One hundred words should add up to no more than one hundred and fifty syllables. You heighten interest when you include at least 6 per cent "personal words." These are names and personal pronouns. Personal sentences—questions, commands, requests—help a lot too. Let them add up to at least 12 per cent of your total.

Notice how your audience pays attention when you apply these suggestions to your public speeches. Notice, too, how easily others understand your directions when you break them up into short sentences, well-known words.

In summary, then, let's ask ourselves some helpful questions.

EXERCISE 66: Gobbledegook Questionnaire

DIRECTIONS: *Ask yourself the following five questions every day for a month. Read the comment after each question.*

1. **Do I use words that reveal me as a sincere, modest person?** Gobbledegook often points to the show-off. That is why people who get along well with others never parade a knowledge of big words.
2. **Do I use words that don't offend?** Here we might list cuss words and low slang, also all familiarities of address that degrade or make unworthy comparisons. Careful speakers remember that *odor* is usually safer than *stink, insides* will do where *guts* offends, etc.
3. **Do I use simple words in short sentences?** Long strings of words put people to sleep with their eyes open or closed. That is why pedantic lecturing is taboo. Have you noticed how often a question or statement of few words brings good results? Short phrases and expressions save time, aid attention, and gain rewards.
4. **Do I use simple words in great variety?** We get tired hearing a man or woman repeat *very* or *nice*. We lose attention when slang crowds out accepted usage. Occasional slang? Yes. But not an unvarying diet of it.
5. **Do I use words that satisfy?** "Pleasant words," according to Solomon's Proverbs, "are as a honeycomb; sweet to the soul, and health to the bones." Simple words winged with imagination are "fair as a star when only one is shining in the sky."

Such questions are close to the hearts of the world's greatest speakers and writers. Abraham Lincoln thought of them as he prepared the immortal lines he spoke at Gettysburg. So did the writers of the Declaration of Independence, among whom were the country's leading orators. Good speakers set very definite standards of word selection for themselves. Many read the Bible for word study. For here is a fountain of simple words. In this way speakers know their thoughts are understood.

Chapter 16: TRY PHONETICS ON
FOR SIZE

Have you ever seen or read Shaw's play, *Pygmalion?* You'll recall it's
the play in which he preaches, ɡʊd spitʃ ɪz ðə θɪŋ ɪf ju wɪʃ tu ɡet tu
ðə tɑp‖ The funny symbols come from the International Phonetic
Alphabet.

Under Professor Higgins's instruction, the raucous cockney-tongued
flower peddler, Eliza Doolittle, learns to speak like an angel. Shaw
implies that beauty is as beauty says it; that if you can hold your own
in polite society's chitchat, you're made.

In their many practice hours, Eliza and the professor undoubtedly
use IPA, abbreviation of the International Phonetic Alphabet, also of
the International Phonetic Association. Promulgated in 1888—two years
after the founding of the International Phonetic Association and almost
a quarter of a century before Shaw set Higgins on his ever-popular
course—IPA is only now really going places.

Shaw lionizes his old friend, Henry Sweet, in the role of Higgins.
Professor Sweet was the first honorary chairman of IPA. He taught
speech at Oxford University. Sweet and his colleagues felt the need
of a world-wide alphabet to represent all the sounds we human beings
make in our babel of countless languages.

And so the IPA—it has more than one hundred and sixty symbols
and modifiers—is used everywhere in the civilized world today. Its
Bible is *Le Maître Phonétique.* The Association publishes this six times
a year for its thousands of international members, mainly teachers.

Printed entirely in IPA—even the Association's financial statements
are, if you please—a representative issue contains articles in many languages. You may find Hindustani, English, Swahili, French, and
Russian all between the same covers. Once you know the entire IPA,

you can pronounce any language. Rather, once you learn to enunciate the sounds represented by IPA symbols, you may become polylingually proficient. The difference is important.

That's why phoneticians emphasize the term *ear words* as opposed to *eye words,* particularly when they deal with the English language. This tough tongue has a bad reputation. It keeps spelling at logger-heads with pronunciation.

A professor of phonetics was asked once, "Could you spell *fish* any other way?"

"Well," he said, "it *might* be spelled 'ghoti.' *Gh* stands for *f* as in *laugh;* *o* stands for the *i* sound as in *women;* and the *ti* stands for *sh* as in *attention.* That's how 'ghoti' spells *fish!*"

English eye and ear words are certainly different. For example, the eye words *alms, glad, ask, ball, coal, gaol,* have widely different vowel values as their ear words reveal: ɑmz, glæd, ask, bɔl, koʊl, dʒeɪl.

The phonetician's business is ear words. He tolerates only one symbol for each sound. He's always consistent; he uses the same symbol each time he represents the same sound. He doesn't use capital letters either, nor orthodox punctuation.

He tells us *General American* contains approximately forty phonemes. A phoneme, he says, is a family of sounds, closely related. For example, each of the *e* sounds in *ten and ten are twenty* is slightly different from the others. Yet all of them belong to the *e* phoneme. Untrained ears can't differentiate them. Professor Higgins trained his ear to identify 130 phonemic variations!

You need forty symbols in broad transcription to represent the forty phonemes. But our Roman alphabet contains only twenty-six characters. To be consistent, the phonetician adds some symbols. He also casts out some others. He does not use *c,* for instance. Why? Because it's pronounced either *k* as in *curtain* or *s* as in *certain.*

This whole business of phonetic symbols is intimately tied up with hearing. Phonetics is the language of the ear. Alexander Melville Bell, relative of the telephone inventor, devised a phonetic alphabet in 1867. He called it *Visible Speech, Science of Alphabetics.* He used it to teach the deaf to speak. Henry Sweet paid tribute to this pioneer work.

But Bell wasn't the first to teach phonetic symbols. Our own eager-minded Ben Franklin proposed a phonetic alphabet a century earlier.

They still use Visible Speech in some of the schools for the deaf. But they use IPA even more to train the hard of hearing.

Psychologists tell us that we hear best when we are fourteen or fifteen. They say hearing gradually tapers off after that unless we develop it.

Here is where the IPA helps. If you learn to associate symbols with sounds, first in isolation and then in connected discourse, you can actually raise the *limen,* or *threshold,* of your hearing. That is, if there's no organic deterioration in your hearing mechanism. IPA training often helps the hard of hearing get used to mechanical hearing aids, too. That's why speech and hearing clinics use IPA along with phonographic voice recording and other laboratory aids.

But IPA is by no means confined to the upper reaches of colleges and clinics. Some training programs for salesmen include IPA instruction. Not long ago a company opened a new territory in the South. They found subconscious resistance to the New England speech of its salesmen. They called the salesmen in from the field and gave them intensive training to soften their dialectal differences. They actually taught them to drawl a bit. It was IPA instruction and voice recordings that did the trick!

In World War II the speed-up programs of language teaching—in and out of the armed forces—demonstrated one of the basic principles of the International Phonetic Association: that the shortest cut to learning a foreign language is to speak it. With the aid of IPA a soldier or sailor could learn to speak Japanese, Italian, German, or some other language within a few weeks. Other enthusiasts of IPA are immigrants. They want to speak the speech of their new homeland. They join with actors, radio announcers, teachers, salesmen, and others in finding IPA a good friend.

Scarcely a day goes by but what Professor Higgins—or one of his colleagues—hears, "But isn't IPA too hard to learn?" And then he replies that even youngsters in the primary grades can take IPA in their stride. He may hand you a nursery rhyme or two, written partly in eye words and partly in ear words, to let you taste the pudding.

EXERCISE 67: Reading Phonetic Symbols

DIRECTIONS: *Read the nursery rhymes on p. 156. Study the ear words. If you have forgotten your nursery rhymes, you may have to borrow a Mother Goose book. After you read them refer to the phonetics key:*

Key Word	Phonetics	Key Word	Phonetics
*a*ll	ɔl	*o*ld	ould
*a*t	æt	*oi*l	ɔil
*a*ce	eɪs	*ou*t	aut
*ai*r	ɛər	*p*ine	paɪn
*a*lms	ɑmz	*r*ace	reɪs
*b*ack	bæk	*s*o	sou
*ch*ain	tʃem	*sh*all	ʃæl
*d*o	du	*t*o	tu
*e*lm	ɛlm	*th*in	θɪn
*ee*l	il	*th*ee	ði
*ear*n	ən	*u*p	ʌp
ear	ɪər	*f*oot	fut
*f*it	fɪt	*f*ood	fud
*g*o	gou	*u*se	juz
*h*urt	hət	*v*ine	vaɪn
*i*s	ɪz	*w*ine	waɪn
*i*ce	aɪs	*wh*ine	hwaɪn
*j*ay	dʒeɪ	*y*ou	ju
*k*iss	kɪs	*z*est	zest
*l*amb	læm	*rou*ge	ruʒ
*m*y	maɪ	*s*of*a*	soufə
*n*ice	naɪs	*littl*e	lɪtl̩
*si*ng	sɪŋ		

| used in place of a comma and for phrase markings.

‖ used instead of a period to mark the end of a sentence.

accent mark used in polysyllables, *in front of* the syllable it stresses. (For example: *remember*, "rɪˈmɛmbər")

secondary accent mark; appears before and *below* the syllable receiving secondary stress. (For example: *cemetery*, "ˈsɛməˌtɛrɪ")

1. A dillar, a dollar,
   ə tɛn əklɑk skɑlər|
   What makes you come so soon?
   ju just tə kʌm æt tɛn əklɑk|
   And now you come at noon.

2. Jack Sprat could eat no fat,
   hɪz waɪf kʊd it noʊ lin|
   And so betwixt them both, you see,
   ðeɪ lɪkt ðə plætər klin||

3. Tom, Tom, the piper's son,
   stoʊl ə pɪg| ənd əweɪ hi rʌn||
   The pig was eat, and Tom was beat,
   ən tɑm wɛnt kraɪŋ daʊn ðə strit||

4. Peter, Peter, pumpkin-eater,
   hæd ə waɪf ən kʊdṇt kip hər|
   He put her in a pumpkin shell,
   ən ðɛər hi kɛpt hər vɛrɪ wɛl||

5. Hickety, pickety, my black hen,
   ʃi leɪz ɛgz fər dʒɛntḷmɛn||
   Gentlemen come every day
   tu si hwɑt maɪ blæk hɛn dʌθ leɪ||

6. Little Polly Flinders
   Sat among the cinders,
   wɔrmɪŋ hər prɪtɪ lɪtḷ toʊz||
   Her mother came and caught her,
   ənd hwɪpt hər lɪtḷ dɔtər
   For spoiling her nice new clothes.

7. Jack and dʒɪl went up the hɪl
   To fetch a peɪl əv wɔtər||
   Jack fell down and broʊk hɪz kraʊn|
   And dʒɪl keɪm tʌmblɪŋ æftər||

8. Little dʒæk hɔrnər sæt ɪn ə kɔrnər|
   Eating ə krɪsməs paɪ||

He put in hɪz θʌm| ən tʊk aʊt ə plʌm|
And said, hwɑt ə gʊd bɔɪ æm aɪ||

9. Hey, diddle, diddle, the cat and the fiddle,
   ðə kaʊ dʒʌmpt oʊvər ðə mun||
   ðə lɪtl̩ dɔg læft tə si sʌtʃ spɔrt|
   ən ðə dɪʃ ræn əweɪ wɪð ðə spun||

10. Humpty-Dumpty sat on a wall,
    hʌmptɪ dʌmptɪ hæd ə greɪt fɔl||
    ɔl ðə kɪŋz hɔrsəz| ənd ɔl ðə kɪŋz men|
    kʊdn̩t pʊt hʌmptɪ dʌmptɪ təgeðər əgen||

11. Three blind mice, see how they run!
    ðeɪ ɔl ræn æftər ðə fɑrmərz waɪf|
    hu kʌt ɔf ðɛər teɪlz wɪð ðə kɑrvɪŋ naɪf|
    dɪd ju ɛvər si sʌtʃ fulz m jər laɪf||
    θri blaɪnd maɪs||

12. Hickory, dickory, dock,
    ðə maʊs ræn ʌp ðə klɑk|
    ðə klɑk strʌk wʌn|
    ðə maʊs ræn daʊn||
    hɪkərɪ| dɪkərɪ| dɑk||

13. Ba-a, ba-a, black sheep, have you any wool?
    jes| sɚ| jes| sɚ| θri bægz fʊl||
    wʌn fər maɪ mæstər| wʌn fər maɪ deɪm|
    bət nʌn fər ðə lɪtl̩ bɔɪ hu kraɪz m ðə leɪn||

14. Jack be nimble,
    dʒæk bi kwɪk|
    dʒæk dʒʌmp oʊvər ðə kændl̩ stɪk||

15. **Old King Cole**
    ould kɪŋ koʊl wəz ə merɪ ould soʊl|
    ənd ə merɪ ould soʊl wəz hi||
    hi kɔld fər hɪz paɪp ən hi kɔld fər hɪz boʊl|
    ənd hi kɔld fər hɪz fɪdlərz θri||

16. This Little Pig
ðɪs lɪtļ pɪg wɛnt tə mɑrkət|
ðɪs lɪtļ pɪg steɪd ət houm|
ðɪs lɪtļ pɪg hæd roust bif|
ðɪs lɪtļ pɪg hæd nʌn|
ðɪs lɪtļ pɪg kraɪd wi| wi| wi| ɔl ðə weɪ houm‖

17. Old Mother Hubbard
ould mʌðər hʌbərd
wɛnt tu ðə kʌbərd
tə gɛt hər pur dɔg ə boun‖
bət hwɛn ʃi keɪm ðɛər
ðə kʌbərd wəz bɛər
ən sou ðə pur dɔg hæz nʌn‖

18. Hark, Hark
hɑrk| hɑrk|
ðə dɔgz du bɑrk|
ðə begərz ər kʌmɪŋ tə taun‖
sʌm ɪn rægz|
sʌm ɪn bægz|
ən sʌm ɪn vɛlvɛt gaunz‖

19. Rock-a-bye, Baby
rɑk ə baɪ beɪbɪ| ɑn ðə tri tɑp‖
hwɛn ðə wɪnd blouz ðə kreɪdļ wɪl rɑk‖
hwɛn ðə bau breɪks ðə kreɪdļ wɪl fɔl‖
daun wɪl kʌm beɪbɪ| kreɪdļ| ənd ɔl‖

20. Ride a Cockhorse
raɪd ə kɑkhɔrs tə bænberɪ krɔs|
tə si ə faɪn leɪdɪ əpɑn ə hwaɪt hɔrs‖
rɪŋz ɑn hər fɪŋgərz| ən bɛlz ɑn hər touz|
ʃi ʃæl hæv mjuzɪk hwɛərɛvər ʃi gouz‖

21. There Was an Old Woman Who Lived in a Shoe
ðɛər wəz ən ould wumən hu lɪvd ɪn ə ʃu|
ʃi hæd sou mɛnɪ tʃɪldrən ʃi dɪdņt nou hwɑt tə du‖

ʃi geɪv ðəm səm brɔθ| wɪðaut ɛnɪ brɛd|
ʃi hwɪpt ðəm ɔl saundlɪ ən sɛnt ðəm tə bɛd||

22. **Mistress Mary, Quite Contrary**
    mɪstrəs mɛərɪ| kwaɪt kəntrɛərɪ|
    hau dəz jər gɑrdən grou||
    wɪð sɪlvər bɛlz ən kɑkḷ ʃɛlz|
    ən prɪtɪ meɪdz ɔl ɪn ə rou||

23. **Wee Willie Winkie**
    wi wɪlɪ wɪŋkɪ rʌnz θru ðə taun||
    ʌpstɛərz ən daunstɛərz| ɪn hɪz naɪtgaun||
    ræpɪŋ æt ðə wɪndou| kraɪŋ θru ðə lɑk|
    ɑr ðə tʃɪldrən ɪn ðɛər bɛds|| fər nau ɪts eɪt əklɑk||

24. **Little Bo-peep**
    lɪtḷ bou pip hæz lɔst hər ʃip|
    ən kænt tɛl hwɛər tə faɪnd ðəm||
    liv ðəm əloun| ən ðɛəl kəm houm|
    ən brɪŋ ðɛər teɪlz bɪhaɪnd ðəm||

25. **Bye, Baby Bunting**
    baɪ| beɪbɪ bʌntɪŋ|
    dædiz gɑn ə hʌntɪŋ|
    tə gɛt ə lɪtḷ ræbɪts skɪn
    tə ræp ðə beɪbɪ bʌntɪŋ ɪn||

26. **Little Boy Blue**
    lɪtḷ bɔɪ blu| kʌm blou jər hɔrn||
    ðə ʃips ɪn ðə mɛdou| ðə kauz ɪn ðə kɔrn||
    hwɛərz ðə bɔɪ ðæt lʊks æftər ðə ʃip||
    hiz ʌndər ðə heɪstæk fæst əslip||
    wɪl ju weɪk hɪm| nou| nɑt aɪ||
    fər ɪf aɪ du| hiz ʃʊr tə kraɪ||

27. **Little Miss Muffet**
    lɪtḷ mɪs mʌfət
    sæt ɑn ə tʌfət|
    itɪŋ hər kɚdz ən weɪ||

ðɛər keɪm ə greɪt spaɪdər|
ən sæt daʊn bɪsaɪd hər|
ən fraɪtənd mɪs mʌfət əweɪ‖

28. Pat-a-cake
pæt ə keɪk| pæt ə keɪk| beɪkərz mæn‖
beɪk mi ə keɪk dʒʌst æz fæst æz ju kæn‖
pæt ɪt| ən prɪk ɪt| ən mark ɪt wɪð ti|
pʊt ɪt ɪn ði ʌvən fər tami ən mi‖

29. Pease-porridge Hot
piz parɪdʒ hat| piz parɪdʒ kʊld|
piz parɪdʒ ɪn ðə pat|
nam deɪz ʊld‖

30. Simple Simon
sɪmpḷ saɪmən mɛt ə paɪmən
goʊɪŋ tə ðə fɛər‖
sez sɪmpḷ saɪmən tə ðə paɪmən|
lɛt mi teɪst jər wɛər‖
sez ðə paɪmən tə sɪmpḷ saɪmən|
ʃoʊ mi fɚst jər penɪ‖
sez sɪmpḷ saɪmən tə ðə paɪmən|
ɪndid aɪ hæv nat ɛnɪ‖

31. Mary's Lamb
mɛərɪ hæd ə lɪtḷ læm|
ɪts flis wəz hwaɪt əz snoʊ‖
ənd ɛvrɪhwɛər ðæt mɛərɪ wɛnt
ðə læm wəz ʃʊr tə goʊ‖

ɪt faloʊd hər tə skul wʌn deɪ
hwɪtʃ wəz əgɛnst ðə rul‖
ɪt meɪd ðə tʃɪldrən læf ən pleɪ
tu si ə læm ɪn skul‖

EXERCISE 68: Transcribing Phonetics

DIRECTIONS: *Transcribe the following passage into IPA and compare your transcription with the second one. Pronounce each word aloud before you write down its sounds.*

"ARGUFYING"

Remember the six blind men of Hindustani who bumped into an ele‧phant? One felt the trunk and yelled, "Look out, it feels like a snake!" Another ran his hand over the creature's side and said it felt like a wall. The third, grasping a tusk, said no, it felt like a spear. The fourth believed he had discovered a treelike animal because the huge leg was like a stump. The fifth touched a flapping ear and was sure the elephant was shaped like a fan. While the sixth was equally positive that the pachyderm re‧sembled a rope because he had grabbed its tail.

Now all of them were right as far as they went. The trouble was— they didn't go far enough, and that's why they fell into a bitter quarrel. *We can never settle arguments so long as we talk about different things.* So the first thing to do when an argument lifts its ugly head is to make sure you are on common ground with your opponent, be certain you and he are talking about the same things. Define your terms.

ˈɑrgjuˌfaɪŋ

rɪˈmembər ðə sɪks blaɪnd men əv ˌhɪnduˈstɑnɪ hu bʌmpt ˈɪntu æn ˈeləfənt‖ wʌn felt ðə trʌŋk ænd jeld| lʊk aʊt| ɪt filz laɪk ə sneɪk‖ əˈnʌðər ræn hɪz hænd ˈoʊvər ðə ˈkritʃərz saɪd ənd sed ɪt felt laɪk ə wɔl‖ ðə θəd| ˈgræspɪŋ ə tʌsk| sed noʊ| ɪt felt laɪk ə spɪər‖ ðə fɔrθ bɪˈlivd hi hæd dɪsˈkʌvərd ə tri laɪk ˈænɪməl bɪˈkɔz ðə hjudʒ leg wəz laɪk ə stʌmp‖ ðə fɪfθ tʌtʃt ə ˈflæpɪŋ ɪər ənd wəz ʃʊər ði ˈeləfənt wəz ʃeɪpt laɪk ə fæn‖ hwaɪl ðə sɪksθ wəz ˈikwəlɪ ˈpɑzɪtɪv ðæt ðə ˈpækɪdərm riˈzembəld ə roʊp bɪˈkɔz hi hæd græbd ɪts teɪl‖

naʊ| ɔl əv ðem wər raɪt æz fɑr æz ðeɪ went‖ ðə ˈtrʌbəl wəz| ðeɪ ˈdɪdn̩t goʊ fɑr ɪˈnʌf| ænd ðæts hwaɪ ðeɪ fel ˈɪntu ə ˈbɪtər ˈkwɑrəl‖ wi kæn ˈnevər ˈsetəl ˈɑrgjumənts soʊ lɔŋ æz wi tɔk əˈbaʊt ˈdɪfərənt ðɪŋz‖ soʊ| ðə fəst θɪŋ tu du hwen æn ˈɑrgjumənt lɪfts ɪts ʌglɪ hed ɪz tu meɪk ʃʊər ju ɑr ɑn ˈkɑmən graʊnd wɪð jʊər əˈpoʊnənt| bi ˈsətn̩ ju ænd hi ɑr ˈtɔkɪŋ əˈbaʊt ðə seɪm θɪŋz‖ difaɪn jʊər təmz‖

You may become so interested in transcribing eye words into ear words that you'll want to spend a few minutes every day recording pronunciation as you hear it. You can get at the anatomy of words that way.

Chapter 17: SAY IT WITH YOUR HANDS

Sɪʀ Rɪᴄʜᴀʀᴅ Pᴀɢᴇᴛ, famous English scientist, says you can make seven hundred thousand different gestures. This is about a hundred and fifty thousand more than the words listed in our biggest dictionaries. Of course, to make that many gestures, you've got to exhaust all the possible movements of your face, arms, wrists, hands, fingers, and postures —and their combinations.

Climb to the roof of your house. Put a penny on top of the chimney. Paste a stamp on top of the penny. Now you have a way to estimate how old gestures and speech are. The height of your two-story house and chimney represents the time it took us to evolve to an upright posture. The thickness of the penny stands for the ages our ancestors communicated by gestures and grunts. The thickness of the stamp equals the time since mankind first pronounced words.

The way speech actually developed is anybody's guess. Some believe it grew out of our attempt to mimic the noises of birds and beasts. This is the *Bow-wow Theory*.

The *Yo-he-ho Theory* suggests that words came when we first worked in groups. Our rhythmic, muscular heaves and pulls brought forth chants. "The Song of the Volga Boatmen" reminds us of this theory.

Max Müller based his *Ding-dong Theory* on the belief that early words were the direct results of our feelings. The phonetics of a word like *rush* give the sense of a stream or wind swishing by you.

Some authorities believe that our first words grew out of emotional exclamations. They call it the *Pooh-pooh Theory* and make much of pain and pleasure, of *Oh! Ah! Ouch!,* etc., as originators of speech.

The theory that makes most sense to me states that the tongue makes the same gesture "while saying *ta-ta* (or something else) as would be made by the hand with similar intention; but you need not wag your hand, your friend hears you wag your tongue to the same effect."

At present we still use gestures to make words mean more. Sometimes words fail us. Then we use gestures only. Why? Because gestures are more basic than speech. Because everybody understands them, whether they speak our language or not.

Have you ever watched Mother, Father, and Junior (aged three) on a train? Mother calls a car advertisement to Father's attention. Before long Junior chimes in. Mother explains the ad to him with a lot of gestures—many more than she used with Father. Junior understands better that way.

Until Junior was about six months old, like all normal youngsters he didn't respond to gestures. You could frown or shake a fist at him, and he would as lief smile at you as anything. A little later he cried when you did such things. From then on he became more sensitive to all kinds of gestures.

A youngster's intuition is sharp because his ability to interpret facial tensions, gestures, and postures is unspoiled. But whether Junior is an American riding on a train or a Hottentot carried on his mother's back or a Hindu on an elephant with his mahout father, he learns the meaning of a thousand common gestures.

When the early explorers crossed the continent they found sixty-five different Indian languages in what is now the United States. All the tribes could communicate with one another by gesture language, or *sign talk*. And the explorers could make known their wants even to the most isolated tribes. All of which proves how basic gestures really are.

Not many years ago, Chief Little Raven, of the Arapahoes, said, "The summer after President Lincoln was killed we had a grand gathering of all the tribes to the east and south of us. Twenty-five different tribes met near old Fort Abercrombie on the Wichita River. The Caddos had a different sign for *horse* and also for *moving,* but the rest were made the same by all the tribes."

The northern tribes use both hands; the southern, mostly one hand. Two-handed gestures make better signals. The Indians use single-handed signs in conversation.

Indian sign language is like the manual language of the congenital deaf. (The latter use more facial expression.) Deaf-mutes from fourteen different countries attended a service in London's St. Paul's Cathedral in 1935. The liturgy, sermon, and the rest was conducted entirely in manual language. Everybody understood it.

Gestures describing a beard, a headdress, a cupped hand raised to the mouth mean "a man," "a woman," "water" among Armenians, American Indians, Russians, Australian bushmen, and the deaf everywhere. Indian gestures for such words as *child, man, no, drink, tears, night* can be traced to the Egyptian, Chinese, and Mayan symbols representing the same ideas.

Boy Scouts attend jamborees from countries all over the world. They use sign talk to carry on their meetings. So you see, meaningful gestures transcend continents, racial barriers, civilizations, and religions.

Sign language differs from *dactylology,* the finger spelling still used by the deaf. Many systems of dactylology are taught. Some of these go back to the seventh century. Abbé de l'Épée, who opened a school for the deaf in Paris in the eighteenth century, is the father of modern dactylology.

His system, popular in France, Italy, and the United States, makes use of one hand. A good finger speller can "sign," or "talk," eighty or more words a minute. Deaf people untutored in dactylology talk among themselves with a "natural" sign language at an even faster rate.

Gesture language has a grammar all its own. Tomkins gives some examples in his *Universal Indian Sign Language:*

English: Two months ago I took two friends with me and went up to start the camp. The day we got there we saw tracks of deer and bear and caught some fish for supper. We were too tired when night came to put up our tents, and we didn't think it would rain anyway. We made up our beds near the fire and lay down to sleep.

Indian: Two moon beyond I with friends go make-rise camp. We arrived little hand; we see track deer, bear; we take fish eat, sunset. Evening come we tired, we want not make-rise tent; we think rain no. We make bed near fire, sleep.

The syntax of sign language is logical. It's much easier to learn than English grammar. First things come first. There are no run arounds, no complicated subordinations.

Since gestures have such basic appeal, only the poor speaker neglects them. The good speaker, on the other hand, avoids overdoing them. He applies Shakespeare's advice to the actors: "Do not saw the air too much with your hand thus . . . suit the action to the word, the word to the action; with this special observance, that you o'erstep not the modesty of nature."

More than two thousand years ago, Quintilian gave us some sound advice about gestures. The dynamic speaker, he said, uses gestures in harmony with the spirit of his remarks. "If our gesture and looks are at variance with our speech, if we utter anything mournful with an air of cheerfulness or assert anything positive with an air of denial, not only impressiveness is wanting to our words but even credibility."

He points out that body movement ought to be graceful. For example, the speaker should turn his face in the same direction as the gesture of the hand—unless he refers to thoughts or feelings of which he disapproves. He shouldn't nod his head too often or gesticulate with the head alone. Any one gesture or movement repeated too often loses its appeal. It annoys the audience. Variety in gestures, as in vocal inflections, keeps the audience awake.

We gesture most with our hands, Quintilian continues.

The action of the other parts of the body assists the speaker, but the hands (I could almost say) speak themselves. By them do we not demand, promise, call, dismiss, threaten, supplicate, express abhorrence and terror, question, and deny? Do we not by them express joy, sorrow, doubt, confession, repentance, measure quantity, number, and time? Do they not also encourage, plead, restrain, convict, admire, respect, and, in pointing out places and persons, do they not discharge the office of adverbs and pronouns?

He says that gestures of the hand should pass from the speaker's left to his right. They ought to begin and end with the sense of the words. Best of all: "The hand should be neither too long inactive nor disturb the speech, as is the practice of many orators, by perpetual motion."

What kinds of gestures do we use most often on the platform?

Literal gestures refer to physical objects. When you point to the microphone, you use a literal gesture. When you suggest the joining of two rivers by bringing your hands together, you use a literal gesture. If you hold up two fingers to indicate the two main divisions of your address, you use a literal gesture.

Figurative gestures are analogies. You use them to express mental or emotional states. If you wish to suggest reverence, you may point toward heaven. This gesture carries an obvious analogy to physical elevation. Suppose you wish to convey a feeling of defeat or degradation. You give the arm a downward movement. To express two opposing sides in a hostile conference, you may bring your hands together and quickly separate them.

Of course, there's no actual relationship between these gestures and their analogies. But the gestures do fortify your meaning. Figurative gestures add vividness to your descriptions.

Good speakers always make their gestures wholly visible to their audience. Perhaps you've noticed a speaker make small movements with his arms and hands close to his body. He seems to want to gesture but is afraid to follow through. We call this an *incipient gesture*. It's a sign of nervousness. Better no gesture at all than an incipient gesture.

When your gestures are good they have a *preparation,* a *stroke,* and a *relaxation.* The preparation brings the hand to the place where the most meaningful move, the stroke, takes place. After you deliver the stroke, you return the hand to your side. This third movement is the relaxation. The problem is to manage all three parts naturally.

Be careful not to drop your arm to your side like a dead weight. Don't let it swing after the stroke. Don't lower it too slowly.

Sometimes you'll want to deliver a series of strokes. Take the sentence: "This thing went *on,* and *on,* and *on.*" Here the relaxation waits upon the last stroke.

A gesture means more to the audience when you give it easily, spontaneously, accurately, and with confidence. By accurately, I mean *timed right.* The stroke comes on the word, or words, you accent with your voice. This is the important word. If the stroke comes too soon or too late, the speaker looks ridiculous.

Suppose someone asks you, "Have you seen my little boy?" And you respond, "Yes, *there* he goes." The stroke must come on *there*.

Let's come back to that point about naturalness. We sometimes see a speaker who delivers his gestures like an automaton. You feel, here's a fellow who took a course in public speaking—the wrong kind. He goes through the motions of gestures. But they're so wooden, so awkward you'd prefer none at all.

And then you remember the speaker who makes his gestures an integral part of his communication. They come at the right time. They come gracefully because he's developed the coordinations and attitudes to make them succeed. And you realize how much his gestures contribute to his platform success. The second fellow is the worthy model.

EXERCISE 69: Formal Gestures

DIRECTIONS: *Recite the following sentences, giving them appropriate gestures. Watch yourself in a mirror.*

1. Put the chair over there. (*location*)
2. No, I can't agree to that. (*refusal*)
3. Why! The man must be crazy! (*incredulity*)
4. And the old missionary blessed the throng. (*reverence*)
5. I dare my opponent to substantiate his charge! (*defiance*)
6. The two armies clashed on the plain. (*description*)
7. If you weigh one against the other you won't find much difference. (*antithesis*)
8. The tall man stooped to help the child up. (*kindliness*)
9. He seemed to be here, there, everywhere at once. (*movement*)
10. From the mountaintop he could see the prospectors toiling in the gulch far below. (*distance*)
11. As woman's education has broadened, her figure has become narrower. (*contrast*)
12. Here we have representatives from the eastern part of the state and, over there, representatives from the western counties. (*contrast*)
13. There are three main families of American dialects: (*a*) New England, (*b*) Southern, and (*c*) Midwestern, or General American. (*enumeration*)

14. I don't like this plan, never have, doubt that I ever shall. (*intense negation*)

15. Ladies and Gentlemen: May I present our speaker of the evening, Mr. John Evans. (*welcome*)

If you feel that your platform delivery is a bit wooden, why not practice gesturing before a mirror? Let your gestures be readily visible to your audience; let them be given in a warm, vigorous way. Put all of yourself behind them—your thought, your conviction, your facial expression, your whole body. But guard against too many gestures, or you will lose your power to attract people.

Chapter 18: A DOZEN TIPS TO MAKE YOU A BETTER CONVERSATIONALIST

Do you really like people? Not only your friends and relatives, but people in general? And do you want to be liked by everyone you meet? Do you enjoy others' company more than your own? If so, you have what it takes to make an excellent conversationalist.

For conversation is the chief art of friendliness, and the good conversationalist is a warm, friendly person. Once friendliness is abiding, the technique of conversation is easy enough to master. The technique boils down to at least a dozen do's and don'ts.

1. Do your fair share of talking but don't monopolize the conversation.

How much talking does a good conversationalist do? That depends upon your definition of a good conversationalist. Old Dr. Samuel Johnson used to hold his circle spellbound by the avalanche of his learned, opinionated talk. He betrayed a selfish attitude when he said, "Unconstraint is the grace of conversation." To him, as to most egotists, conversation was pretty much a one-way affair.

The great Thomas Babington Macaulay, whose vast memory encompassed the New Testament, *Paradise Lost,* and lengths of other literature, wore you out with his word flow. This led someone to remark, "Macaulay has occasional flashes of silence—perfectly delightful!"

Can you imagine Abraham Lincoln or Robert E. Lee or the great scientist, George Washington Carver, monopolizing the conversation? They were too gentle, too humble of spirit, too considerate of others. They loved their fellow men too deeply to commandeer attention. They were genuinely eager to learn from everyone.

If, then, our definition of a good conversationalist is acceptable, he is one who gives others equal opportunity to talk. He bears in mind that *conversation* means "talking with," not "talking to." Effervescent individuals, whose word flow gushes, need to cultivate the *Share-the-talk Plan.* Once they become generous, once they give others a turn to converse, they experience a new growth in their human relations.

2. Be a good listener—be helpfully attentive.

This means studying the speaker's whole personality, not simply looking at him passively. Passive attention absorbs only sounds and surface behavior. But close attention probes the speaker's whole meaning. It seeks subtle depths, interprets the expressions of his eyes, posture, gestures, pitch of voice, and inflections, the selection and progression of his thoughts.

When your companion says something amusing, why not smile appreciatively? If his remarks meet with your approval, your corresponding nod will encourage him. You may discover an uptake in your popularity as you increase your facial responsiveness to the surprise, humor, disapproval, and other feelings mirrored in a friend's conversation. A shy, hesitant speaker especially deserves such a responsive attitude because it makes him feel important.

People in the act of speaking are such complex creatures that they offer a world of fascinating study. Prominent men and women say that whatever success they achieve in conversation grows out of their study of and interest in others.

A good conversationalist is a sponge. He sops up all the wonderments of the speaking personality. He cannot afford to feel bored, superior, or negatively critical. If the circle is large, he guards against the urge to chat with a neighbor while someone else is speaking. As he grows he realizes that charm of conversation consists less in display of his own wit than in his power to draw forth the resources of others.

3. Avoid the extremes of forwardness and reserve.

"While familiarity may not breed contempt," said the great essayist, William Hazlitt, "it takes the edge off of admiration." All of us meet the breezy fellow who is so forward we doubt his sincerity. He is probably an exhibitionist. With his first words you feel you know him as well as you will ever know him. He may buttonhole you or hold you by the arm to make you hear him out—against your will.

He usually lacks the sixth sense of propriety. Sometimes he tells off-color jokes at first meeting. Nothing more surely kills a nascent admiration; nothing causes more distaste or sense of affront than to have an improper story, no matter how funny, forced on you by one from whom you are not ready to hear it.

On the other hand, one of the heightened moments in the relationship of urbane people is the telling of the first slightly risqué story. It usually marks a step forward in a friendship. You often take it as a sign of confidence. A good conversationalist, therefore, if he must tell a shady joke, reserves it for acquaintances prepared to accept it.

Then there is the cold, reserved person whose conversation is limited to single words of assent or negation. Occasionally he grunts. He tires you. You have to work too hard to get responses from him. But the good conversationalist doesn't underestimate him. His reserve may hide deep feelings or rich experience. Sometimes you can melt it with a question or an encouraging smile.

Somewhere between the two extremes is the golden way trod by the good conversationalist. The safest path may be cultivated by checking forwardness and breaking down reserve through contacts with happy, kindly people.

4. Tell your stories well.

Once upon a time there was an old actor who spent his days of retirement at New York's famous Lambs Club. He had specialized in roles of Abraham Lincoln and affected Lincoln's beard, speech, and mannerisms. He bored some of the members. One of them said, "If he doesn't stop acting like Lincoln, he's going to be assassinated."

Recently Tommy Richardson, famous after-dinner speaker, told the story and made a member of the audience the character. Result was, it got more laughter than would otherwise have been the case. A good storyteller always tries to improve upon a story by making it pertinent to his audience.

He also practices the ten commandments of a good storyteller:

a. Make the story your own. If you put it into your own words, transpose a phrase here, add one there, it takes on your personality. Printed stories often need drastic editing.

b. Don't be the first to laugh at your own jokes. All of us have had to smile grudgingly at the speaker who laughs too soon at his own stories.

c. Don't tell a story until you really like it. Unless you think it is funny, you will have a hard time selling it to others.

d. Work for surprise. Laughter is a release from nervous tension built up throughout the story. If you defer the point to the very last word, the tension will reach the laughing point at the best time.

e. Master at least one dialect. You may become a specialist in Irish stories. If so, you will want to make them click with a brogue. Good storytellers often become competent in many dialects, like Peter Donald of radio fame.

f. Make it conversational. Mere recital is wooden, but live conversation, direct and in a selection of language geared to the characters, is sure fire. If the story involves more than one person, change your voice and position to identify the various characters.

g. Overlearn your stories. Know them so well that you won't muff them. A mangled joke falls hard.

h. Don't tell too many stories. Always leave your circle with the wish to hear more. A good storyteller has to guard against the temptation of virtuosity. Two or three first-rate stories pay better dividends than six or seven that overflow the cup.

i. Tell one on yourself. One of the best ways to captivate an audience is to get them to laugh at you. This gives them a feeling of superiority. It's good psychology.

    j. Change your stories now and then. Good stories travel so rapidly these days that they soon become hackneyed. An excellent story has a life span about as long as a juke-box song. A good storyteller therefore changes his repertoire several times a year.

5. Don't be a one-subject conversationalist.

    Too many times you meet the person who can only talk intelligently about his favorite interest. No matter where you see him he brings it up *ad nauseam*. He may talk shop if he is wrapped up in his work or golf if that is his game or Western lore if that is his sole reading. The first time he converses about it, you find him quite diverting. And then with subsequent contacts you realize that he is not interested in talking about anything else. He tries to obtrude his pet subject on you. It is a kind of obsession with him that alienates him from everybody.

    The good conversationalist, when occasion demands it, can talk like an authority on at least one subject. But he is careful not to lecture or to repeat his tune before the same group. He develops a wide assortment of interests—all of them grist for his conversational mill.

    He is like a successful newspaper reporter. He senses a story in almost everything he sees or hears. He reads much and regularly to keep abreast of current events. He's interested in science, literature, sports, movies, fashions, and what not. He makes a habit of carrying a magazine or book to turn to in spare minutes. He studies self-improvement books, like Douglas Lurton's *Make the Most out of Your Life*. He capitalizes on the interests of others. He draws them out —to make them feel good, to add to his own store of knowledge.

    You may say, "Is good conversation superficial?" And the answer is, "Yes, ordinarily." Isn't small talk the lifeblood of conversation? For conversation is width rather than height; it is whimsical instead of profound; it is light, not pedantic; it amuses oftener than it instructs. Its purpose is to bind casual contacts closer together. Thus, the more things we are interested in, the easier we find talking to others.

6. Look at all the members of the conversational circle.

We can forgive many a conversational sin so long as the speaker looks at us while he talks. The commonest cause of the avertive glance is shyness. When General Grant became President he learned to combat his embarrassment while conversing with diplomats; he looked at the end of their noses. Noses, curiously enough, are easier to dominate than eyes. The secret? The person at whose nose we gaze assumes that we are looking him squarely in the eye. For even at short range, he can't tell the difference. If, then, you dislike to look at eyes, why not try noses instead?

Another common barrier to good conversation is the tendency of many of us to look at inanimate objects while we are talking. A famous professor of philosophy invites his advanced students to meet in his New York home once a week. They discuss the progress of their dissertations. Whenever the professor talks, he looks out of the window and loses all the interest he might otherwise sustain. He ought to glance from one student to another as he converses. His is a bungling act. It betrays more interest in the tree outside the window than in his guests.

We also meet the man or woman who looks at only one person when others are present. The good conversationalist says with his roving glance—that neglects no one—"I am grateful to each and every one of you for listening, and I am showing my appreciation by looking directly at you on my right and you on my left and you opposite me." When we observe the good conversationalist in action we put him down as a person who holds the group in unity by the direct gaze he offers every pair of eyes (or every nose).

7. Don't lay down the law.

Gelett Burgess, famous conversationalist and author of that delightful bit of nonsense, "The Purple Cow," points to the Japanese tea ceremony as perhaps the most refined social form ever practiced. He calls it a cult of self-effacement, because a tacit rule of the Japanese prohibits any definite, decisive statement. They deem all flat-footed pronouncements vulgar in polite society. You may speak about almost any subject, but never with an expression of finality. Your remark is left up in the air for your neighbor to enlarge upon. In that way no one is guilty of forcing his personal opinion upon the social circle.

Even good conversationalists occasionally ask disarming questions, such as, "Isn't it possible that . . . ?" "May I tell you about . . . ?" Woodrow Wilson as an undergraduate at Princeton University traced the cause of his unpopularity to his demand for proof, no matter how inconsequential the statement was. Once he learned to be more diplomatic in his conversation, his friends multiplied.

A group of New York social workers met to arrange a round-table discussion. Someone suggested the name of a famous doctor as the leader of the program. An excellent candidate in many respects, was the consensus: an illustrious reputation, a ready speaker, nice-looking. These were some of the traits put on the right side of his ledger.

And then someone said, "But he always knows all the answers, never gives anybody else a chance. He lays down the law too glibly." And they turned to someone else, perhaps not so well known but having that choice gift of self-effacement, tolerance for the other fellow's point of view.

8. Avoid derogatory remarks.

When Will Rogers used to say, "I never met a man I didn't like," he didn't mean he liked *everything* about every man he met. He meant that he always looked for likable qualities in men and women. He never failed to find them. The outstanding reason for his popularity was this ability to see the good in others and to draw it forth in conversation.

Many of the men who have attempted to fill his shoes as America's most beloved humorist and public speaker have failed because they lacked the same ability. Their humor was too brittle and biting. They didn't have Will's sympathetic understanding of people, his readiness to listen and respond to words sympathetically. They were as quick as he was to detect the weaknesses and frailties that beset all of us. But they stopped there. They didn't try to temper their words and balance their criticism with an understanding of the individual's good points. It was his gentle understanding that made Will Rogers's humor so mellow, so human and sympathetic that his conversation never carried the sting of dislike.

How easy it is to find fault! To see shortcomings! Cynicism may be clever, but the laughter it generates somehow leaves a bitter taste. Oscar Wilde's epigrams were admittedly brilliant, but too often they were bolts of lightning aimed at his listeners' self-esteem.

Ridicule, unnecessary criticism, vicious gossip are all destructive, signs of personal maladjustment. The good conversationalist avoids them. Rather, he emphasizes wholesome, constructive attitudes.

9. Be ready to disperse the doldrums.

Have you ever observed that conversation lags at times, even in congenial circles? Good conversation seems to run in cycles. A lull occurs about once every ten minutes. This is the time for the good conversationalist to come to the aid of his party.

Dr. Victor Heiser, famous physician and author of *American Doctor's Odyssey,* uses nine words to dispel the conversational doldrums. He asks, "Who can spell *inoculate, supersede, rarefy, plaguy, desiccate, picnicking, innuendo, vilify, embarrass?*" Wherever he goes, he finds the question an excellent pickup. Almost everybody is interested in orthography, and very few can spell all nine of these words. Sometimes he asks if you know five adjectives that end in *dous.*

Alexander Graham Bell, inventor of the telephone, once entertained a group of young scientists who were obviously overawed by the great man. He broke the ice by asking, "How many of you have ever been arrested?" All but one had been in hot water with the law at one time or other. The recital of their peccadilloes saved the occasion.

Other questions that usually pay good dividends in fallow periods are: "What would you do if you had a million dollars?" "Where would you go first if you were an invisible man?" "What five books would you want on a deserted island?"

If you experiment with questions, riddles, and stories you will discover the kind that suit your personality. The most successful are marked by universal appeal and good taste.

10. Don't throw verbal monkey wrenches.

What are the most ruinous verbal monkey wrenches? Good conversationalists mention these three: (*a*) interruptions, (*b*) flat contradictions, (*c*) abrupt changes.

A word or two of approbation, such as, "Isn't that interesting?" or "My goodness!" is not, of course, a monkey wrench. Often it encourages the speaker. But to insinuate thoughts while he is speaking or to take the words right out of his mouth disconcerts him. Needless to say, it's impolite, too.

We allow contradictions in that rather outmoded form, the *formal debate,* particularly during the tail-end speech known as the *rebuttal.* Here a speaker tries to convince the audience to accept his contentions rather than his opponent's. But in conversation there should be no sense of competition, no wild-eyed eagerness to impose one's thinking on the group. The good conversationalist knows that *A man convinced against his will is of the same opinion still.* If he feels deeply about something someone has just said, he may put in, "I wonder whether we ought not add that . . ." But this kind of remark, uttered in kindly sincerity, is not a flat contradiction.

Closely related is the attempt to divert the subject under discussion to something entirely different at an inappropriate time. Polite circles are often embarrassed by the rude person who dams a lively stream that everyone is fishing in only to divert it to his own ends. The right time to change a subject soon becomes obvious; no one wishes to say anything further about it.

11. Don't get too personal.

Not long ago I submitted a questionnaire to 100 individuals of good conversational ability. I invited them to jot down their pet peeves in conversation. They agreed pretty generally on ten:

a. Personal questions (such as, "Mind telling me how much you paid for that?").
b. Talking about a husband (or wife) behind his (or her) back.
c. Talking about the precocity of one's children.
d. Surgical operations.

e. Poor health.
f. *I, me, mine.*
g. The weather.
h. Religion.
i. Love affairs.
j. Politics.

Polite society frowns upon questions and allusions of a highly personal nature. Nor does the good conversationalist boast about or vilify members of his family. Young parents particularly have to guard against stressing baby's precocity. Most of us are delighted to hear that a youngster is getting along well. But when we inquire about his welfare, we don't expect an interminable recountal of his wise sayings and profound actions. We may even enjoy seeing a snapshot or two of him, but a perambulating album is just too much.

The good conversationalist also steers away from the enjoyment of poor health, surgical operations, and other gloomy topics. Those who enjoy such subjects are ordinarily self-centered hypochondriacs. They leave a pall on the atmosphere, hard to dispel. Then you meet people with a proclivity for retrospect—"the good old days when I was young."

Good conversationalists use *I, me,* and *mine* sparingly. They substitute *you* and *yours*. Better still, they encourage subjects of wide and general interest, things of some intellectual content.

The weather, as a sustained subject of conversation, is usually deadly. The French, perhaps the most conversation-minded of all people, put the weather among *banalités de jour,* the hackneyed, trite subjects of little lives. "My, but it's a beautiful day, isn't it?" is a good enough opener in a passing chat, but from there on the weather serves little purpose as a subject of conversation.

Religion, love, and politics are inherently dangerous conversational topics because they involve very personal convictions. When these are ruffed the wrong way, hard feelings develop. As a discerning person, you will avoid such subjects.

Bruyère summarized the whole point of tact in conversation when he wrote, "There is speaking well, speaking easily, speaking justly, and speaking seasonably. It is offending against the last to speak of entertainments before the indigent, of sound limbs and health before the infirm, of houses and lands before one who has not so much as a dwelling—in a word, to speak of your prosperity before the miserable. This conversation is cruel, and the comparison which naturally arises in them betwixt their condition and yours is excruciating."

12. Speak clearly.

When you study the technique of the conversationalists you admire most, you undoubtedly discover that they speak distinctly. You don't have to strain to understand their words. Moreover, they sustain a pleasant voice.

Everyone knows the loud talkers who can't keep the interest and attention and, conversely, the low, pleasantly tuned voices on which you hang with avid ears.

If we have anything worth saying, doesn't it deserve considerate phrasing, acceptable pronunciation, and flexible voice? For there is no sterner test of civilized man and woman than the art of conversation.

When we consider such tips as we have reviewed here and apply them in our daily contacts—around the luncheon table, over a cup of tea or a cocktail, in the railway car, before the fireplace, and wherever else men and women of good will congregate in friendly intercourse— we grow in assurance and pleasure in the companionship of others. And that is what conversation was made for.

Why not check up on your conversational technique every once in a while? Perhaps this questionnaire will help you.

EXERCISE 70: Conversational Inventory

DIRECTIONS: *Here is a check list to help you become a better conversationalist. A good score is 200. A perfect score is within the reach of all of us.*

	Yes	No	?
1. Do I avoid monopolizing the conversation?	15	0	5
2. Do I watch the speaker all the time while he's talking?	15	0	5
3. Do I avoid overfamiliarity?	15	0	5
4. Have I learned to tell my amusing stories well?	15	0	5

	Yes	No	?
5. Am I the first to laugh at my own jokes?	0	15	5
6. Have I mastered at least one dialect to heighten interest in my stories?	15	0	5
7. Am I a "one-subject" conversationalist?	0	15	5
8. Do I avoid forcing personal opinions upon others?	15	0	5
9. Do I avoid derogatory remarks about others?	15	0	5
10. Do I assume responsibility for dispersing the conversational doldrums?	15	0	5
11. Do I have the bad habit of interrupting a speaker?	0	15	5
12. Am I given to flat contradictions?	0	15	5
13. Do I like to change the subject abruptly?	0	15	5
14. Do I avoid talking too much about myself?	15	0	5
15. Do I speak clearly and slowly enough to make myself understood?	15	0	5
16. Do I listen carefully?	15	0	5
17. Do I consciously look for ways and means to improve my conversational ability?	15	0	5

TOTAL

Chapter 19: CULTIVATE YOUR SPEECH PERSONALITY

GREEK ACTORS—hundreds of years before the birth of Christ—wore masks. You knew the hero, villain, and the others by the type of masks they wore. Later on, the Romans called these masks *personae*. (To this day we print *dramatis personae* on our theater programs to announce the play's characters.) From *personae* comes our big, buzzing word *personality*. The psychologists have a hundred and one technical definitions for it.

But you and I use it every day in such expressions as, "Mary Smith has a wonderful personality," "Good scout, Tom Brown—lots of personality!" We mean that Mary and Tom are nice to be around. We like them. They make us feel happy, important.

Heywood Broun, famous newspaper columnist, used to say, "Personality counts more than prowess in the professions." He might have added, "In most other walks of life, too."

Your personality is the impressions you make upon others. Your clothes, facial expressions, gestures, moods, the way you talk—these and many more things make up your personality. Did you know that Webster's *New International Dictionary* lists more than seventeen thousand words that describe personality? You see, it's quite complex.

Yet the building blocks of a pleasant personality are within reach of most of us. Let's consider the most valuable of them here—those closely linked with the act of talking.

Take clothes, for instance. They make up more than 90 per cent of what you see of a man. And what he wears and how are surely a part of his speech personality. Someone said, "Your *presence* largely determines your future." You usually see a speaker before you hear him. If he's untidy, if he wears unsuitable clothes, he may ruin the effect of what he says. Everyone bent on speech improvement needs to ask himself, "Am I making the most of my personal appearance?"

Remember always the *you* others see first. Don't think yourself vain when you improve your appearance. It makes you a more distinctive, worthy person. It brings you closer to others. They'll like you better that way.

I once sat on a committee appointed by a department of education. Our job was to pass or fail teacher candidates on the basis of personality. We rated them on a long list of traits—appearance, pronunciation, voice, etc. Before we parted we gave our judgment blanks to a statistician. He told us later that the candidates we failed because of poor speech also had been rated below average on appearance. Had our first impressions (visual) unconsciously influenced our judgment of what we heard? Probably.

See yourself as others see you is almost as difficult as *Hear yourself as others hear you*. When you look into a full-length mirror, what do you see? How about that suit, that tie, those shoes? The ideal of good dress is to be neat and conservative. That way you blend into your surroundings, offer no clashing contrasts, no points of irritation, no focus for distracted attention.

The ladies are careful to get the most out of their clothes. They seek expert advice in the stores, through magazines. Men are likely to be more casual. One easy way for a man to check up on his appearance is to observe how leading actors dress. If you're stout, you may get some tips from Edward Arnold. If you're streamlined, Gregory Peck or Walter Pidgeon may serve as models. Television and movies can teach us a lot about clothes, posture, courtesy observances, and speech.

A speaker may be well dressed without necessarily looking well. Does he need a shave or a haircut? Maybe a shoe shine would help. His pants may need a pressing. Details? Yes, but tremendously important ones. Emerson used to say, "What you are speaks so loud, I can't hear what you say." Clothes tell us a lot about the fellow who wears them. Good clothes, neatly worn, increase the speaker's confidence. They give him a justified superiority feeling.

Perhaps the strongest impression we get from a speaker is his sincerity or lack of it. We forgive him a swarm of shortcomings if he's sincere. Sincerity springs from the heart. It's hard to mimic. You know it by the speaker's voice, the way he looks at you. No personality trait is so important to a speaker. All speakers of high purpose are sincere. Aristotle defined the great orator as a good man, a sincere one.

Yes, the way he looks at you. The indirect glance is a barrier to good communication; so are nervous tics and twitchings. But a warm smile helps a lot.

The physiologists tell us we use the *risorius* and twelve other facial muscles to smile. These muscles tug in all directions to give various meanings. That is how we get the vacant smile, the smile of contempt, the sardonic smile, the feigned smile, and many others.

The best smile of all—the one that wins the speaker's audience—is the friendly smile. We know it at first glance. The mechanical smile, often a nervous mannerism, never fools anybody. Neither are we taken in by the posed smile that sometimes grimaces at us from advertisements. The most beautiful model in the world may be trained to use her smiling muscles in the "right" way, yet if her smile lacks spirit it doesn't quite come off.

The friendly smile springs from affection for these fascinating things called human beings. It grows with sympathy and understanding. A friendly smile involves body and soul. This doesn't mean overdoing it. It does mean gentleness. It means smiling without reservations.

Mothers are chiefly responsible for teaching us to smile. At two months Baby first smiles at others. At five months he may cry if Mother frowns at him. Mothers and nurses ought to cultivate the friendly smile. They should take care to iron out stern facial tensions. For their facial expressions influence their youngsters, in the tender years and throughout life. Mothers may be inspired by the beautiful smiles of Joan Crawford, Judy Garland, Jeannette MacDonald, Kate Smith, Mary Margaret McBride, and other American sweethearts.

When you meet a fellow who is stingy with the friendly smile, forgive him. He probably got that way in his crib. Remember, he's never too old to change. Why not help him? If you smile on him with all the penetrating rays of friendship, his heart must melt. He'll catch the friendly smile's sweet contagion. Don't forget, it helps to make your speech persuasive too. General Dwight D. Eisenhower, Joe DiMaggio, Arthur Godfrey, and Bill Robinson are good examples of persuasive men. They know and practice the art of the friendly smile.

"Smile and the world smiles with you," goes the old poem. How true it is, particularly when the smile is friendly! When you can count on it in good times and bad! And, by the way, did you know that it takes just about 100 per cent less energy to smile than frown?

I wonder whether we stop often enough to count the blessings that flow from laughter also?

1. Laughter crowds tension out of our lives, brings worry to a halt, gives the personality a chance to stretch.
2. Laughter brings refreshment, courage to try again; it adds joy to our work and play.
3. Laughter builds strength, aids digestion, develops the lungs, frees the vocal cords for kind and gracious tones.
4. Laughter feeds our sense of humor, turns away barbed words and unkind thoughts, puts our personal problems in the proper perspective.

5. Laughter quickens the mind, feeds on wit, grows strong on the sense of the ridiculous.
6. Laughter mellows the soul, renews faith in our fellows, makes a philosopher out of a man or woman.
7. Laughter is contagious, spreads contentment, helps the heartsick take new hope, makes friends, and converts enemies.
8. Laughter is always *with* rather than *at;* it costs nothing yet brings handsome dividends.
9. Laughter lightens the daily load, greases life's axles, helps us to run uphill.
10. Laughter is the mark of the positive spirit, of the warm and understanding heart, the badge of the person who gets along well with others.

Its close relatives are the friendly smile, the infectious chuckle, the hilarious guffaw. It can be musical, raucous, loud or soft, high or low. It should come quick and be sincere. When it comes at the right time it's a great help to a speaker.

We must not forget to include the handshake as part of the speech personality either.

In Caesar's day, whenever you hailed a friend, you extended both hands as he came toward you, and he did likewise. Upon meeting, you and he grasped each other's forearms—a quaint custom surviving the days of the caveman when everybody distrusted everybody else. So it was, the habit of grasping arms—to make sure no attack was forthcoming—grew up. In those faraway days the father of the modern handshake was a negative sort of thing, a precaution.

But as our confidence in others grew, we developed the habit of putting forth the right hand in friendliness. The warm and gracious handshake is now a part of the personality of every person who gets along well with others.

Yet all of us know men and women who shake hands in a slipshod sort of way. They lose an ocean of good will. We know the "pumper"; he takes too long to let go. The fellow who swings you off your balance. The woman whose grip is so tepid it dries up your spirit. The man who forces an unwelcome handshake upon you. Then there's the child who hesitates to respond to your kindly proffered hand.

What, then, is a warm and gracious handshake?

1. It is firm but not bone-crushing.
2. It fits comfortably into the palm without any cramped resistance.
3. It does not touch gingerly at the finger tips nor lie limp and boneless in the other fellow's hand.
4. It is not tense with eagerness to make a grand impression, yet it's eager enough to convey sincerity.
5. It is not extended in chilling formality with a stiff bow, but like the crook on the shepherd's staff leads the way to comradeship.
6. It is not given too promiscuously.
7. It is accompanied by the pleasant facial expression, the steady eye, and the good posture.
8. It comes at the right time with due consideration of the fitness of things.
9. It is withdrawn slowly across the palm as if reluctant to leave a good friend.
10. It springs from the heart and mind of him or her who wants good will to flourish like the green bay tree.

The warm and gracious handshake is a sign of excellent human relations.

How high on your list of desirable speech traits is *composure?* It's near the top of my list. We occasionally notice a speaker who seems to be out of joint psychologically. He may have *autistic gestures.* These are recurrent movements of the body, limbs, and face that he's not aware of. They crop out every time he talks, particularly with strangers.

The psychologists list more than a hundred and fifty of these. They ruin direct communication because they distract attention. They make you, the audience, jittery. For tension, like composure, is catching.

At the National Institute for Human Relations we wanted to know what sales managers think of autistic gestures. Do they interfere with business? We asked a group of sales managers to write down the autistic gestures they observed. We then listed the hundred autistic gestures they mentioned most frequently. Then we submitted the list to fifty buyers for industrial concerns. We invited them to check the twenty-five most annoying autistic gestures. Let's make use of their choices as an exercise.

EXERCISE 71: Check Up on Autistic Gestures

DIRECTIONS: *If you suspect that you have autistic gestures, use the following check list as the first step in doing something about them.*

1. Continuous blinking of the eyelids
2. Nose-picking
3. Twitching the eyebrows
4. Cracking the knuckles
5. Biting or chewing the lips
6. Scratching the head
7. Shrugging the shoulders
8. Smacking the lips
9. Protruding the tongue
10. Licking the lips

11. Jerking the head
12. Pulling an ear
13. Tapping the floor with the foot
14. Swinging a crossed leg
15. Corrugating the brow
16. Twiddling the thumbs
17. Finger-tapping
18. Stroking the chin
19. Lacing and unlacing the fingers
20. Tugging at the collar or tie

21. Pursing the lips
22. Moving the chair ever closer
23. Swaying the body while sitting or standing
24. Twitching the cheeks
25. Shuttling the eye (*nystagmus*)

You may be interested in the results of a questionnaire we asked the buyers to fill out, too:

1. They noticed autistic gestures more than twice as often among young as among seasoned salesmen.
2. They judged autistic gestures to be three times as frequent among "mediocre" as among "successful" salesmen.
3. They linked autistic gestures to "nervousness," "poor sales training," and "fear of not making a sale."

4. They said autistic gestures build sales resistance because they distract attention and make the buyers feel uncomfortable.

Why not look at yourself as you talk to others by glancing in the mirror in some public place? Do you have any distracting mannerisms? If so, you will want to shed these demons. True, they may be hard to get rid of. But you can probably manage it with sustained effort. If you can't, why not seek the help of a psychologist? But harry the twitches out of your speech personality. The rewards are worth much more than the effort.

Is self-consciousness your worst enemy? If so, move over and make room for about one out of every three men and women. Dr. A. A. Roback, the eminent psychologist, studied the worries of American adults. He discovered that 35 per cent of all American men and women believe self-consciousness is their main handicap, their chief source of worry. The others said they were self-conscious only on occasion.

Much of our self-consciousness comes from a foolish compulsion to conform to standards. Many women are self-conscious because they can't afford the latest styles. Men sometimes become self-conscious if their advancement doesn't conform to a preconceived schedule. They make unworthy comparisons between themselves and others—and come out at the little end.

Some of us feel self-conscious in social gatherings. We wonder whether our speech is pleasant, or we feel we have nothing to talk about. We're afraid we aren't following certain rigid rules of etiquette. We forget that true courtesy springs from consideration of others—not necessarily from using this fork or that one.

The point I want to make is we often become self-conscious about trivia, about matters over which we have no control. We often try too hard to make our lives conform to "what will other people think?" We neglect to follow the paths indicated by our heads and hearts. The great dramatist, Ibsen, stressed in his realistic plays that we head for trouble when we ignore *Be yourself!*

Break precedents rather than remain self-conscious. "A foolish consistency," says Emerson, "is the hobgoblin of little minds." The outstanding men and women—those you admire most—are not self-conscious. They respond to the inner urge of individuality. Franklin Roosevelt broke away from formal addresses to hold fireside chats with the nation. They fitted his personality better.

Constant self-consciousness is negative. It limits your expression. It makes inferiority feelings multiply. It destroys good human relations. It can eat your heart out. It's the thing to heave out of your life once and for all. How?

Lose yourself in the subject under discussion. Lose yourself through interest in others. Forget about the impression you are making. Let yourself go. Here's how a friend of mine cured himself of self-consciousness. He was an insurance adjuster as a young man. His job was to call on business executives. He didn't like the job, but he couldn't get another. There was the depression.

One morning he said to himself, "This will never do. I must do something about my self-consciousness." It came to him in a flash: "Every time I call on a big shot, I'm going to imagine he's got soap in his eyes. And he's reaching for a towel that isn't there." It did the trick.

Confidence comes from not taking ourselves too seriously. It comes from improving our abilities. All of us have an Achilles' heel. No one is perfect. Besides, people are very much alike everywhere. (The oldest bit of writing in the world, the *Prisse Papyrus*, is in the municipal museum at Constantinople. It dates from about six thousand years ago. The first sentence reads, "Alas, times are not what they used to be. Everyone wants to write a book, and children are no longer obedient to their parents.")

So don't let the most awesome person you meet destroy your self-confidence. When you build sturdy habits of central breathing, good posture, right pronunciation, and all the other bases of good speech, you arm yourself in confidence.

Some of us hide our tensions behind loud and boisterous actions. Or we may protest our shyness by talking too much about ourselves. The psychologists call this *egocentric speech*. About 68 per cent of all the talking done by a youngster may be egocentric speech. It brings him attention. It helps him to feel secure. But in later life we consider it an infantilism. It's hard to enjoy the companionship of an egocentric person.

My colleague, Dr. Bertram Pollens, has a simple cure for egocentric speech. He suggests to a man (or woman) that he (or she) *make* himself talk about himself—when he doesn't want to—for a fifteen-minute stretch. Try it. Put *I* in every one of the sentences. It's quite hard to do. This device helps to center attention on the number of times we use *I, my, mine* in our speech. It encourages us to shift to *you, yours, our.*

Now let's talk about the impression we make over the telephone. You hear the phone ring. You pick up the receiver and say hello. Immediately you give the person at the other end of the line a definite portrait of yourself.

Professor T. H. Pear, of England's University of Manchester, proved that radio audiences attribute all sorts of personality traits to a speaker they've never seen. They'll guess his weight, whether he is an extrovert or an introvert, and so on.

So it is with the telephone. People come to important conclusions about you through your "telephone personality." How, then, can you make a favorable impression on the stranger at the other end?

The Bell Telephone Company prepared twenty questions to measure your telephone rating. Want to try them?

EXERCISE 72: How to Measure Your Telephone Personality

DIRECTIONS: *Fill out the following questionnaire. If you score 80 on this exercise, you are above average.*

	Yes	No
1. Do you answer your telephone before the third ring?	5	0
2. Do you identify yourself—that is, give your name and department—when you answer?	5	0
3. Do you talk without a pipe, cigarette, or cigar in your mouth?	5	0
4. Do you speak in a natural tone, directly into the mouthpiece?	5	0
5. Do you make an effort to make your telephone voice sound pleasing and friendly rather than curt or indifferent?	5	0

	Yes	No
6. Do you ask necessary questions in a nice way?	5	0
7. Do you avoid transferring calls whenever possible?	5	0
8. When you want to recall the operator, do you move the hook up and down slowly so that she receives the signal clearly?	5	0
9. Do you courteously ask the other party to hold the line when you leave the telephone to obtain desired information?	5	0
10. Do you thank the other party for waiting when you return to the telephone?	5	0
11. Do you offer to call him back later in cases where it requires some time to secure the necessary information?	5	0
12. Do you arrange to have someone else answer your telephone when you are away from your desk?	5	0
13. When you answer the telephone for someone else do you give his name, as "Mr. Brown's telephone, Mr. Smith speaking"?	5	0
14. Do you courteously ask the party to hold the line, and do you avoid shouting "Hey, Joe" when you call others to the telephone?	5	0
15. Do you express regret when the person called is out?	5	0
16. Do you offer to take the message or the telephone number of the person calling?	5	0
17. Do you thank the party for calling?	5	0
18. Do you say good-by or otherwise definitely close your conversation?	5	0
19. Do you wait for the calling party to hang up first?	5	0
20. Do you always replace the receiver gently and thus avoid giving the other party a bang in the ear?	5	0
TOTAL		

If you get a perfect score, you may want to join TOPS (Telephone Order of Personality and Smiles), founded by F. Darius Benham of New York, to promote happy telephoning.

They who have attractive speech personalities speak many kind words throughout the day. They never underestimate their power but strive daily to repay acts of service and fellowship with kind words as well as kind deeds. What is equally important, they are aware of the most prevalent of life's minor tragedies: *We find it hard to say kind words to those deserving them most.*

Why don't we form a society for cultivating the habit of saying nice things to people while they are still with us? Why defer them until they are gone forever? Why not make a motto of King Solomon's "Pleasant words are like the honeycomb: sweet to the soul, and health to the bones."

Isn't it strange that a passing courtesy extended by a total stranger— one whom we may never see again—brings forth profuse thanks? Even more constant and helpful courtesies showered on us at home and on the job often go unacknowledged. Perhaps the fault lies in our attitude of "taking things for granted." But the kindly acts of everyday life must never be taken for granted; they are far too precious in building good human relations.

It isn't that we are ungrateful. We just allow a habit of awkward silence to develop, and this acts like a barrier between our appreciation and our expression of it. Words are the wires between heart and mind. Unless we express our messages of good will they are lost forever. The world then becomes a poorer place in which to live and work.

Phillips Brooks hit the nail on the head when he said, "You are letting your friend's heart ache for a word of appreciation or sympathy which you mean to give him someday. If only you could know and see and feel, all of a sudden, that the time is short, how it would break the spell! How you would go instantly and do the thing which you may never have another chance to do." In the better world each of us must help build, the greatest value will be placed on the habit of repaying the common, "unremembered" acts of everyday existence with kind words.

How much brighter the day for the wife who receives a word of recognition for cooking a good breakfast! What an uplift for a little child when he is encouraged with a kind word! How we like to work beside those who let us know they are grateful for the helping hand! So, the cue is easy enough to take: If we get a thrill from words of recognition spoken at the right time, we can also get a thrill from giving others kind words more often.

Once the ice is broken, the rest is easy. We develop good will toward our associates by speaking words of good will. We strengthen our personalities each time we sincerely express our gratitude. Have you ever noticed that the really strong and respected people you know are those who make a practice of saying kind things? They cannot afford to do otherwise. It would compromise the value they place on their fellow men. So why not be on the lookout for the nice things people do for you and repay them with like deeds? And never forget kind words of recognition.

People who get stirred up about little things don't usually have attractive speech personalities. They make their listeners feel uncomfortable. They may use unkind words too much. You never know when they're going to fly off the handle next. On the other hand, those who have human relations of the right sort check the impulse to let their tempers run wild. They learn to count ten and take a deep breath before they blurt out harsh words. As a result, their lives become easier and happier. Their blood pressure goes down, and good luck bobs up all over the place.

This problem of getting wrought up about little things brings us to the question, "What are the marks of emotional maturity?" First, we might place the habit of using the head instead of the solar plexus in our dealings with people. Have you ever seen someone just miss the bus and cuss and fume about it, getting his whole day spoiled right from the beginning? "It's invariably the fault of somebody else," he says. But you and I know the commonest reason why we miss buses is that we don't get up in time to meet them. So the first mark of emotional maturity is using our heads to solve the little everyday problems on the job and at home. Once we make this a habit, the big problems take pretty good care of themselves.

Second, the emotionally mature person is one who can keep a secret. Have you ever had an unpleasant experience because someone wasn't old enough emotionally to repress the urge to break a confidence? Information is of three kinds—that to be shared with everybody, that to be shared with nobody, and that to be shared discreetly. The second and third types test emotional maturity. For unless we can control the impulse to break a confidence, unless we can keep a secret, we are not grown up emotionally.

Someone called *blame* and *fame* "those twin impostors." Now the emotionally mature person isn't thrown off balance by undue praise or unfair censure. He knows that words are often uttered with little regard for facts. While attempting to correct the situation, he plods his resolute way and holds to his accustomed course. This, then, is our third mark of emotional maturity.

There are many other characteristics of emotional maturity, but the three we mention here are among the most highly valued by the world at large. To cultivate them, to make them habits, is a noble and rewarding pursuit. By using our heads instead of our solar plexuses, by keeping confidences, and by being impervious to "those twin impostors," we shall not only get along well with others but rise in our own estimation as well. *Growing up emotionally is a lot of fun that all of us can indulge in.*

All our illustrations point to the fact that the speech personality doesn't really exist until you have an audience. You must be with people to exercise it. That means speech is inseparable from human relations. Let's close this chapter by taking a human-relations inventory.

EXERCISE 73: Your Human-relations Inventory

DIRECTIONS: *Circle the number in the column that most closely answers each question. Then total the numbers. If your score is 150 or below, your human relations should be above average. Zero is a perfect score. But that doesn't mean you can't try to reach it.*

	Yes	No	?
1. Is there someone I wish to get "even" with because he has treated me unfairly?	50	0	25
2. Do I get angry at a person who steps in front of me in a line of people?	10	0	5
3. Can I adhere to the issue in an argument without resorting to sarcasm or denunciation?	0	20	10
4. Do I get a secret pleasure from listening to the misfortunes of others?	20	0	10
5. Do I believe that those who have made amends for their mistakes should be given another chance?	0	20	10

	Yes	No	?
6. Would I vote for a qualified candidate for the governorship if he were of a different race from my own?	0	20	10
7. Do I enjoy passing along unkind gossip?	25	0	15
8. Would I be willing to pay additional taxes to stamp out undernourishment in my community?	0	25	15
9. Have I established the habit of giving a soft answer to an excitable question or remark?	0	20	10
10. Do I set a good example for children in the way I speak and act?	0	20	10
11. If I hear another maligned in his absence, do I suggest he have a chance to defend himself?	0	20	15
12. Have I learned to rule out or minimize fear?	0	25	15
13. When good fortune comes my way, do I share it?	0	20	10
14. Am I actively associated with at least one welfare organization?	0	25	15
15. Is my reputation for helping to spread feelings of security and good will stoutly established where I work and live?	0	20	10
16. Do I budget my income so as to donate a portion of it to charitable causes?	0	20	10
17. Have I developed faith in man's ability to improve himself?	0	30	15
18. Am I popular by virtue of making others feel better in my company?	0	30	15
19. Do I treat the members of my family as graciously as I do strangers whom I wish to impress favorably?	0	25	10
20. Have I learned to accept defeat without bitterness?	0	30	15
21. Whenever possible do I avoid people and things that irritate me?	0	20	10
22. Is my vocational goal marked by the desire to give more than I receive?	0	30	15
23. Am I stronger in mind or body today than yesterday?	0	30	15

	Yes	No	?
24. Am I now adding only constructive interests to my life?	0	30	15
25. Am I hesitant to say kind words to those who merit or need them?	20	0	10
26. Do I keep my promises?	0	50	25
27. Am I now engaged on a program of self-improvement?	0	30	15
28. At least once daily do I consciously yearn for deeper understanding?	0	20	10
29. Do I keep my head when others about me become excited?	0	30	15
30. Do my hopes exceed—both in number and intensity—my regrets?	0	25	10
TOTAL			

Chapter 20: HOW TO PREPARE A SPEECH

WASHINGTON HIGH SCHOOL

DAYTON, OHIO

October 2, 1948

Mr. Joseph T. Brown, President
Brown, White, and Black, Accountants
26 Main Street
Dayton, Ohio

Dear Mr. Brown:

At the excellent suggestion of the President of our School Board, Mr. Edward Breen, we are arranging a series of assembly programs for our senior students at Washington High School. These programs will be devoted to information about occupations that may hold opportunities and interest for our boys and girls.

We are asking leaders in various fields to speak about their work at these assemblies. In this way we hope to help our graduating class think realistically about the selection of a life work.

We would be deeply grateful if you would inaugurate the series on Tuesday, November 16, at 10 A.M.

You would be helping us achieve our objective if you would speak for twenty-five or thirty minutes on the subject, "What It Means to Be an Accountant." Our students would like to know what are the abilities and education necessary to become an accountant, what opportunities exist in accountancy and related fields, and what is the compensation in the beginning and later on. Any other information that you know would be helpful to them would be most welcome.

At the conclusion of your speech, there may be some questions that the students would like to ask from the floor, if you would be kind enough to entertain them.

We are hoping that you will have the time and interest to accept this invitation.

With every good wish, I am

Sincerely yours,
Albert Ovalle, Principal

Let's suppose you just received this letter. Your first reaction is, "How in the world could I keep several hundred youngsters quiet for a half hour?" But you want to help. After all, your firm is a leader in the accountancy field. There'll undoubtedly be something said about your speech in the local papers, some free advertising. Ned Breen is an awfully nice chap, one of your best friends; you can't let him down. And so you write Doc Ovalle, one of your brothers in the Kiwanis Club, that you accept.

Then you begin to think about the fateful assembly—your speech and how you're going to deliver it. You get out your notes on the public-speaking course you took some years ago. You prepare your speech with the help of your notes. Here they are:

1. Give a gracious salutation.

Smile as you acknowledge the chairman's introduction. Don't forget to include special guests and the audience in your first words.

2. Make them sit up at your introduction.

There are many ways to do this:

a. Be direct. Tell the audience what you are going to talk about. When Thomas E. Dewey was New York's famous racket-busting prosecutor, he went on the air with *The Inside Story of a Racket*. Here's how he began: "Tonight I am going to talk about the alliance between crime and politics in the County of New York. I am going to tell you about a politician, a political ally of thieves, pickpockets, thugs, dope peddlers, and big-shot racketeers. . . . Tonight we turn on the spotlight."

b. Startle them. Winston Churchill opened a speech in Parliament in 1934 with, "To urge the preparation of defense is not to assert the imminence of war. On the contrary, if war were imminent preparation for defense would be too late. I do not believe that war is imminent, and I do not believe that war is inevitable."

c. Tell a story. In this way you appeal to a very basic interest in people of all ages. Choose a story which has some connection with your subject. For instance, a speaker at a high-school graduation talked about "Intelligent Kindness." This is how he began: "An elderly Negro was carrying two heavy valises across Forty-second Street in New York City. Someone touched him on the shoulder and said, 'I'm going your way. Let me carry one of these.' Booker T. Washington said, 'That was the first time I ever met Theodore Roosevelt.'"

d. Ask questions. These arouse curiosity. For example, "Why does a cowboy dress as he does? What's the ten-gallon hat for? Why do his boots have high heels? What's the reason for his chaps? When we answer these and other questions, we'll see that he is a creature of his environment, that there's a whole lot of common sense in back of his clothes. . . ."

e. Use a quotation: "In the Book of Job, Chapter 39, appear these words about the ostrich: 'She is hardened against her young ones, as though they were not hers. . . . Because God hath deprived her of wisdom, neither hath He imparted to her understanding.' Job was a little harsh in his judgment upon this faithful servant of the ladies, his decorator of millinery. Let's look at her habits and character. . . ."

There are many other ways to begin a speech, but these five get immediate attention. They are the most popular. Masterly speakers use them oftenest.

3. Hold them with a logical plan.

Once you catch your audience's attention with a good opening, or *exordium,* hold their interest with a plan which is easy to follow. Brown decides that he can present his material under this plan: (*a*) what the job of accountant is like, (*b*) what abilities and personality traits make for success in accountancy, (*c*) what is the present and future need for accountants. He then decides to open his speech something like this:

Principal Ovalle, Members of the Faculty, and Seniors of Washington High:

Accountancy is the first of the vocations; it begins with *A.* That's why I have the pleasure of being your first speaker. It is a wonderful vocation, interesting and full of service—else I wouldn't have chosen it. And I've not regretted my choice.

Some of you have already planned to be accountants. Others of you may decide to join us. May I then chat with you about three important aspects of the job of an accountant. Here they are:

1. What the job of accountant is like.
2. What abilities and personality traits make for success in accountancy.
3. What is the present and future demand for accountants.

4. Develop your ideas with variety.

Don't let your ideas fall flat because you lack ways to develop them. Here are seven sure-fire ways to put across your ideas:

  a. Use examples. Let's listen to Harry Emerson Fosdick talk about "Being Civilized to Death." Here is his first paragraph:

In a western New York community stands a house, still occupied, the original portion of which was a log cabin. That log cabin my great-grandfather built. Hardly three generations are represented in the years that have passed since then, and yet how startling have the changes been! When my grandsire played as a lad about a log cabin, there was not any-

where in the world a railroad or a telephone or a telegraph. There were
no matches to light fires with or gas or coal ranges to light them in. There
were no elevators or refrigerators, no plumbing, no electric lights, no sew-
ing machines, no furnaces. Letters were written with quill pens because
steel pens had not been invented and were dried with sand because blot-
ting paper did not exist. And of course there were no victrolas, radios, type-
writers, bicycles, automobiles, or airplanes. With what absorbed preoccu-
pation during three generations has mankind been engaged in inventing
and producing the paraphernalia of civilization!

How many examples do you count?

b. Use definitions to make sure they know what you're talking about.
Here's how:

My dictionary says that *democracy* came originally from the Greek language and meant the rule of the people. Today it means practically the
same thing: "government in which the supreme power is retained by the
people and exercised directly or indirectly."

But democracy means much more. Professor Arthur M. Schlesinger, Jr.,
of Harvard University, recently defined it this way: "Democracy, we may
agree, implies government by discussion and consent under law. As one
surveys the workings of the democratic impulse in the American past, one
discerns, I would suggest, two fundamental characteristics. One characteristic is the belief in the inalienable rights of the individual. The other is
the belief in the necessity for democratic control of political and economic
life. These two articles of faith constitute the premises of our democratic
tradition."

c. Use contrasts and comparisons.

Someone said, God made the country, man made the city, and the devil
made the suburbs. I've never lived in the suburbs, but I have lived in a big
city, and I am now living in the country. Which do I like better? The
country. And I'll tell you why.

There is a peace and quiet among the fields and hills you never find
in the crowded, dusty streets of a metropolis. In the country you have all
the conveniences that city dwellers are always boasting about. You have
telephones, electric lights, radio, and television. In addition, you have
cleaner, purer air. You don't have all the infernal din of Main Street. In
the country you can cultivate your garden. What have you in the city?
A window box.

Don't tell me city schools are better. We now have central schools in the country. A bus picks up my youngsters, takes them to a pretty, well-educated teacher. My youngsters have small classes. They play in a large, open playground. No hard cement pavements, no crowded courts such as their city cousins have to put up with.

I live cheaper and better in the country. My brother in the city is always complaining about the high price of butter and eggs. We produce our own. Our vegetables are garden fresh and we put away lots of them in our deep freezer. You mean to tell me the city slicker can do these things?

d. Develop your ideas by reasons. Henry A. Wallace, when he was Secretary of Agriculture, delivered "The Community of Interest Between Labor, Capital, and Agriculture." He began to develop it by reasons:

There are many reasons why I am glad to come to Pittsburgh. In the first place, my grandfather, Henry Wallace, was born on a farm about twenty-five miles from here and in his autobiography tells many stories about this part of Pennsylvania. In the second place, Pittsburgh typifies more dramatically than almost any other city the close relationship which exists between farmers, industrial workers, and capitalists. . . .

e. Say it in a conversational style. Listen to Franklin Delano Roosevelt hit the conversational note in his Victory-dinner Address of May 4, 1937:

A few days ago a distinguished member of Congress came to see me. . . . I said to him, "John, I want to tell you something that is very personal to me—something that you have a right to hear from my own lips. I have a great ambition in life."

My friend pricked up his ears.

I went on, "I am by no means satisfied with having twice been elected President of the United States by very large majorities. I have even greater ambition."

By this time my friend was sitting on the edge of his chair.

I continued, "John, my ambition relates to January, 1941."

I could feel just what horrid thoughts my friend was thinking. So, in order to relieve his anxiety, I went on to say, "My great ambition on January 20, 1941, is to turn over this desk and chair in the White House to my successor, whoever he may be, with the assurance that I am at the same time turning over to him as President a nation intact, a nation at peace, a nation prosperous. . . ."

f. Say it again and again. The professors call this device *parallelism*. Notice how Arthur H. Vandenberg kept them awake at a Memorial Day ceremony in 1938 (the italics are mine):

Mr. Chairman, fellow citizens, at this sacred moment, dedicated to the memories that have preserved America, we stand on hallowed ground. *It is hallowed* by the heroisms of one of the decisive battles of all times and history. *It is hallowed* by a victory which prophesied the end of civil war. . . . *It is hallowed* by the human sacrifice of brave men upon both sides. . . . *It is hallowed* by the echoes of the Emancipator's great yet simple oration. . . .

g. Say it in vivid words. Francis Cardinal Spellman spoke at the dinner given by the Friendly Sons of St. Patrick on March 17, 1948. Notice how he aroused his audience with words of strong emotional appeal:

Once again the world hangs crucified on its cross of sin—crucified by nails of greed, anarchy, cruelty, and atheism. And in this hour of dreadful, desperate need we have permitted Soviet Russia to continue her policy of persecution and slaughter, dooming our neighbor nations and ourselves to reap a rotted harvest of appeasement. Once again, while Rome burns, literally and symbolically, the world continues to fiddle. The strings on the fiddle are committees, conferences, conversations, appeasement—to the tune of no action today. . . .

5. End like a lion.
Don't forget to come to a definite conclusion.

The best way to do this when you give a speech explaining something is to tell again what you have been talking about. Summarize it. Brown, for example, might say:

So I've tried to tell you something about (*a*) what the job of accountant is like, (*b*) what abilities and personality traits make for success in accountancy, and (*c*) what is the present and future demand for accountants.

If there are any questions I may be able to answer at this time, I'll be very happy to answer them.

Be sure, too, to make your last sentence a memorable one. Give it the flavor of a *peroration,* a sentence or two that carries the main idea of your speech. When Daniel Webster spoke for more than two hours in his famous "Reply to Hayne," he summarized his whole meaning in the last sentence: "Sink or swim, live or die, survive or perish, *the Union must be preserved."*

Sometimes a famous quotation will serve your needs. You may wish to appeal for action. A question will do the trick, such as, "Will you help us put the Community Chest drive over in a big way?"

The point is, don't leave your audience in mid-air. Bring them down to earth with a summary and a final sentence they can easily remember.

Of course there are many other ways to develop a speech. But you will find the speech that succeeds invariably has a definite beginning, development, and conclusion. Do you remember the bishop's speech in *The Bishop's Wife?* Composed by Cary Grant and spoken by David Niven, here it is—thanks to Samuel Goldwyn's kindness. It's a good speech because it starts off well. It's developed by examples all of us can see and hear. It ends with an appeal to the heart.

Tonight I want to tell you the story of an empty stocking.

Once upon a midnight clear there was a Child's cry, a blazing star hung over a stable, and wise men came with birthday gifts.

We haven't forgotten that night down the centuries. We celebrate it with stars hung on the Christmas tree and the cry of bells and gifts. Especially with gifts.

We buy them and wrap them and put them under the tree. You give me a tie, I give you a book, Cousin Martha always wanted an orange squeezer, Uncle Harry can use a new pipe. Oh, we forget nobody. Adult or child. All the stockings are filled. All, that is, except one. We have even forgotten to hang it up. A stocking for that Child born in the manger. It's His birthday we're celebrating. Don't let us forget that. Let us ask ourselves what He would wish for most, then let each put in his share: loving-kindness, warm hearts, and the stretched-out hand of tolerance— all the shining gifts which make up peace on earth.

From now on, as you listen to speeches, you will have a more critical ear. You may wish to analyze how well speakers succeed on the platform by using the check list below. For, the more analytical you become, the easier it is to do a better job preparing your own speeches.

EXERCISE 74: How to Evaluate a Public Speaker

DIRECTIONS: *Below are twenty items with which to estimate a speaker's effectiveness. Study the items before you listen to a speaker and then check his proficiency in regard to each one during or after his speech.*

	Excellent	Good	Fair	Bad
1. Personal appearance				
2. Posture and stance				
3. Facial expression				
4. Articulation				
5. Pronunciation				
6. Voice				
7. Vocabulary				
8. Grammar				
9. Gestures				
10. Opening remarks				
11. Plan of speech				
12. Concluding remarks				
13. Flow of words				
14. Reasoning				
15. Examples				
16. Interest				
17. Energy				
18. Audience contact				
19. Value of content				
20. Total impression				

Remarks: (What the speaker has taught me to do and not to do as a public speaker.)

Chapter 21: CONQUER THE PLATFORM JITTERS

MARGARET LEE RUNBECK, author of *Time for Each Other* and other best sellers, tells about her high-school graduation. She was scared as her turn came to speak. She admitted her stage fright to the visiting commencement speaker, seated at her side.

"I'm scared too," he said, "I've got a speech written down, but I don't think it's much good, and besides . . ."

"But *you* don't have to be afraid," she interjected.

"Neither do you," he replied. "I'll tell you a secret; then you'll never need be scared again. Everyone on earth is shy, self-conscious, and unsure of himself. Everybody's timid about meeting strangers. So if you'll just spend the first minute you're in the presence of a stranger trying to help *him* feel comfortable, you'll never suffer from self-consciousness again. Try it."

She thought of that when her turn came, and it worked! The program told her who he was: "Commencement Address, by the Honorable Franklin D. Roosevelt, Assistant Secretary of the Navy."

Did you ever have an experience like Miss Runbeck's? Do you ever wish you could feel as much at home before a formal audience as you do talking with a friend? Perhaps you've wanted to take part in a discussion from the floor but somehow couldn't make yourself stand up and start talking. If so, you have plenty of company, for fear of an audience is a common experience, even among able talkers.

Many brilliant conversationalists get cold feet every time they think about getting up to deliver a formal speech. Those old butterflies flutter around the solar plexus. (Sometimes they feel like eagles.) Perspiration—hot or cold—is the rule. Life gets on the unpleasant side.

Seasoned public speakers and actors testify to the "qualms." The late Otis Skinner, renowned star of *Kismet,* tells us in his autobiography that after fifty years on the stage he still feared his first entrance.

One of America's highest paid business executives told me that he suffers agony just before he acknowledges the chairman's introduction. Yet he's a spellbinder.

So stage fright is a problem every one of us must face if we wish to succeed at public speaking. You have two ways to solve it.

A psychologist can help you if yours is an extreme case. Take the vice-president who was given the added responsibility of reorganizing the sales department. He could talk around a conference table, hold an interview, speak over the telephone without any trouble. He spoke well in such situations. But the thought of standing before his salesmen or any formal group sent him into an emotional tailspin. He had to do something about it.

The psychologist explained that perhaps the difficulty could be traced to a forgotten experience. He gave the man the Rorschach Diagnostics Test, a series of ten ink-blotted cards. As the man described the images he saw among the blots, he revealed a deep-seated resentment. It all went back to the time he was five years old—when his mother forced him to recite pieces before guests and at church sociables. She was a domineering woman who alienated her son's affections.

His stage fright was a protest against his mother's domination. In other words, his buried animosity cropped out as fear of audiences after he reached manhood. Once he understood the cause, his resentment disappeared. And so did his fear of getting up before formal groups. Today he is an accomplished public speaker.

Such cases aren't numerous. Perhaps fewer than 10 per cent of those suffering from stage fright need this kind of help. It's called *deep therapy.*

The others can learn and apply the eighteen ways successful speakers use to control stagefright:

1. They always keep in mind that fear of failure before an audience is shared by the best public speakers.

Professor Charles W. Lomas studied (*a*) speakers who had no stage fright whatever, (*b*) speakers who had stage fright before they started to speak. The first group made the worst speeches; the second group, the best!

Speakers who don't fear a formal audience give a poor account of themselves. Hard to listen to, they lack the feeling that good public speaking demands. They're so sure of themselves that they lose much by not trying to be better. They look on public speaking as humdrum business rather than as a challenge to share thoughts and influence others.

Why not keep in mind that platform jitters are the rule rather than the exception? That all good public speakers are in the same boat—afraid of failure? That the audience is on your side, hoping you will give a good account of yourself? Or put it this way: "My nervousness before making a speech is pretty good evidence that I will succeed."

Then let the platform jitters come if they will and resolve to give a good account of yourself despite them.

2. They overpractice.

This means practicing after you can say the speech to yourself without forgetting any part of it. Overpractice puts the speech into your bloodstream. It gives you the kind of self-assurance you need. The idea is to know your speech so well that you can deliver it backwards and forwards. You can say it without hemming and hawing. You don't need to mutter to yourself: "Let me see now, how does that next point go?" Repeat your speech until you are sick and tired of it. Then you can be sure it is yours, even after that sea of faces swims before your eyes.

3. They do not memorize the speech word for word.

Experience teaches a bitter lesson: rote memory increases the jitters. What if you should forget a phrase or sentence? Your whole speech might fly out of the window. Moreover, you can't hoodwink an audience. You can't make them believe a memorized speech is extemporaneous. A memorized speech asks to be declaimed. It betrays a written style. There is something wooden about it. Good public speakers *converse with* rather than *recite to* their audiences.

4. They prepare an outline.

The best speakers take care to plan a beginning, list the various thoughts to develop the body of their speech, and include a summary in their concluding remarks. They "think out" the speech logically. Then, when they face the audience, they give their attention to putting the thoughts into words. This makes for a conversational style.

You too will notice that practice teaches you to phrase your thoughts in many different ways. By increasing your facility you develop self-confidence as a public speaker.

5. They prepare good notes.

Notes are good friends when they serve your purpose. But don't obtrude them upon the audience's attention. Many outstanding speakers type their notes on 3- by 5-inch cards to fit nicely into the hand or lie flat on the speaker's stand. They take a hint from broadcasters who underline important ideas with colored pencil. They make their notes easy to read. They type them in capitals and use triple spacing. They reduce their notes to the bare essentials so that their thoughts are easy to find. Good notes go a long way to build confidence.

6. They practice before a full-length mirror.

This allows them to see themselves as their audience sees them. They can study their facial expressions. Have you ever noticed how your words take on persuasiveness when you say them with a nod or facial gesture? Don't be afraid to exaggerate somewhat, because a formal audience can't see fleeting shades of expression. You may also want to check up on your appearance. Perhaps your gestures look a bit clumsy in a buttoned coat. Once you're satisfied that you do the right thing, that you put your best foot forward, your confidence grows.

7. They use gestures.

Gestures, when they are given right, add meaning. They help the audience understand the important points of a speech. That's why you'll want to rehearse your gestures before the mirror. You'll want to see what you actually do with your hands, arms, and body. Be sure to check up on the *autistic gestures* that we took up in Chapter Twenty.

They reveal tensions and embarrassment. They distract the audience. But the right kind of gestures—timely, delivered with purpose and ease—help to channel your jitters into dynamic action. Good gestures give you freedom from fear.

8. They hear themselves as others hear them.

Sometimes they rehearse their speeches in a small, enclosed space, like the bathroom. They cup their ears to catch the same voice quality the audience hears. Or they make a recording of their speech and play it back—with a critical ear cocked. Once they know how their speech sounds to the audience, they can heave a sigh of relief if it pleases them. Or they can do something about it if it doesn't. In either case, this is a way to dispel your nervousness.

9. They pronounce their words right.

They use a dictionary and a vocabulary builder. They know their confidence increases every time they pronounce and use words correctly. Sometimes an unusual pronunciation reminds us we have pronounced a word incorrectly for years. Are you satisfied with the way you pronounce words like *irreparable, route, harassed, luxury, forehead?* You'll want to learn the right pronunciation of the chairman's name and other proper names for the occasion. Good public speakers needn't fear the impression they'll create on a discriminating audience if they mind their pronunciation and usage.

10. They sometimes make use of a stooge.

One successful public speaker I know arranges with someone seated in the last row to raise his hand every time he can't hear. The speaker then doesn't have to worry about his "voice projection." When you speak in a good, loud voice, you show audience- and self-control. Speaking in a confident tone is like whistling in the dark. It bolsters your courage.

11. They learn how to use a microphone.

Speakers before large groups these days ordinarily use a microphone. But if your voice is strong enough and the acoustics good, don't use the microphone. It limits your actions and audience contact. You may wish to use the loud-speaker only when really necessary. In order to feel comfortable and self-assured, why not speak a few words over the public-address system before the audience gathers? Make sure the microphone isn't too high or too low. Keep it below your chin line, so your face is completely visible to the audience. Don't adjust it after you begin to talk. Any fumbling around with gadgets during a speech irritates the audience. Practice until you can speak convincingly without turning your head too far away from the microphone. Precautionary measures like these build up your composure.

12. They study their audience.

As you wait your turn, take it easy. Don't wiggle in your chair. Breathe deeply, even if you have to count to do it. Look at various parts of the audience in a calm way. Don't rush to acknowledge the chairman's introductory remarks. Turn to him deliberately. Then fasten your eyes on the audience before you start to speak. Hold your gaze until the audience quiets down. Such arbitrary rules of thumb help you control nervousness. And the audience thinks, "He's not a frightened speaker."

13. They practice autosuggestion.

Some years ago Stuart Chase—you've probably read some of his books on economics—had to speak before a schoolteachers' convention in Milwaukee. He'd never faced anything like that before.

The upturned faces seemed to flow to the horizon. As there was no retreat, I had to pull myself together. Taking a long breath, I reminded myself sternly that here was something new and exciting. Not everyone has a chance like this. You know what you have to say, my boy. So I stepped firmly up to the microphone, determined to enjoy the remarkable new sensation. And I did enjoy it!

Why not repeat to yourself, just before you get up to speak, "I'm going to succeed because I have practiced faithfully and well," "The audience wants me to succeed," "I'm growing in confidence all the time." Unless you sell yourself on the idea that you'll succeed, how can you sell the audience?

14. They lose themselves in their subject.

A speaker with a hundred oratorical faults can be a huge success if he gets all wrapped up in his subject. To put your message above your ego is a wonderful way to conquer platform jitters. We're all astonished from time to time by a shy, quiet fellow who makes a good speech. He gets excited about his subject. He loses himself in real eloquence. "Good speech, Joe. I didn't think it was in you," I heard a man say at the Chamber of Commerce the other day. Most of us find fluency when our feelings are deep enough to tap it. So get immersed in your subject and let yourself go.

15. They look at their audience all the time.

Ever notice how good speakers control their audience's attention? They don't glance at the floor or ceiling or out of the window. For they know that attention must be constantly coaxed along—by eye as well as ear. *Keep your eye on them every second* is a good motto to practice. Remember, you're in the best position of anyone in the room to dominate. You're standing while the others sit. You have been singled out for recognition. Look at the audience squarely as you realize your steady gaze helps you to be calm.

16. They keep on the move.

The *Vigorous-action Technique* is one method to combat the platform jitters. There's none better. Whenever you prevent your nervous energy from being pent up, your jitters lessen. So why not change your position from time to time? Give your audience those gestures you rehearsed. Shake and nod your head to let them know how you want them to feel about your thoughts. Be active and dynamic—but don't overdo it—and your tensions will subside.

17. They apply the law of empathy.

This two-story word means "feeling oneself into." The audience identifies itself with the speaker. When he steps too close to the edge of the platform, they fear they will fall off. When he feels nervous, they do too. And an apprehensive audience in turn increases your nervousness. Your job is to prevent the vicious circle from developing. That's why you, as the speaker, are called upon to give every outward sign of calmness. For it is bread cast upon the waters.

18. They accept every invitation to speak.

You, like the professionals, can grow into an admirable public speaker. Begin in a modest way, if you like. Make routine motions at business meetings. Join a service club where you have a chance every week to say a few words. You may wish to enroll in a public-speaking class. The coaching you receive there will give you confidence. Then, as your wings grow stronger, try them out on every invitation that comes your way. Before long you will soar to the peaks.

You will discover other ways to get rid of the platform jitters through self-discovery and trial and success. But these eighteen suggestions help many a speaker. Why not give them a chance to prove their value? Why not try them out as you speak on simple subjects, such as:

1. What I like about my job.
2. How to talk to a Communist.
3. My wife's the boss.
4. Should radio programs be censored?
5. Country life—that's for me.
6. What I plan to do when I retire.
7. Golf is a good game.
8. How to pick a mate.
9. The dominant sex.
10. Gardening is a fine hobby.
11. Children should be spanked.
12. The little red schoolhouse was all right.
13. The marks of a good father.
14. How to find a good job.
15. Automobiles—now and then.
16. People are more neurotic than they used to be.
17. What it means to me to be an American.
18. How we can help lower the divorce rate.
19. The greatest general of all time.
20. How to get along with people.

21. Should we have lotteries?
22. The best sport in the world.
23. How we can improve our schools.
24. One picture is worth ten thousand words.
25. Career women.

Chapter 22: TWO DOZEN WAYS TO KEEP YOUR AUDIENCE AWAKE

Back in 1923, when I was in college, our chemistry professor captivated us the first day. After we found our places, he looked calmly over the amphitheater. That's where he held his lectures. And then he did something rather strange.

He took a thimble out of his watch pocket. He held it up for all of us to see. He looked at it intently. Then he walked over to the laboratory table. He turned the spigot and filled the thimble with water. As he held the thimble between his thumb and index finger, he said—these were his first words—"Gentlemen, the time is not far off when we will discover the secret of atomic energy. We'll know how to release the energy from this thimbleful of water. Then we'll capture that energy. We'll harness it and perhaps use it to drive an engine from New York to Chicago."

From then on we were in the hollow of his hand. He made a wonderful impression on us. Here was a professor who didn't begin like all the rest—roll call in a singsong voice. Rather, he put on a good show. He piqued our interest. We never went to sleep in his course. And we learned a lot.

The moral of this story is: Keep your audience awake by being a good actor. Say and do attractive things. Start strong. For that is the time to win them over. The old saw, *A good beginning is half the battle,* is never truer than on the platform. Let's go through a list of do's and don'ts seasoned speakers keep in mind to hold their audience. If you follow these you too will keep your audiences awake.

1. Speak extemporaneously.

Don't read your speech. Let's make sure we understand the difference between *impromptu* and *extemporaneous*. The former means "offhand, without preparation." The other means "spoken without the use of a manuscript, not memorized." (*Declamation,* in which you deliver a speech memorized word for word, is passé.)

If your listeners expect a speech, don't disappoint them by reading instead. You'll find it difficult to read from a manuscript with a lively sense of communication. Reading destroys audience contact. Written speeches don't sound like speeches anyway; they sound like essays. If you have to present a formal "paper" for the record, prepare enough copies for press release. But speak your speech extemporaneously. Your audience will find it easier to stay awake that way.

2. Don't apologize.

According to my tabulations—tabulations made over many years—more than 98 per cent of the apologies speakers make are uncalled for. They attract attention to minutiae. They are signs of narcissism. They bore the audience. Have you ever heard a speaker apologize for a cold when his voice sounded all right to you? Perhaps he thinks we'll believe he could do much better, that we'll give him credit for being better than he is. If a speaker has a cold, apologies won't help it.

Which apologies do audiences find most boresome? We have some data on that: (*a*) excuses for unpreparedness; (*b*) calling attention to poor public-speaking ability.

Be therefore of stout heart. Do the best you can without apologizing. Your audience will admire you for it.

3. Get down to brass tacks.

The most popular kind of speech with audiences is clear exposition. Here you take a subject. You define it. You tell your audience what you are going to talk about. You talk about it—in necessary detail.

Finally, you summarize it. This is workmanlike. It makes sense, is easy to follow. It takes the audience somewhere.

The other evening I listened to a pleasant fellow get started in three different, unconnected ways. First, he referred to another speaker's remarks. Second, he told a story he had just heard—it had nothing to do with his subject or the occasion. Third, he gave his prepared *exordium*. It was a good one, if only it had come at the right time—in the beginning.

All this kind of beating about the bush is what the old rhetoricians called *prefatory generality*. Let's get going on the subject as soon as the chairman says go. Let's not shadowbox.

4. Stay within your time limit.

Remember the speaker who takes a half hour when the program announces a twenty-minute limit? Even able speakers sometimes break this commandment—to the chairman's embarrassment and the audience's sighs.

You see, time-blindness is a sign of many ills. It means poor preparation. Voltaire once inscribed a novel of his to a lady friend. The novel was printed in two volumes. His inscription went, "To ———— with love and apologies. If I had had the time this story would have been written in one volume." Thorough preparation implies keeping your speech within the time agreed upon.

It may mean egotism. The time hog is discourteous. He loses his head, is carried away by his own voice. If you suspect yourself of developing time-blindness, why not ask the chairman to give you a signal a minute or two before your time is up? Then you can give your conclusion and come in on a photo finish.

When you act as chairman, particularly of a program of more than one speaker, you will be kind to announce the time limits. Give your warning signal overtly enough so that everybody can see it. This way you discourage the time pirates.

5. Handle your notes well.

Notes—unlike little children—should be heard and not seen. Winston Churchill tells us in his *War Memoirs* how glad he was to sit with the party in power in Parliament. Then he had the advantage of laying his notes on the lectern. You see, he didn't want his notes to detract from his delivery. Yet he needed them for reference to statistics.

May I give you one man's experience? I prepare my notes on 3- by 5-inch white cards. I mark the first card "Introduction." On it I jot down a few words to remind me of the opening remarks and the plan of my speech. Then the next two or more cards I give over to the points to be covered in the body of the speech. Each of these I mark "Body." I number each point, using subheadings if necessary. The last card, marked "Conclusion," carries my notes on the summary and my *peroration.*

I use these notes to rehearse my speech. Each successive rehearsal differs somewhat from its predecessor, because I extemporize rather than memorize. But after a few rehearsals I find the notes aren't necessary any more. They've served their purpose.

However, if you feel you must have notes by your side, by all means keep them there. They may add to your confidence. So long as they don't obtrude, so long as you don't give them too much attention, your audience won't mind.

6. Speak up.

How many wearisome times we suffer through speeches, seeming more long-winded than they really are, simply because the speaker doesn't make himself heard! Public-address systems help—when they work. When they aren't available or break down, the speaker of un-trained voice is at a loss.

Some of us use a microphone only when absolutely necessary. Most of our audiences are small enough to hear the natural voice. Why rely on a microphone when it isn't necessary? Most amplifiers distort the voice anyway. To use one right, you have to speak steadily into it. Now the good speaker must feel free to move about when necessary. He may want to look this way and that when he gestures. He ought to nod or shake his head once in a while. Each time he does so he breaks the steady stream of voice into the microphone.

But if you improve your voice and articulation you won't need to depend upon the microphone. You'll be able to speak in a "20-foot voice," "40-foot voice," "100-foot voice," etc., to accommodate a variety of audiences and acoustics. You'll increase your adaptability. Don't forget also it's better to err on the side of loudness than softness. Audiences that hear you easily don't fall asleep.

7. Keep a steady eye on them.

Most novices give themselves away by looking out of the window as they talk. They may shift their eyes from the floor to ceiling. They don't look steadily at their audience.

Notice how good speakers never lose sight of their audience. They bind the various sections into a compact mass by looking first in one direction and then in another. But they always look at people. When you turn your eyes away from your audience you break an important psychological bond. *Hold them by eye as well as by ear* is a winning motto.

8. Don't lose them in a chart.

Ever notice an audience "get lost" because the speaker stops in the middle of his discourse to set up a visual aid? Or talks to the blackboard while demonstrating a point? Visual aids may be used to great advantage if the speaker blends them in nicely with his oral presentation and doesn't allow them to break his audience contact.

9. Hold on to yourself.

Movements and gestures that attract attention to themselves rather than help to carry meaning intrude upon the audience's attention; and the audience doesn't like them. They disclose the speaker's nervousness. Speakers should learn to control such gestures with the aid of an instructor. Remember to visualize yourself as your audience sees you.

10. Deliver good gestures.

If your gestures are poorly timed and lack variety, if they are stiffly given, if they appear isolated from the speaker's whole body, they irritate the audience. Better no gestures at all than distracting ones. You pique your audience's attention when you use good gestures.

11. Don't ignore the chairman.

Speakers are sometimes so intent upon getting the first words out that they forget to acknowledge the introduction. Almost as bad is the speaker who acknowledges the chairman in a condescending manner. A deliberate acknowledgment marked by facing the chairman and thanking him by gesture or word is impressive. If the chairman is particularly gracious, the audience will sit up when you thank him by shaking his hand. It's good showmanship and good courtesy. Done right, it immediately arouses the audience's attention. By the way, you will want to avoid, "Mr. Chairman *and* Gentlemen."

12. Tell appropriate jokes.

Not all good speeches begin with jokes. Audiences are quick to make snap judgments. If the joke has nothing to do with the subject or occasion, if it is inappropriate to the sensibilities of the gathering— no matter how good the joke may be in itself—don't tell it. There are many other ways to begin with a bang, as we saw in Chapter Twenty.

13. Don't use a singsong voice.

An excellent way to induce sleep, according to the hypnotists, is to speak in a monotonous voice. Why not color words with vocal inflections? Why not keep the audience on the edge of their seats by frequently changing your pace? Why not pause slightly before important words? You create suspense thereby and prevent slumber—with or without closed eyes.

14. Pronounce them right.

Tiresome, particularly to educated audiences, is the speaker who mispronounces words such as *amateur, drowned, mischievous, deaf, orgy.* These are not unusual words, and when they are mutilated audiences make deductions—often unfair, but they make them just the same. "Why don't they give us speakers we can learn from?" they say, before slumping a notch or two farther down on their backbones.

15. Don't use too much slang.

A bit of slang here and there may heighten interest, may hit the nail on the head. But the speaker who is entirely dependent upon the current argot, who obviously doesn't know the difference between slang and accepted usage, makes some audience's gorge rise. Overuse of slang makes inroads into good taste.

16. Cast no slurs.

Ever hear a speaker say "dint" for *didn't*, "gumt" for *government*, "jeet" for *did you eat*, "miyon" for *million?* In this category also goes the speaker who trails off or smothers the final words of his sentences. Such habits, easily corrected, exasperate good listeners. Slurred words are hard to understand.

17. Get rid of the nasal twang.

We hear nasality because speakers don't chew their words. Unless the speaker can put two fingers between his front teeth without feeling tension in the cheek muscles, he is probably speaking with a clamped jaw. Result: his voice is nasal. He'd better do something about it if he wishes to influence his audience on the positive side. He may want to review Chapters Four and Five.

18. Make your explanations clear.

"There are three sides to this problem which we will want to consider" is a good straightforward way to pique an audience's attention. They expect, logically enough, that the speaker will then explain each before going on to the next. Speakers who throw out pearls of wisdom in a crazy-quilt pattern are deucedly hard to follow—so hard, that 68 per cent of the average audience won't even try. If you want to hold your audience without tying it with a rope, plan the progression of your ideas and stick to it. They'll love you for not making unpremeditated excursions.

19. Don't sell good grammar short.

Most of us these days like to hear colloquial speech. "It is I" sounds a little too precious. Even the Churchills have adopted "It's me." But on the other hand we still look down upon the speaker who uses a double negative or doesn't take the trouble to make his subject agree in number with his verb, etc. Every public speaker should mind his grammar lest it mar his fortune.

You will, of course, avoid the most common errors, such as, "you *was*," "he *don't*," "that *there*," "this *here*," "*them* chairs," "*more* happier," "I *can't hardly* wait," "*Me* and *him* were just like that," "*Them* and *us* should join forces," "You must *learn* him better," "I *ain't* going," "Let's *not* think of it *no more*," "I *seen* him there a hundred times," "They defended *theirselves* pretty well."

You'll want to review your grammar from time to time. It will give you confidence.

20. Use word magic.

Don't be afraid to use your imagination. Get in the habit of making bold comparisons. Billy Rose calls his chorus girls *long-stemmed beauties*. Study advertisements. The good copywriters know a trick or two. Listen: "A warm shirt warms you inside like a cup of coffee," "Smooth as cream pouring from a pitcher," "Slide into sunny-warm sheets. No scrooching around to get comfy," "Sharp as the bark of a wire-haired," "Made of plump, choice nuts—the kind squirrels fight over." If you lighten up your speech with expressions like these, their magic will keep your audience wide awake.

21. Pitch it right.

When the speaker's voice is pitched too high, the audience's Adam's apple moves up and down in sympathy to relieve his strain. When it is pitched too low, a funereal overtone often results. Once a speaker finds his normal pitch level he ought to make his voice play between his upper and lower vocal limits. Much can be done by experimenting with a voice recorder; more, with the aid of a speech teacher. The average audience can be held by the deft use of vocal pitch. The right pitch has a way of hypnotizing the higher critical powers. A wretched pitch can ruin the best thoughts.

22. Don't let "antis pantis" show.

Sometimes known as *termitus trouserus,* this malaise is noticed in speakers who lack platform composure. They don't stand foursquare to the winds. They can't sit still on a chair. Their gestures are oftener incipient than full-blown. *Antis pantis* is contagious among an audience. Any speaker afflicted should learn to control it lest his audience's attention run away from him.

23. Be enthusiastic.

The great English writer Bulwer-Lytton said, "Nothing is so contagious as enthusiasm; it moves stones; it charms brutes. Enthusiasm is the genius of sincerity, and truth accomplishes no victories without it." Audiences do not forsake the enthusiastic speaker. If you know your subject, if you find it interesting, if you really want to share your message, your audience must surely stay awake.

24. Don't forget to tie the knot.

Speakers often start with a bang and do a nice job of exposition, but then they forget to summarize or come to a conclusion. Thus the audience is left dangling. Audiences do not have the speaker's notes or thoughts to refresh a flagging memory. They need reiteration. Why not give it to them at the end of your speech?

There are many other ways to keep an audience awake, but these twenty-four are among the most useful. Once you adopt them you grow in power. All of us should check through them from time to time, because even the masters may forget them on occasion.

Chapter 23: BE A GOOD CHAIRMAN

YOUR FRIENDS and colleagues will soon recognize your growth as a speaker. They will sense your deep interest in public speaking. So don't be surprised if they elect you to arrange programs for business clubs, fraternal organizations, sales meetings, testimonial dinners, or conventions. You will want to accept such responsibility. It will add to your growth. Your immediate decision will be, "I'm going to make a huge success of it."

One of your jobs will be to get a good speaker. Then you'll have to introduce him. And, of course, you'll want to send him away happy. When you do these three things well, you come through with flying colors. Result: your stock goes up among your friends, at home, and —most important—in your own heart.

Let's go through the mill, a step at a time. Certain adaptations of course you will want to make. But the procedure we shall review is tried. It gets results. Let's suppose it's a dinner meeting.

1. Get a "big name" AND a good speaker.

Because the two aren't always found in the same person, make sure of the latter qualification. There are ways of finding out.

Program Counsel Bulletin, established in 1946, is a periodical addressed to program chairmen and group leaders. It gives impartial estimates of speakers and speeches much in the same way a journal reviews books.

Program, a monthly magazine, tells you what is going on in the lecture field. It carries advertisements of the leading lecture agencies. Your public library may subscribe to it.

2. Begin your selection by drawing up a list.

Choose the speakers you would like to have, any one of whom would bring distinction to your program. Don't be afraid to list topnotchers. Write the first man on the list far enough in advance of the occasion to accommodate his crowded schedule. If he doesn't accept, you still have time to invite an alternate.

Big men are easy to approach. They are humble of spirit. They want to help. They have attained their eminence because of these and other admirable traits.

Let me tell you of just two instances, recently brought to my attention. A small group of New York speech teachers hold several dinner meetings a year. They wanted to learn what speech training is given to salesmen in the metropolitan area. The chairman read an article in *Sales Management* on the subject by B. J. Todd, Vice-president of Orthopharmaceutical Corporation, a subdivision of Johnson and Johnson. The chairman wrote Mr. Todd and invited him to address the group—few in number but intensely interested in the speech course that his company gave its salesmen. Mr. Todd accepted, gave an excellent speech, and participated in a question-and-answer period.

A class wanted to hear Mr. Ody Lamborn, Director of the Sugar Research Foundation, give his views on public relations. One of them had heard him at a convention. Mr. Lamborn said yes to their letter and gave the class a whole evening of his time. These two cases may be multiplied.

If your invitation is well written you lessen the possibility of refusal. Here is a sample letter, one that brought an acceptance from a well-known business executive. It is disguised and may be adapted to your needs.

Mr. John Smith, President
Mars Manufacturing Company
New York 16, N. Y.

Dear Mr. Smith:

Last evening your name was unanimously selected as the speaker the Bingson Advertising and Sales Executives Club would like to hear at its twenty-fifth anniversary dinner, October 16, 1948.

Our membership is composed of fifty-two sales and advertising executives of Bingson and neighboring communities. We meet eight times a year to discuss ways and means to increase our service to the community. To the annual dinner meeting we invite an outstanding speaker and more than two hundred guests. These represent local business and industry.

We can assure you a capacity audience in the ballroom of Bingson's largest hotel. You may also be assured of every effort on our part to make your visit pleasant. Arrangements are now being made to broadcast the speech of the occasion over KWZX.

When our modest budget was prepared in January, one hundred dollars was earmarked as a token of our gratitude to the speaker of our anniversary meeting. We would also want to defray your expenses to and from Bingson.

This will be a memorable event for us, particularly if we may welcome you as our guest of honor and speaker of the evening.

With every kind regard, I am

Sincerely yours,
Frank Jones, Chairman
Program Committee
Bingson Advertising and Sales
Executives Club

3. Reply to the speaker's acceptance.

Thank him and request the title of his speech. If your broadcast time is limited, inform him of the time limit.

4. Begin to send out publicity.

Plan with your committee to send out several releases: announcement of the date of the occasion, story about the speaker, etc.

5. Write the speaker about two weeks before the event.

Tell him of transportation, hotel reservation, whether it will be a formal affair, etc. If you need his photograph—perhaps his public-relations department has mats—for the newspapers or printed program, now is the time to request it. Ask now also for a copy of his speech or a summary of it, also for publicity releases.

6. Meet him at the depot.

Then take him to his hotel room. He may wish to lie down to rest before dinner or take a drive or inspect the place where he will speak. Give him a free hand.

7. Make sure when you leave him he understands that you—or your deputy—will call for him at a definite time.

8. Let him know if there will be a reception line for him to join, cocktails with the officers, etc.

9. Call for him early enough to show him the speaker's table.

Get his approval of the arrangements. Would he like to speak from a lectern? If the acoustics are poor, let him know it. Rehearse with him the matter you intend to mention in your introductory speech for his approval. And ask him whether he would like to have any other items mentioned. (He's probably in *Who's Who in Commerce and Industry*.) Is there any question in your mind about the way he pronounces his name? If you're not sure, ask him.

10. Ask some friends to stand when applauding the speaker at his conclusion.

The rest of the audience will then follow suit. (You can make these arrangements before the day of the dinner.)

11. Start on time.

If the program states "Dinner at seven," don't begin at seven-thirty.

12. Seat the speaker on your immediate right, if you are the chairman.

Custom has made that the place of honor down the ages.

13. Place a good conversationalist-listener to the speaker's right.

This will free you from being solely responsible for talking with him. You'll doubtless have other things to think about some of the time.

14. Instruct the photographer to take his pictures during the dinner or after the speech.

If he insists on having a shot of the speaker in action, let it be done after the speaker warms up, not at the beginning when the flash bulb may disconcert him. You don't want to ruin his initial contact with the audience.

15. Watch the clock.

Perhaps you have to meet a radio spot for the speaker's address. If there are other speakers, be sure they understand how long they should talk. Hold them to their time limit by prearranged signals.

16. Get ready to begin the program as soon as the speaker's table has been served dessert and coffee.

Any time lag is a psychological letdown. Keep things moving, like a ringmaster. Often announcements can be given while the diners are finishing up. (Arrange beforehand with the management for the waiters to keep quiet and stop moving about once the guest speaker begins.)

17. Take a sip of water and clear your throat if necessary before standing up.

Why not say to yourself silently, "I've taken every precaution, worked hard, prepared my remarks carefully, so everything's going to be all right." Positive autosuggestion helps a lot in spots like these.

18. Don't look scared.

Glance deliberately over to the right, then to the left, then to the rear, and finally to the front to get attention. If the audience is not quiet after that, tap for attention.

19. Begin in a confident voice.

Remember how you spoke when you practiced your speech of introduction. A good beginning sets the pace for the whole program.

20. Know what you want to say so well—but don't recite it parrotlike —that you can dispense with notes.

21. Don't take too much time to introduce the speaker.

You can speak about a hundred and fifty words a minute without rushing. If your speech of introduction takes more than two minutes, it's probably too long for most formal programs. (Remember the speaker who was praised so loud and long that he opened his speech with, "Ladies and Gentlemen: The toastmaster has praised the speaker so highly I can hardly wait to hear myself talk.")

22. Let your remarks be pertinent to the occasion.

A joke just for a joke's sake, without any relevancy, had better be omitted. But an appropriate pleasantry is in order.

23. Don't embarrass the speaker.

Flattery or praise of his speaking ability may make the audience expect too much. Then the speaker begins with a mental hazard. Let your sincerity make him feel important.

24. Don't steal his thunder.

Ever hear a chairman or toastmaster "anticipate" the speaker's message?

25. Don't forget to announce his subject exactly.

Be particularly careful if he specified the wording.

26. Conclude your introductory remarks.

One good way is to pronounce the speaker's name as you turn toward him with a smile or inclination of the head.

27. Give him enough elbow room.

You may wish to push back your chair from the table. It's more comfortable for the speaker that way; for you, too.

28. Don't whisper or move about while he is talking.

Give him your full attention; it helps the audience to do likewise.

29. At the conclusion of the speech, give him time to acknowledge the applause.

The audience may wish to call him back for a second bow. Some clubs have the gracious custom of offering a vote of thanks to the speaker at this time.

30. Bring the meeting to a close with a few words of gratitude to the speaker.

You may shake his hand if you feel like it. If a question-and-answer period was announced, now is the time for it. You may recognize speakers from the floor. Or, by prearrangement, have the questions written on cards to be sent up. You then read the questions aloud. Some chairmen "plant" a question or two before the program begins. This starts the ball rolling.

31. Don't leave the speaker in the lurch.

Stay with him as he leaves the dais or platform. Guard against over-enthusiastic guests cornering him or you. He's probably tired and would like to leave soon.

32. Ask him whether he would like more entertainment.

If he indicates that he'd like to retire or catch a train or plane, don't try to dissuade him. Comply with his wishes.

33. When he does leave, escort him unless the hour is very late.

In this case he probably won't want you to take the trouble.

34. Write him a letter within two days.

Express the gratitude of your organization. Try to make it something more than a simple sentence of thanks. The following letter was supplied by a speaker for this chapter.

Mr. John Smith, President
Mars Manufacturing Company
New York 16, N. Y.

Dear Mr. Smith:

The phone calls started early this morning and have continued throughout the day. Every call brought us the hearty thanks of our members and guests on the excellence of the material you gave us and the very fine way you presented it.

Thanks to you, our meeting was a huge success. We shall always be grateful to you for making such a worthy contribution to our program.

With every good wish, I am

Sincerely yours,
Frank Jones, Chairman
Program Committee
Bingson Advertising and Sales
Executives Club

35. Send him newspaper clippings.

Any that mention his contribution to the occasion will be welcome. Don't forget to attach to the clippings the names of the papers in which they appeared.

36. Why not send the speaker a phonographic recording of his speech, especially if it was broadcast.

Such recordings are not expensive and since none of us can hear ourselves as the audience does they are usually appreciated.

37. Don't let him forget you.

The Advertising and Sales Executives Club of Montreal, Canada, sends its speakers a certificate of honorary membership in its club. It is beautifully illustrated with the speaker's name inscribed. It makes an attractive decoration, somewhat like a framed diploma.

The Study Club of International Business Machines sends its speakers a leather notebook. The speaker's name is embossed on it.

Such courtesies are never forgotten.

38. Be ready to disregard any of the above suggestions.

They may not fit. Above all, the good chairman and introducer of speakers is plastic and adaptable.

Of course many of us have to preside at meetings throughout the week. You may be the chief steward of your local union. You may be a foreman or department head. Or the president of a club. In each case your ability to lead the group depends on your knowledge of parliamentary procedure. Also on your knack of inspiring the group to work together toward wholesome ends. You may want to read Ordway Tead's *The Art of Leadership.*

Recently I was invited by Mr. Frank Dennis, Personnel Director of Hooker Electro-Chemical Company, to sit in on two meetings at the home plant in Niagara Falls. The president of the union called a meeting of his seventeen representatives. He was evidently an excellent leader, for he came with well-prepared agenda. He generated a spirit of friendliness and cooperation. There were disagreements. But they were resolved by open discussion, deftly kept in order by the group's elected leader.

Later on in the day, I met with the company's supervisors. Here again you felt that democracy was really functioning. Is it any wonder that the company has always had excellent labor-management relations?

I came away from both meetings with the conviction that our great system of free enterprise has still unlimited possibilities. Yes, unlimited so long as management and labor have sense enough to elect worthy leaders—leaders who know and practice the art of conducting conferences. For our misunderstandings can be resolved by playing the game around the conference board according to the rules laid down by decent men of good will. You can't legislate good will, but you can incubate it through free and open discussion.

A really good chairman must have all the qualities that will convince his group he is worthy of their confidence. They must like him. They must respect him.

From there on his presiding duties are fairly simple. Just as a dietician prepares her menus, so our chairman lines up his *agenda,* or order of the business to be brought before the formal meeting. Here is the established order:

1. Calling of the meeting to order
2. Calling of the roll (This may not be necessary.)
3. Reading and approving the minutes
4. Reports of officers
5. Reports of committees
6. Old (unfinished) business
7. New business
8. Adjournment

You may say, "But as a department head of Such-and-such Company, should I be as formal as all that?" Perhaps not. Yet even in an atmosphere of informality you can get a lot accomplished *if you encourage your staff to follow a definite procedure.* Once this is established and you encourage them to express their opinions, you'll get more and better work done.

One of my friends is a department head in the executive offices of a bakery chain. The department meets in the chief's office at least once a week. Twice a year the department elects a secretary who keeps the minutes of all the meetings. "The Chief" is a real leader. He does not fear open discussion. He is wise in the knowledge that through these meetings the department continues to grow in responsibility and teamwork.

Of course parliamentary procedure can become complicated. You may even want to study it, against the time you have to preside at very formal meetings. But by and large you and I need only the rudiments for our common responsibilities as presiding officers.

Here is a simple quiz to test yourself on your abilities as a chairman.

EXERCISE 75: Your Rating as a Chairman

DIRECTIONS: *Circle the answers that fit you best. Then total them. The higher the score, the better. You should make a score of at least 125 to be a good chairman.*

	Yes	No	?
1. Do I prepare the agenda before presiding?	15	0	5
2. Do I read and study *Roberts' Rules of Order* or some other recognized authority on parliamentary procedure?	15	0	5
3. Do I follow the regular order of business?	15	0	5
4. Do I "take sides" while presiding over a debate on a motion?	0	15	5
5. Do I recognize speakers in the order in which they signal their wish to speak?	15	0	5
6. Do I refrain from making unnecessary comments?	15	0	5

	Yes	No	?
7. Do I suggest that someone offer a motion to bring aimless discussion to a point of action?	15	0	5
8. Do I rap for order when the audience is inattentive to a speaker?	15	0	5
9. Do I encourage a mumbler to speak louder if the fringes of the audience can't hear?	15	0	5
10. Do I ask the audience's pleasure about time of adjournment if the agenda takes more time than I anticipated?	15	0	5
11. Do I "favor" overeager discussants to the detriment of the less forward?	0	15	5
12. Do I have the reputation of suggesting worthy compromises when impasses are reached?	15	0	5
13. If I feel the need of taking sides in a debate, do I call upon the vice-chairman to take over the chair while I speak from the floor?	15	0	5
14. Do I encourage the spirit of friendliness and good will by the way I conduct myself?	15	0	5
15. Do I enjoy the art of conducting a meeting well?	15	0	5

TOTAL

Chapter 24: BE A CREATIVE LISTENER

Do you ever get tired of "What did you say"? We hear it oftener than any other question in human relations. Why? There are five reasons.

1. Too many of us mumble.

We speak too fast, too indistinctly. We're careless about our articulation. We often talk with a cigarette, cigar, or pipe between our teeth. We run our words together, and our listeners have to work too hard to separate them.

2. We fall into the habit of not paying attention.

We become deaf to certain voices. I know a woman who hears everyone except her husband. Years ago she and he ceased to be good friends. She "learned" to crowd his criticisms out of her life by being deaf to him.

3. Some of us get subconscious pleasure when we make others repeat words.

It tickles the ego to get repetitions on demand. We ask, "What did you say?"—or its cousin from the other side of the tracks, "Whajasay?" —when we heard the first time. The question helps us to get attention we don't deserve. You find it a favorite with frustrated youngsters— grownups, too.

4. We converse in noisy places.

Many a voice tires by the end of the day because its owner shouts *above* rather than speaks *under* the din. How often we neglect to close a window or a door! How often we fail to lead someone to a quiet nook for a chat! When we take such common-sense steps, we cut down on the wear and tear of communication.

5. We have hearing losses we don't know about.

Almost 2 per cent of us have hearing losses we don't suspect. We hear common noises and *most* speech sounds. A door closes. We look up. Someone whistles. We turn around. We may hear words like *good* but miss some of the sounds in *mister*. (Dr. Harold Westlake, of Northwestern University, discovered *strawberry* is one of the hardest words for most people to hear.)

Not long ago the National Institute for Human Relations gave hearing tests to a large group of salesmen. It found ten types of symptoms among those who didn't hear sharply enough. Yet not one suspected that he had a hearing loss, and neither did his divisional manager. Here are the ten types.

You may have a hearing loss:

1. If you develop a very loud, metallic voice.
2. If you develop a very soft, whisperlike voice.
3. If you are in the habit of asking others to repeat questions or statements.
4. If you get ringing noises in your ears.
5. If you get earache.
6. If you lisp because you can't hear the high-frequency sounds like *s*.
7. If you find it hard to remember a telephone number long enough to jot it down.
8. If your attention wanders during an interview.
9. If you develop a monotone in speaking.
10. If you can't seem to understand unless you see the speaker talking.

Charles Darwin, the great evolutionist, used to say he shuddered every time he described the human ear. It's so delicate, so marvelous. It's so precious to us. We ought to recall how it works.

Did you know you have seven ears? Here's how to count them: three physical ears on each side of the skull, plus the *auditory center,* or *central ear,* in the brain. The three physical ears on each side are the *outer ear,* the *middle ear,* and the *inner ear.*

The *outer ear*—the one the girls hang earrings on—collects sound waves. Our friends, the dog, the horse, and other animals, cock their outer ears toward the source of sound. But only parlor tricksters wiggle theirs. A sort of tube, the *meatus,* leads to the eardrum, or *tympanum.* The eardrum draws inward and holds taut. Attached to it is one of our three smallest bones, the *hammer.* This is supported by a tough little muscle, the *tensor tympanum.*

The *middle ear* is an air-filled chamber. It lies right behind the eardrum. From the middle ear to the air passages of the nose goes the *Eustachian tube.* (You are right if you pronounce it "yoo STAY ki 'n.")

Have you ever noticed that you swallow when you go up or down fast in an elevator? Or open your mouth at a loud sound? These are reflexes to equalize air pressure on both sides of the eardrum, via the Eustachian tubes.

We sometimes become hard of hearing temporarily, when the tubes are clogged by a cold or inflamed tonsils. Not long ago they discovered many hard-of-hearing children and adults had vitamin deficiencies.

The Eustachian tubes often perk up, get freer air passages, once the missing vitamins are supplied.

The hammer moves every time the eardrum vibrates to sound waves. The hammer actually strikes another tiny bone, the *anvil*. The anvil touches a third bone, the *stirrup*. The footplate of the stirrup presses against a small membrane, the *oval window*. This oval window seals the inner ear. Ear specialists tell us that the commonest disease of the middle ear is *otosclerosis;* the three little bones become calcified together so they can't move freely.

The *inner ear* is a bony and membranous labyrinth. It houses the *semicircular canals*. These are the organs that control our sense of equilibrium. (Did you know that deaf people can't balance themselves as well as those who hear all right?)

The inner ear also contains the *cochlea*. This is a tube shaped like a snail's shell. The auditory nerve lies in it. It has thousands of hairlike endings. They make up the end organ, or *organ of Corti*. The commonest theory of how we hear states that each one of these "hairs" responds to a particular vibration. The *Harp Theory,* they call it, because the hairs are arranged somewhat like the strings of a harp.

The inner ear is immersed in a fluid. The fluid covers the oval window at all times. It receives all sound pulsations that beat upon the oval window. Deafness results when the oval window becomes too rigid. Then the ear surgeon may decide to perform the *fenestral operation*. He actually makes another oval window and shifts the stirrup's footplate. He says it is a successful operation about 50 per cent of the time.

Now let's sum up: We catch sound waves with the outer ear. These are channeled to the eardrum. The eardrum vibrates and moves the hammer. The hammer strikes upon the anvil. The stirrup picks up the vibrations from the anvil and passes them on to the oval window. The moving oval window creates ripples in the inner ear's fluid, and these stimulate the organ of Corti. With the aid of a nerve, the organ of Corti conveys the message to the central ear in the brain.

Just as we have a *cyclopean,* or mental, eye to fuse the images of both physical eyes, so we have a central ear. For example, let's suppose my right "ears" can hear *s* but can't hear *o*, and let's suppose my left "ears" can't hear *s* but can hear *o*. My central ear combines the *s* and *o* vibrations. Result: I can hear *so* just about as well as if I heard both sounds on both "sides." The important thing is to preserve our central hearing for all speech sounds.

How well do you hear? The best way to find out is to take an *audiometric examination*. (An *audiometer* is a machine that measures hearing.) Schools, speech-and-hearing clinics, and *otologists* (ear specialists) usually have audiometers for your use.

Dr. Harvey Fletcher and Dr. Edmund S. Fowler some years ago invented the *4b Audiometer* at Bell Telephone Laboratories. You can test from one to forty individuals' hearing at one time with it.

It's quite simple. There's an ordinary platter-type phonograph. It has a magnetic pickup needle with wires attached to it. The wires lead to plugs and so to earphones.

You put an earphone to your right ear. The record starts to play. You hear a voice read off numbers of two or three digits. After each number there's a pause. During the pause you write down the numbers you just heard on a printed form, the *audiogram*. Gradually the voice is *dampened*. That is, it becomes fainter by three *sensation units* with each succeeding number.

After your right ear is tested, you shift the earphone to your left ear. Then you listen to other numbers on the reverse side of the record. Of course the room must be quiet to get the right kind of results.

They use the *2a Audiometer* for careful testing. Instead of numbers a tone is played at many different pitches. You take your 2a audiometric test in a soundproof room alone with the *acoustician*.

Audiometric-test results describe various hearing losses, or *hypacusia*. Take the case of Mary Smith. Her problem is *monauralism*. She hears in one ear only. She can't locate the source of sound very well. And of course she's handicapped when someone talks close to her deaf ear. Otherwise she hears pretty well.

Tommy Jones is seven and doing badly in school. The otologist says that Tommy can hear all the speech sounds but can't retain their auditory images long enough. Because he can't remember sounds you might judge him to be feeble-minded. Can Tom be helped? Yes, usually. A competent speech teacher can help him to a comfortable memory span.

Mr. Brown can't hear you much of the time because he's got *tinnitus,* "head noises." It's vastly distressing; it keeps him awake, drowns out what you say to him. The otologist perhaps can help him.

Mrs. Green's voice is loud and monotonous. She speaks all her words with the same stress. She can't understand you, especially when you change your inflections. Speech reeducation and lip reading will help her a lot. Her next-door neighbor can't hear very well either. But she talks in a soft, breathy voice and swallows many of her words.

Mr. White's deafness gradually became worse over twenty-five years. At last he couldn't hear you unless you shouted close to his ear. Last week he tried on a bone-conduction hearing aid. And presto, he heard very well! Now he wears the receiver clamped to his mastoid bone. This conveys the sound vibrations to the inner ear, bypassing the middle ear, where the seat of his deafness is.

Surveys made by fellows of the American Speech and Hearing Association give some frightful facts about how widespread poor hearing is. Aside from the totally deaf (there are about ninety thousand of these in the United States), we have almost three million men, women, and children who ought to use hearing aids. But only eight hundred thousand do.

One reason is the cost. Another reason is vanity. Too many of the hard of hearing hate to admit it.

Many manufacturers of hearing aids worry less about the price angle than this psychological one. They are making receivers smaller and less noticeable. One company goes after women customers with a receiver that looks like an earring. The receiver matches an earring on the other ear. The earring is connected with a 7-ounce instrument which is concealed in the bosom or strapped to the thigh. By catering to the women's preference for miniatures, the one hundred odd manufacturers are confining themselves more and more to small mechanisms.

Laryngoscope, journal of the American Otological Society, reports that "fitting [of hearing aids] is wasteful. . . . The differentials between instruments that are indicated by most current tests are largely illusory." But because of the different hearing impairments and the "psychological problem of teaching the patient how to make use of his remaining faculties . . . the selection of an aid may still call for expert advice. But it is likely to turn less on acoustic and more on economic (price) factors."

Many excellent hearing aids are now on the market. If I were buying one, here's how I'd go about it. I'd get an audiometric test at some qualified clinic or from a specialist. I'd then take my audiogram to the local League for the Hard of Hearing or university speech clinic. Here you ordinarily find different makes of aids for fitting. I'd talk over with the acoustician the nature of my hearing loss. "What does my audiogram mean?" "Will I hear better with bone or air conduction?" I'd try on many or all of the aids and listen to voices and many common noises. I'd then go to the distributor of the aid I liked best and buy it. With hearing aids as with so many other things, *what's one man's meat is another man's poison.*

I would not expect the impossible from the aid. I would not be disappointed to discover:

1. My aid reproduces the human voice with a metallic timbre and with very little difference in voices.
2. A buzzing fly may sound like a buzz saw.
3. Adjustments take a long time to learn—several months or more.
4. Batteries have a way of going dead at crucial times.
5. Speech training is usually desirable.

But I'd be happy because machine-made hearing is better than deafness. Bernard Baruch, adviser to Presidents Wilson, (Franklin) Roosevelt, and Truman, and many other leaders, are enthusiastic about their hearing aids.

Although most of us don't need mechanical hearing aids, we can improve our hearing capacity, particularly after we are fourteen years old. Remember, along about that time our hearing reaches its highest acuity. Later there is a slight tapering off *unless* we use props.

One prop is ear training. Dr. Krikor Kekcheyev, of the Moscow Academy of Pedagogical Sciences, recently made an important discovery about ear training. You can temporarily increase the acuteness of your hearing if you think of bright lights. Psychologists tell us all the sense organs do their best work when emotionally pleasant ideas flit through the mind. This means that if we would make the most efficient use of our hearing (and our other senses) we must be happy, optimistic people. They also say that if we wear glasses we hear better with them on than off. So, if you wear them, be sure to put them on when you practice your ear-training drills.

EXERCISE 76: Tuning Up Your Ears

DIRECTIONS: *Sit by an open window. As you think about the brightest lights you ever saw:*

1. Listen very intently for a faint noise—far off.
2. Try to hear it better, clearer; "bring" it closer to you.
3. Now listen to a nearby sound.
4. Now alternate your attention between the faraway sound and the near one.

When you take a walk in the country, listen for the various birdcalls and insect noises. Identify voices on the air. Spend some time each day listening to radio commentators' speech sounds rather than their ideas. This helps you to become phonetic-conscious. On the train or bus, try to catch pieces of conversations in front or back of you. This kind of eavesdropping is one of the best exercises. There's a lot of human interest in it, too.

You may want to increase your auditory memory span. Here's one way:

EXERCISE 77: How to Lengthen Your Memory Span

DIRECTIONS: *Take a pencil and paper. Have someone stand behind you and read the numbers below from left to right. Your examiner should read the numbers at the rate of one digit a second, and he should utter each number distinctly and loud enough for you to hear easily. When he comes to the end of each number, he waits one second before he says, "Write." Then you write the entire number.*

6 1 9
5 2 8 6 (Youngsters between four and six can usually reproduce this group.)

2 0 3 7 4

6 3 9 4 2 7 (Sixteen year olds ordinarily can do this one.)

8 1 2 3 6 5 9 (Eighteen-year-old norm. Most people can't remember a longer number than this one after one repetition.)

4 2 7 9 3 1 6 0

7 1 0 6 8 2 9 3 5

3 6 1 8 7 4 2 0 9 5

5 4 2 7 3 9 6 0 1 9 7

DIRECTIONS: *Follow the same directions for consonants. (Be sure your examiner says sounds, not words:* s *not* es, r *not* ar)

s t p

z d b g

k g t d sh

zh n v f l ng (as in *king*)

ch m t r d k z

v f w th r b p k

j g s sh z th k t p

A second prop is lip reading. Of course all of us do some lip reading whether we know it or not. Even in a small room, you always find it easier to understand a speaker who faces you than one who turns his back.

Phoneticians assure us that all human speech in all languages can be narrowed down to seven basic lip functions. Teachers of lip reading, who train the deaf to hear through their eyes by watching speakers' lips, teach these seven basic lip functions to their pupils. Their names don't mean very much without a lot of explanation, but here they are anyhow, with some examples:

1. Extended vowel movements: as in *ee*l, *e*ll, *a*t.
2. Consonant lip movements: as in *m*y, *p*ie, *b*y, *f*ive, *v*ie, *w*ay, *wh*at, *r*oot, *s*ip, *z*ip, *sh*ut, *ch*ow, *J*oe, a*z*ure.
3. Relaxed vowels: as in *i*tch, *u*nder, *a*lms.
4. Puckered vowels: as in h*oo*t, b*oo*k, *aw*l.
5. Consonants of the tongue: as in *th*in, *th*en, *l*aw, *t*o, *d*o, *n*o.
6. Diphthongs: as in *ou*ch, m*o*ld, *u*niverse, *oi*l, *ai*sle, fr*ay*.
7. Consonants of context (they take place so quickly you seldom see them): as in *y*es, *k*in, *g*o, ki*ng*, i*nk*.

If you have studied the chapters on articulation and phonetics, you already have other props. Watch yourself talk in a mirror. Put your hands over your ears and see how much you can understand of what your friend says. With a little regular practice, you'll do a much better job of lip reading. This may come in handy when you have to listen to others talk in a noisy place.

A third prop is concentration. Don't let your mind wander. Hold on to the speaker's words. Get in the habit of repeating silently whole sentences that you hear. When you attend a formal lecture or address, jot down notes and review them. Train yourself to become deaf to all sound except the speaker's words. Type, or classify, his voice. Analyze his inflections: is he guttural, orotund? Repeat the words of the news item you just heard on the radio.

The fourth prop is gracious listening. People who get along well with others listen graciously. They are composed and relaxed. They believe with Epictetus that, "Nature has given to men one tongue, but two ears, that we may hear from others twice as much as we speak." For there is nothing so complimentary to a speaker—and to what he has to say—as the eager eye, the responsive face, the deferential ear.

Creative listening is a fine art. It's fun. You have to work at it. Its rewards are like King Midas's touch. A star salesman, who last year earned thirty-one thousand dollars, attributes his success to the way he listens to his clients. It flatters them. He can recall anything they say in an interview. Often he quotes them to his advantage. He never feels he loses the upper hand in an interview when he stops talking. His creative listening dominates better than words.

The best teacher I ever had did little talking, surprisingly little. He'd throw out a question here, a leading sentence there. He'd lean forward in his chair. He'd give you all his eyes. It was contagious. The class paid attention. His students were grateful for his courteous manner. He inspired you. He made you feel you were as important as a grown-up. He led your thoughts forth—an *educator*.

Are you ever irritated by someone—an acquaintance perhaps or an unhappy clerk—who reeks of boredom? His is the vagrant eye, the superior attitude, the restless shrug that tells you he already has a pert answer for you, isn't paying the slightest bit of attention.

Now all of us can develop creative listening. Here is a check list to help:

1. Get an audiometric examination at least once a year.
2. If you are deaf and a hearing aid will help, why not get one?
3. Work on an ear-training program.
4. Become a better lip reader.
5. Develop more concentration power.
6. Associate with gracious listeners, for they will inspire you (and me) to listen graciously also.
7. Speak distinctly to make listening easier on the other fellow.
8. Finally, put your shoulder to the wheel. Help worthy programs for the prevention of deafness, better education of the deaf. Help your local school buy an audiometer for the youngsters' use.

If you want proof of how a deaf-mute can be helped, see or read the play *Johnny Belinda*. Warner Brothers' movie of that play is one of the best I have ever seen. They deserve our gratitude for focusing attention on speech problems of the deaf.

You may want to take the following quiz several times a year to make sure you continue to develop your listening ability:

EXERCISE 78: How Good a Listener Are You?

DIRECTIONS: *Many of us with good hearing don't exercise it efficiently. We're not good listeners. Yet good listening ability is one of the main highways to vocational and social success. How good a listener are you? If you get 175 on this quiz your listening ability is probably average; anything higher is excellent.*

	Yes	No	?
1. I can repeat a series of six digits after hearing them read off once.	15	0	5
2. I have to ask people to repeat what they say more often than others seem to.	0	15	5
3. I get my hearing tested regularly.	15	0	5
4. I make a practice of repeating to myself what others say.	15	0	5
5. I study the lips of the speaker as he talks to me.	15	0	5

	Yes	No	?
6. I find myself daydreaming when others address me.	0	15	5
7. I find myself cutting off a speaker before he has time to finish.	0	15	5
8. I enjoy talking more than listening.	0	15	5
9. I am bored with what most people say.	0	15	5
10. A slow talker gives me the jitters.	0	15	5
11. My vocabulary is large enough to permit me to understand almost everybody.	15	0	5
12. I get enjoyment from listening to the "quiet" sounds of a woods or pasture.	15	0	5
13. I have always found it easy to mimic another person's vocal inflections.	15	0	5
14. I can identify well-known radio voices easily.	15	0	5
15. An error of grammar on the part of the speaker distracts my attention so that I lose his thought.	0	15	5
16. I can't pay attention to a speaker with nervous mannerisms.	0	15	5
TOTAL			

Chapter 25: WHY STUTTER?

ONE OF OUR three largest networks employs a radio announcer who stutters. He stutters everywhere except in front of a microphone.

"How in the world did you ever get an announcer's job?" I asked him.

"Oh, I married the boss's daughter. I knew long before I tried it that I'd never stutter over the air."

Most stutterers speak all right in certain places. A pretty debutante I know never stutters at a dance. Youngsters sometimes stutter at home, not at school—or vice versa. Perhaps you too know an eloquent public speaker who stutters in conversation. I know several smooth-talking interviewers who always stutter on the platform.

One of the oldest known facts about stuttering is that it comes and goes. Stutterers have their good and bad days. Psychologists tell us some other strange facts about stuttering:

1. It always begins in childhood, especially (*a*) when speech first develops, (*b*) between five and seven years, (*c*) in adolescence.
2. About 85 per cent of all stuttering begins in the first ten years.
3. Stuttering may disappear, only to come back again later on. A captain in the last war told me he stuttered until he was eight, was corrected, and began to stutter in Sicily while under fire. He had to undergo treatment again.
4. More children than adults stutter. This accounts for the common belief that "you outgrow it."
5. Some stutterers can't read aloud. Others read very well. A few stutter when they read and talk.
6. All stutterers can sing without blocking on their words. Most of them read aloud all right in unison with others.
7. Stutterers say they can speak smoothly when alone—or when they talk to a dog.
8. Many stutterers speak fluently before a younger person or a subordinate. One stutterer I know talks all right with his workers, but he stutters a lot before the plant superintendent.
9. Some stutterers talk fluently only while they crawl on their hands and knees.

Here is an interesting experiment, first performed by my distinguished colleague, Professor Robert West, of the University of Wisconsin. Choose a hundred stutterers at random. Match them with a hundred nonstutterers—for age, intelligence, and occupation of father. Then find out how many of the ancestors of both groups stuttered. You'll find stuttering six times more frequent among the ancestors of the stutter group than of the nonstutter group. This experiment points to heredity as a cause of stuttering.

Why do more youngsters stutter than adults? My friend, Dr. Mack Steer, out at Purdue University, discovered stuttering is normal among very young children. More than 40 per cent of very young stutterers speak all right by the time they go to school.

Dr. Charles Bluemel's theory of *primary* and *secondary stuttering* explains why so many boys and girls don't continue to stutter. He defines *primary stuttering* as the *gross speech symptoms*. You and I recognize them as gasping breath, blocks, repetitions, and twitchings that often mark first attempts to speak. In those tender years, the boy or girl is not aware that stuttering is undesirable.

Bluemel tells us that *secondary stuttering* comes with the child's realization that his speech is different from his playmates'. Secondary stuttering is a frame of mind—of frustration and inferiority feelings. It overtakes the child with a bang when he goes to school. There his classmates mimic him. Or his teacher may force him to recite when he can't. And if his parents scold him, make him repeat, or ask him why he doesn't talk like Susie, they bring on the secondary phase even before he goes to school. If they use common sense, the stutter is likely to disappear. You can easily see why secondary stuttering is harder to correct than primary stuttering.

That's why all authorities agree the stuttering youngster needs help as soon as the first signs appear. His parents ought to take him to an expert for careful advice. In my experience those youngsters who stop stuttering before they go to school have wise parents. They often practice unknowingly the kind of advice the expert gives.

If you force a left-handed child to write with his right hand, does that make him stutter? Those who believe in the *Handedness Theory* tell you these facts: (*a*) the left side of the brain controls the right side of the body, the right side of the brain controls the left side of the body, and (*b*) the same side of the brain that controls your preferred hand also controls your speech.

If, then, you make your left-handed child use his right hand, you may cause him to stutter—they say.

But surveys don't bear out this theory—that stuttering comes from forced change of handedness. In one study of eighty-nine thousand St. Louis schoolchildren "the vast majority of our left-handed pupils who have been taught to write with the right hand had not developed any speech defects. . . . 81.4 per cent of the children . . . began to stutter before they were given any instruction in writing in the schools."

Even so, most psychologists advise you not to change your youngster's preferred hand. "Let nature take its course," they warn you.

Did you ever feel that stutterers are slow to catch on? That they are of below-average intelligence? If so, you, like most of us, put fluency high among the marks of good intelligence. As a matter of fact, stutterers as a rule have normal intelligence at least; most of them are above average.

Here's how we prove it. The feeble-minded have all sorts of speech defects *except* stuttering. Havelock Ellis, great authority on the mysteries of genius, finds "the abnormal prevalence of stuttering among British persons of ability." In my book, *The Personality Structure of Stuttering,* I present the results of speech examinations given in colleges and universities all over the country. We find stuttering more than twice as common among these students as among the noncollege population. Stutterers have larger vocabularies than nonstutterers. They make higher-than-average scores on intelligence tests. All this evidence proves stutterers aren't dull. As a group they are mentally gifted.

But their high intelligence doesn't guarantee them freedom from personality problems. They can't look on their stuttering calmly. Often they accent regrets: "What might I have done if I hadn't stuttered!"

We have to sell them the idea that they can succeed even though they stutter. The great novelist, Charles Kingsley, and many others climbed to the top right over their stuttering—maybe because of it.

If you add up the totals of the deaf, the blind, and the insane, the sum is much smaller than the number of men, women, and children who stutter severely. Of course, all of us hesitate or repeat words at times, but only a small percentage have the recurrent blocks and spasms known as *stuttering, stammering,* or *dysphemia.*

They call stuttering a *sex-factor disorder*. Statistics on sex-factor disorders tell us three times more women than men have gallstones. There's scarcely any *Daltonism,* or color blindness, among females. *Hemophilia,* the bleeding sickness, is a so-called *male disease* because only boys and men have it. Seven times more males stutter, on the average, than females. At two years of age the ratio between boy stutterers and girl stutterers is two to one. This ratio gradually widens until at maturity it stands at ten to one.

Once we understand the reason for the disparity, the problem of stuttering may be solved. But to date we have only speculations, some easier to understand than others.

Some authorities believe that women don't stutter so much because they have a smaller obscene vocabulary. Stuttering, they say, comes from a subconscious fear of saying naughty words. "The idea is that the boy develops a street-corner vocabulary not appropriate to the fireside. In the presence of his parents he starts to use an obscene word, reacts with fear, and interrupts the word. Fear becomes attached to the syllable, and fear always interferes with its use."

Other experts believe the sex ratio is due to faulty breathing habits. They stress the fact that females favor chest breathing and males diaphragmatic breathing. Stuttering, they say, results from poor breath control. The cure lies in learning to control the chest and diaphragm.

The best explanation seems to me to be this. The speech centers in the brains of females grow faster. They become stabilized sooner. Girls speak earlier than boys, have larger vocabularies and fewer speech defects. Girls and women use secret languages oftener. In other words, it is the nature of the female of our species to talk better than the male. Better speech, like longer hair, sets her apart.

The Egyptian, Greek, and Roman civilizations knew stuttering and had "cures" for it. In the last century surgeons still tried to relieve stuttering by surgery. In France they operated on more than two hundred stutterers in one year. They cut wedge-shaped portions from the back of the tongue and severed various tongue muscles. Your tongue was sometimes pierced with needles and cauterized. They put wooden wedges between your teeth.

Some doctors believed the vocal cords were the seat of the disturbance. They prescribed smoking as a cure. Much earlier, Francis Bacon said that the stutterer's real trouble was a cold tongue. He believed stout wine was as good a cure as any. These and many other cure-alls were popular. They looked upon stuttering as an organic disease. Today we don't believe that.

Whatever causes stuttering, the effects are painful. The listener sometimes suffers as much as the stutterer. Here are a few excerpts from stutterers' diaries.

As a stutterer I experienced a rather consistent bodily and mental state. The defect does not exist merely as an obvious inability to express myself adequately in speech; it involves a generally complicated bodily tenseness as well, and mental uneasiness, a real fear which is apparent as a rule in my halting, shrinking manner of expressing myself, my thoughts, my emotions. I tend to hold myself in because I am afraid I shall stutter.

Although I believe I was as physically attractive as most of the girls I went with, I never had the invitations they did to go to dances and other affairs with fellows. I always had a suspicion that they made fun of my stuttering behind my back. Consequently I never married. No one ever proposed to me.

I was terribly shy around them (girls) when not in the classroom. However, I do not think I would have been if I had not stuttered. When I saw other boys talking to some of the girls I liked, I felt envious and even hated myself because I could not talk to them too.

My only enjoyment was to work alone in the fields and dream of what a success I was going to be. My success pictures always had the foundation of perfect speech. I disliked working with anyone. That called for conversation and would not let me dream.

Soon I'll be fifty years old. I have much to be thankful for. A good wife and two fine youngsters. But I feel I've been a failure because of my stutter. As the years rolled along I saw many fellows, without as much ability as I have, pass me in rank and salary. Without exception they spoke well. Why isn't something done for the stutterer before he gets too old?

These confessions tell us only a little about the torture stutterers feel —until they learn a basic truth of mental hygiene: your attitude toward stuttering is much more important than the stutter.

Think of the stutterers in the United States—estimated at one million, four hundred thousand men, women, and children. Then add their relatives and associates, and you find a large section of the population interested in this problem.

But there is a bright side. If the stutter was neglected in childhood, the stutterer may still learn to speak well. Stuttering may be corrected at all ages. There are many helpful procedures, though no simple formulas.

You have to study the stutterer's temperament, keep his age in mind, know something about his home life before you begin. Psychological tests like Rorschach Psychodiagnostics, Thematic Apperception Test, Minnesota Multiphasic Personality Inventory can help you know what makes him fail to tick.

The stutterer needs to beware of anyone who guarantees a cure or uses only one simple exercise in working with all stutterers. Each case is too complicated to warrant rash promises of complete solution.

When the stutterer is a youngster, you work through his parents. For example, Mary, three years old, was an only child. She began to stutter when her mother was taken to the hospital. Before that time she was protected from outside contacts, wasn't allowed to play with other children. She was entirely dependent upon Mother.

During Mother's illness, Mary lived with an aunt, uncle, and three cousins. These were four, six, and seven years of age. By the time Mary came home she stuttered. She said she didn't want to go to her aunt's again. She probably was homesick there.

Mother and Father were advised to put Mary to bed for two days, to keep her quiet. The radio was disconnected. ("Something was wrong with it.") Romping and contacts with outsiders were ruled out for the time being. The parents were cautioned not to speak about the stutter, not to suggest to Mary that she speak smoothly or slowly or to make sympathetic facial expressions. Rather, we encouraged them to ignore the stuttering symptoms and speak calmly. We asked them to wait for Mary's words with disarming patience.

Within two weeks Mary was speaking with her former fluency. Then they encouraged her to play with robust, happy youngsters whose speech was smooth and fluent.

If Mary had been put in a class with other stuttering children or given speech lessons, she would have become too speech-conscious. Then her stutter might have become really severe. The approach was indirect, as it should be in the tender years when primary stuttering takes place. Then the child doesn't know the value others put on fluent speech.

We use direct means on the adult stutterer. He needs first to decide between alternatives: "I am going to correct my stuttering," or "I stut-

ter; so what? I'm not going to let it get me down." In either event,
he will probably get help from certain positive thoughts (the kind of
thoughts almost all of us can profit from). He ought to turn them
over many times throughout the day.

EXERCISE 79: Positive Thoughts

DIRECTIONS: *If you are a stutterer, you will probably get help from reading
the following thoughts until you commit them to memory.*

1. I like everybody and do not hate anybody.
2. I am humble of spirit, eager to give myself away in helping others.
3. I live in the spirit of abundance; I think prosperity and generosity.
4. I share my joys to make them increase; I share my sorrows to make
   them decrease.
5. I speak only pleasant words to and about others.
6. Whatsoever things are true, whatsoever things are just, whatsoever
   things are pure, whatsoever things are lovely, whatsoever things are of
   good report—I think about *these* things.
7. Everybody has personal problems to solve throughout life. My most
   important problem now is to correct my speech, and I can do it.

Such thoughts relieve tension. They grow in meaning. They help
us solve irritating problems in human relations. They encourage us
to think other wholesome thoughts. They help free us from doubts
and worries. They build faith in ourselves and in higher powers. They
make up the kind of thinking psychologists call *mental hygiene,* from
which stutterers derive much help.

Take the case of the forty-year-old executive, whom we shall call Mr.
Smith:

After helping him to understand himself better, the psychologist
explained that only Smith could help himself, that his stutter could not
be cured by any magic. But if he relearned to speak through conscious
control, if he built new ideas about himself and others, his chances
were excellent. The psychologist gave him the Rorschach Test to determine whether he had any deep-seated conflicts. No, there weren't any.

Smith then visited the psychologist every morning before he went to work. He learned *rate-control,* a way of speaking based upon phonetic analysis and designed:

1. To awaken aural consciousness.
2. To diagnose his own poor speech habits.
3. To relax his organs of articulation.
4. To encourage mental ease while speaking and reading.
5. To improve vocal quality.
6. To develop conscious control of articulation.
7. To enlarge his breath capacity and control his breathing coordinations.

He applied these speech principles to reading sounds, then syllables, and finally words, phrases, and sentences. Once he mastered the technique in reading aloud he used it for impromptu speaking too. Mr. Smith first talked about pictures flashed to him. Then he learned to talk impromptu about all sorts of subjects: first, simple subjects about everyday life, then ones that required more concentration. He always used a tempo slow enough to allow him to speak smoothly. He finally applied the technique on the telephone and in a public-speaking class.

Smith required a year to get mastery over his stutter. He visited the psychologist every day, including Sunday, for the first two weeks. Then followed a month of visits on alternate days. Then he came twice a week for the subsequent five months and once a week thereafter until his speech was completely under control.

Along with the speech reeducation went discussions about himself and his associates. Mr. Smith, like so many stutterers, had developed typical quirks. He felt sorry for himself. As his speech improved, he liked himself and others much better. He became optimistic. His victory was assured as soon as he believed he could control the symptoms of stuttering and practiced the suggestions like a good fellow.

Mr. Brown, another business executive of like age, got help from *voluntary stuttering.* Out of Dr. Knight Dunlap's discovery that "repetition may be employed in dissolving or breaking habits as well as in the formation of habits" came voluntary stuttering. What's voluntary stuttering?

You assume that stuttering is a collection of bad habits, that the stutterer can eliminate them by consciously reproducing them. Psychologists who use this technique have the stutterer repeat the first sound in each word distinctly, clearly several times. Each time the stutterer varies the number of repetitions to avoid learning a set pattern.

Whenever the stutterer has a block, he repeats, or *volunteers,* the word until he can say it smoothly. Long words are volunteered by syllables. Each syllable is assigned different sound combinations: for example, "s-s-s-tutter-r-r-ing" or "st-st-st-st-stu-ter-ter-ing." If he has tics or other nervous mannerisms, he learns to control them by volunteering them before a full-length mirror.

Rate-control and voluntary stuttering are only two of many techniques the experts use. I describe (superficially) the two techniques here to illustrate the good old adage: *The fire that melts the butter hardens the egg.*

Mr. Smith found help in rate-control, not voluntary stuttering; Mr. Brown's experience was the exact opposite. That's why the psychologist needs to know many techniques and select the most helpful for each case. Sometimes he employs a combination of techniques. For example, Smith and Brown took progressive relaxation exercises every day, along with their speech reeducation drills.

Like most other therapy, speech correction is an art as well as a science. The important thing for us to remember is that each case of stuttering deserves individual attention.

What's the most important thing in the correction program? The stutterer's confidence in his correctionist. You can't stress *rapport* too much.

If you live or work with a stutterer you can help him a lot by following twelve easy rules:

1. Don't stare at him as he stutters.
2. Relax your facial expression.
3. Speak slowly and easily.
4. Don't upset him with abrupt questions and exclamations.
5. Be composed in your sitting and standing postures. (That way you influence him to relax.)
6. Say pleasant words to him.
7. But don't be condescending.
8. Don't refer to his stuttering.

9. Gain his confidence by keeping your promises to him.
10. Listen to him in a leisurely way.
11. Practice intelligent kindness in your dealings with him.
12. Hold the thought that he'll improve.

The stutterer must take on responsibilities too. He must not feel sorry for himself. He ought to meet and know many accomplished men and women—in all walks of life—who stutter or have stuttered. He should remember that many achieve success despite stuttering.

Aren't all of us handicapped in some respects? Stuttering, like chronic indigestion, or nearsightedness, or deafness, or procrastination, or shyness can often be completely corrected, diminished in severity, or compensated for—if only the stutterer gives himself the chance and the nonstutterers help make that chance possible.

The stutterer's safest procedure is to work directly with an expert. For stuttering cannot be corrected by mail. To make sure that the expert, or institution, is accredited, he can write to the American Speech and Hearing Association, whose secretary, Dr. George Kopp, is located at Wayne University in Detroit, Michigan. Dr. Kopp keeps a list of recognized institutions and individuals who correct stuttering in the United States and Canada.

Once the stutterer knows that he is in competent hands, then he should give his whole cooperation. He shows that his heart is in the right place by following instructions. My grandmother used to tell us, "Beauty is as beauty does." That holds for all of us, doesn't it? For by plugging away in the right direction, the stutterer can also learn to talk well.

INDEX